Water Gardens

Water Gardens

Building, planting and maintaining water features

BEN HELM KELLY BILLING

CONTENTS

A QUARTO BOOK

First published by Apple Press
in the UK in 2008
7 Greenland Street
London NW1 0ND
www.apple-press.com

ISBN 978-1-84543-250-8

This book was designed and produced by
Quarto Publishing plc
The Old Brewery
6 Blundell Street
London N7 9BH

QUAR. WAG

EDITORS: Liz Dalby and Donna Gregory
COPY EDITOR: Diana Chambers
ART DIRECTOR: Caroline Guest
ART EDITOR: Natasha Montgomery
DESIGNER: Elizabeth Healey
PHOTOGRAPHER: Paul Forrester
ILLUSTRATOR: John Woodcock
PICTURE RESEARCH: Claudia Tate

CREATIVE DIRECTOR: Moira Clinch
PUBLISHER: Paul Carslake

Colour separation by Modern Age
Repro House Ltd, Hong Kong
Printed by 10/10 Printing
International, China

2 4 6 8 10 9 7 5 3 1 hardback

Whether it is due to an inbuilt desire to return to the fluid-filled womb or is related to the fact that our bodies consist predominantly of water, the evidence is clear – we are irresistibly drawn to water.

Holidays by the sea or at a lakeland retreat or walks along hillside torrents can fill us with a sense of fulfilment. So strong is our need to be close to water that as gardeners, our instinct is to bring our own piece of water home where we can relax and enjoy it every day.

Water in your garden

Any garden will benefit in many ways from the addition of a water feature or ornamental pond. A pond offers the gardener so many different opportunities, from complementing the rest of the garden's design to attracting wildlife. A water garden adds another dimension to your garden, with the sights and the sound of moving water, as well as providing the challenges of gardening in water and keeping fish.

This practical guide is all you will need to be able to plan and install a pond, through to planting, stocking, and maintaining it into its mature years. The emphasis is on building a pond that is close to nature, using the diverse life within it to help balance and maintain an attractive and healthy pond. Where pond equipment is used, it is done so sympathetically, while also recognizing how such equipment can make a water gardener's life easier.

A holistic approach

Ponds offer the gardener many opportunities and challenges. A successful water gardener must combine several different disciplines, from design and physical construction, through to biology and even some chemistry.

To enable you to take a holistic approach, the book introduces you to the philosophy behind maintaining a stable and balanced pond and understanding the key role that water quality plays. The more you can understand the principles behind certain water gardening fundamentals, the better equipped you will be to control and shape the development of your own pond at every stage.

The creative process

At every stage of creating your pond, you will be faced with many interesting choices, each with their own challenges and benefits. Be led by your own creativity, budget, and instinct to create an aquatic feature that reflects your inspiration. You start with a clean slate, so let your imagination take over. Read on, and enjoy the journey…

ABOUT THIS BOOK

This book is arranged in six sections. The first covers planning and constructing your water garden. This is followed by information on stocking your pond and solving common problems that may occur. There are useful directories of plants and fish, including information on suitability and compatibility, and finally a section on pond management, with vital information on the processes that keep your pond healthy.

Inspirational photographs show examples covered in the text

Clearly illustrated step-by-step instructions take you through tasks and processes

Authoritative text provides a wealth of accessible information

Specially commissioned diagrams and illustrations explain key points and techniques

Panels highlight important information and handy tips

Bulleted panels and checklists provide quick summaries

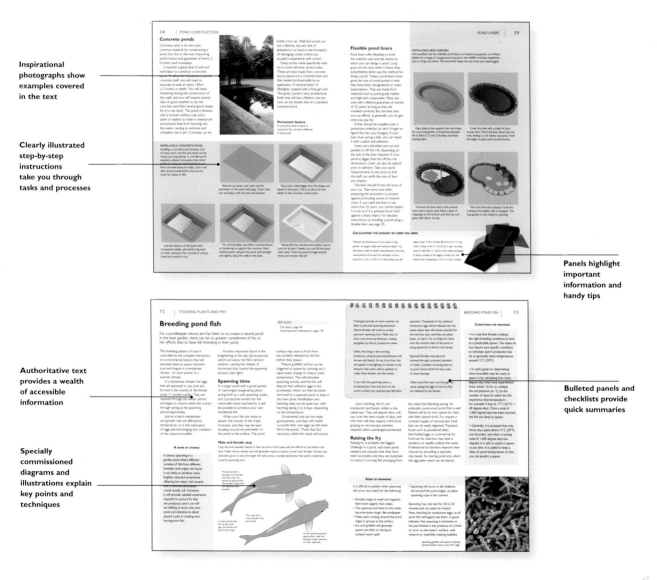

Top ten tips

The creation of a successful and beautiful water garden depends on the understanding and implementation of a few basic principles.

1

Do not try to create an instant pond

A pond will take several months to become established because of the natural processes that are involved. If you try to create a pond any faster than that, then your pond, its plants and the fish are likely to start to encounter problems (see pages 62 to 63).

2

Follow nature's example

Whenever possible, use the example of a natural pond as your guide for success as to how a pond should look, be landscaped and be stocked with fish and plants. The more you choose to deviate from the natural model, the greater your challenge to keep the pond balanced (see pages 158 to 159).

3

Build as large as possible

When planning your pond, bigger is definitely better. Larger ponds are easier to keep clean, create a more stable pond environment for your fish and give you greater scope in design and planting. Many pondkeepers regret not having created a larger pond in the first place.

Harmonious design

A successful water garden will incorporate a range of different, appropriate planting types, as well as carefully chosen fish and ornaments or features.

6

Watch your fish regularly

How your fish behave will give you an instant indication of the pond's water quality. Spend time watching and feeding them to confirm normal behaviour. Any abnormal behaviour should be quickly followed up with water tests to identify problems (see page 168 to 169).

7

Supervise children around your pond at all times

The sights and sounds of a pond can prove irresistible to children, endangering them in and around the water. Keep them supervised at all times, especially if they are not familiar with your garden and pond (see page 94).

8

Take care with electricity

It is inevitable that electrical pond equipment will come into close contact with water, posing some potential risks. To prevent serious accidents, install and use all equipment safely and use the standard safety devices (see page 94).

4

Stock the pond gradually

Even though your pond is an artificial creation, it will still mature at the rate set by nature. So when adding fish, do so gradually over several months to avoid causing water-quality problems. The first 3 to 6 months in a pond's life are by far the most crucial (see pages 174 to 175).

5

Test the water regularly

A pond's water quality has the greatest influence on how it will perform – the better the water, the more stable and successful the pond. Test the water regularly to learn what is happening in your pond, and intervene when necessary (see pages 168 to 169).

Night-time transformation

With careful attention to lighting design in your garden, a pond can become a stunning visual feature to be enjoyed at night as well as during the day.

9

Think long-term with plants

Give plants plenty of space to grow into when adding them to your pond. Plant your pond with the future in mind, paying particular attention to any species that will grow vigorously. Choose suitable sized plants to keep your pond from becoming overgrown (see pages 44 to 45).

10

Keep pond plants in place

Do not be tempted to introduce any of your plants into the wild when thinning them. Many pond plants are nonnative and invasive and will soon take over natural habitats. Likewise, ornamental pond fish belong in ponds and should not be released into natural streams or wildlife ponds.

PLANNING, CONSTRUCTION AND INSTALLATION

Your mind is likely to be buzzing with ideas of how you would like your pond and water garden to look – but first things first. Before embarking on your aquatic creation, you will need to assess the plot of garden that you have got to work with. This will help to determine your pond's size, shape and position – and help you to compile your shopping list, within the limits of your budget. Having established what you hope to achieve, you will need to know how to construct it, and the various materials that are available to use.

Planning the site

Your garden is the blank canvas onto which you will plan your new pond. Every garden is unique, with opportunities and constraints as to where you can site a pond.

A pond should be placed where it will be viewed and enjoyed. If you have been contemplating a pond for some time, you may have already decided on your preferred position. If you are planning a formal, geometrically shaped pond, the existing structure of your garden will determine the pond's position. If you prefer an informal and irregularly shaped pond, then to look convincing, it should appear as if it was placed there by nature. The final position of any pond in an existing site is likely to be a compromise between aesthetic and practical considerations. These will not only determine where the pond is finally located, but will also affect its eventual size and shape and even its performance.

Sunlight: Position the pond so that the sun falls on it for half of the daylight hours. This will help it to achieve a stable temperature that will benefit the aquatic life. Plants will also thrive in a sunlit pond. But if a pond receives too much sun, it will develop algae problems, as well as undesirable swings in temperature.

Roots: If, during the excavation, you encounter tree roots, you will have no option but to cut through them. You should try to avoid this.

Evergreens: Evergreen trees and shrubs drop small leaves or needles all year round. These are stubborn to break down and can be so fine that they will even pass through pond netting. Avoid willow, holly, horse, chestnut, walnut and laburnum, because they are potentially toxic to fish.

Tree growth: Your pond and any existing trees are likely to coexist for many years. As the trees grow, they will deprive the pond of essential sunlight, affecting the life and growth of the plants within it.

Viewing point: Unless your pond is to be a secret aquatic oasis, hidden away for the benefit of wildlife, it is installed as a definite feature of a garden, to be viewed and enjoyed. Whether your preferred main viewing point is your favourite garden bench or through your kitchen window, you need to establish where it will be.

Trees: In nature, you will often find trees next to a pond, but in a garden, placing a pond immediately adjacent to a tree is less desirable. Overhanging trees will drop leaves, fruit and twigs into the pond, which will decay and adversely affect the water quality, reducing dissolved oxygen levels and encouraging algae.

Neighbours: It is quite likely that your pond will include the sound of running water. This is one of the many sensory benefits of adding a pond to a garden. But do consider your neighbours; try installing a separate pump for a fountain or waterfall that can be switched off at night, leaving a pump circulating the water through a filter.

Waterfall: The sound produced by a waterfall may be therapeutic and appealing to you, but to a neighbour, it could prove to be an intrusive annoyance.

Footings and foundations: Make sure when planning the position of your pond that you allow sufficient space to avoid disturbing the foundations of nearby buildings during excavation. Excavating close to adjacent buildings can also encourage subsidence.

Electricity and drains: The closer you excavate to a building, the greater the risk of intercepting existing immovable services. Do as much preliminary investigation as you can at the planning stage and especially before you start to dig.

Temporary buildings: If you would consider moving a temporary building such as a shed or greenhouse to get your pond in the best position, then do so. It's better to build a pond of the desired size and position than to compromise on those factors, potentially affecting its performance for its lifetime.

TIP

If your site is unavoidably sunny for the majority of the day, you could consider erecting a pergola to give it shade.

Lie of the land

Most gardens are flat, presenting you with the challenge of how to incorporate a waterfall or stream. A convenient way of using the soil from the excavation is to pile it behind the pond and use it as a raised area for siting one of these features. There is a big risk that an isolated raised area could look contrived (and very unnatural), especially if it is placed in a central location. A good solution is to pile the soil in a heap and site the waterfall or stream against a garden wall or boundary. If you choose not to have a waterfall or stream in a flat garden, you will be faced with the arduous task of removing the excavated soil from your garden.

If you are fortunate enough to have a sloping garden, this natural feature can be used very effectively. With the high ground sloping down toward the viewing point, the naturally occurring gradient will allow you to construct a plausible stream that appears in a spring-like fashion and then feeds a pond cut into the slope of your garden.

Naturally sloping garden
Here a garden's natural shape is used to good effect in creating a waterfall.

Services

Once you have narrowed down your location, you need to discover the position of existing services (electricity, gas, drains and so on) that might travel under your proposed pond. If they do, establish whether they can be moved, otherwise site the pond elsewhere. You will also need to get an electricity supply to your pond to power the pump and even some lighting. You should be satisfied that the location of your pond allows the safe laying of a new electrical line to your pond.

Visualization

Having taken on board all the aesthetic and practical considerations, you should plan the desired size and shape of your pond in situ in your garden. Lay a rope or garden hose on the ground, walk around it and view it from every angle for several days. Look at how it may be affected by undesirable reflections in the water. Plan where the power will run, and make allowances for where any excavated soil may go. You also need to plan where the

Good for viewing but may get too much sunlight.

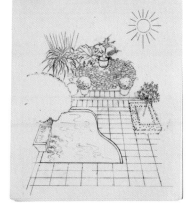

Easily viewed from the house. But be careful about the house's foundations.

Pond will not enjoy much shade here. Geometric shape could work well with a similar shaped terrace.

Not easily viewed from the house – may be difficult for electricity supply – but would make a quiet aquatic oasis.

pond's filter will be situated. Having had a few days to tweak and reconsider your plan, seeking advice from the family, you are ready to begin the hard work of excavating the pond.

Experiment with ideas

Consider more than one site for your pond, weighing the pros and cons of each. The perfect site may not exist – you may have to make a compromise.

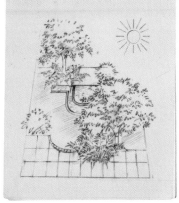

Too close to trees. May suffer from excessive leaf fall in autumn – but will enjoy some pleasant partial shade.

Site checklist

Viewing point: Locate the pond where it can be viewed frequently. Construct waterfalls on the opposite side from the usual viewing point. If your land is sloping, to look natural, an informal pond will be best sited at the lowest point.

Trees: Tree roots can cause problems during excavation and may pierce the pond liner in years to come. Trees may also drop leaves all year round but especially in autumn. These will break down in the pond and may unbalance the natural ecosystem you are trying to create. Avoid siting the pond near willow, horse chestnut, walnut, laburnum, holly or any evergreen trees, as these can be toxic to pond life.

Sunlight: Sunlight is an essential component for success. If there is too little sunlight, the pond will not thrive. Don't site your pond too close to anything that will cast permanent shade (a fence, shed, house or trees). Check the shadows across your garden when the sun rises and sets. Avoid a north-facing garden that is shaded from the sun. Lay a garden hose or rope on the ground to mark out the shape and position of your pond. Check during the next few days that the pond has received sufficient sunlight and can be easily viewed from your favourite viewing points.

Services: Once you have established the best place for the pond, check that there are no services (such as gas, water, drains, telephone or electricity) running underneath. Confirm that it is also feasible for electricity to be taken to your pond safely to work the pump and lighting.

Pond shapes

It is best to adopt a simple approach to the shape of your pond. Taking the example of natural pools, you will notice that they are shaped very simply, with sweeping curves and edges.

Water within a pond must be allowed to circulate freely, mixing the volume of the whole pond and preventing any stagnant areas. Tight channels or dead ends do not allow the free mixing of water and will encourage undesirable debris and silt to settle in the pond. These "dead spots" will also encourage warmer and cooler areas in a pond, where a consistent temperature should be your aim.

Large, sweeping curves not only lead to better water quality and help to reduce maintenance but are also easier to install when using a flexible liner. Dig your pond to suit the area of the land available, keeping the perimeter smooth and gently sweeping, perhaps shelving gently to form a beach area. More intricate designs and shapes mean that the liner will need to be folded or creased, which will create pockets and allow debris to accumulate in the pond rather than pass through to the filter.

Pond size

The size of your pond will ultimately be determined by the size of the space available in your garden and your budget. The pond must complement the scale of other features in the garden so that it is neither "lost" nor dominating. Experience shows that you should plan for as large a pond as possible; in simple pond language, big is certainly best. It is very common to meet pondkeepers who have extended their existing ponds because they wished they had made them bigger in the first place (especially when they realized the vast array of fish and plants that are available).

It is difficult to add a pond liner to (or make use of existing pumps and filters from) a previous small pond, so making a pond too small in the first instance can be an expensive mistake. Similarly, when viewing a display of deceptively sized preformed ponds stacked up in a retail display, it's quite common to believe that they will be too large for your garden. But once sunk into your garden, a preformed pond will seem to shrink, filling you with regret that you did not choose a larger one.

Water quality

A pondkeeper's priority must be the water quality, just as successful gardeners pay a lot of attention to the quality of the soil. If the medium in which the fish are growing is in top condition, success will follow. If the water quality is well understood and managed, you do not have to be an expert in fish or the diseases that affect them, as their good health will follow automatically.

Fish prefer stable water conditions, and if any changes do occur within the pond, they must be gradual. It is far easier to keep fish in a large pond, as it provides a greater volume for diluting any problems (the solution to pollution is dilution). This is especially true in the first months of a pond's life, with a larger body of water being more stable and forgiving. Larger ponds are easier to keep healthy and well balanced, resulting in less maintenance. For example, the risk of algae becoming a problem decreases. Large ponds are also less likely to suffer from extremes of temperature. For more about water quality, see pages 78 to 80.

Choosing a shape

The shape of your pond is crucial to its success. Eccentric pond shapes, sharp curves, or inlets may look interesting on paper but should be avoided.

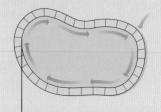

Ideal pond shape
The open shape with sweeping curves makes this pond shape ideal.

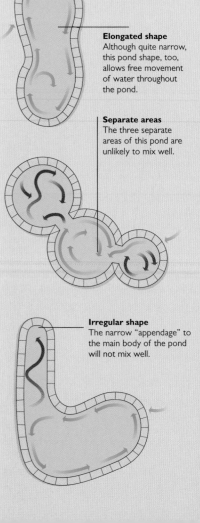

Elongated shape
Although quite narrow, this pond shape, too, allows free movement of water throughout the pond.

Separate areas
The three separate areas of this pond are unlikely to mix well.

Irregular shape
The narrow "appendage" to the main body of the pond will not mix well.

Water quantity

It is essential to know the volume of your pond so that you know what size pump and filter you should install and, if the pond needs treating, the correct dose that should be added.

The bigger the better
This huge pond will be much more stable and easier to maintain than a smaller pond. It also gives you more opportunity for landscaping, planting and fish selection.

AREA, DEPTH AND VOLUME

SURFACE AREA
A pond should have as large a surface area as possible in relation to its volume, while maintaining a depth of 1m (3 feet). A large surface area will benefit a pond by encouraging an excellent two-way gas exchange, with oxygen freely dissolving from the atmosphere and carbon dioxide (and other waste gases) escaping from the pond back into the atmosphere. A large surface area will also provide a pond with essential sunlight, warming it more than if an equivalent pond had a smaller surface area. You should be aware that a good proportion of the area dedicated to a pond on paper is, in reality, likely to be shelved and covered with planted baskets, quickly reducing the real surface area of the whole pond relative to the deep centre.

DEPTH
Depth is important for providing fish with protection during the winter. All pond fish will overwinter on the bottom of the pond and require a minimum safe depth of 1m (3 feet), but, ideally, it should be deeper. In extreme cases, where ponds are built specifically for koi that grow to a great size, pond depths of over 1.5m (5 feet) are more common. When considering the pond depth, remember that children can drown in any depth of water – however shallow. **No pond is child-safe unless it has some kind of rigid safety covering.**

VOLUME
The volume is a function of the width, length and depth of a pond. The greater the volume, the easier it will be to maintain the pond, as it will be more stable and less likely to suffer from adverse water conditions. To establish the volume of your pond, measure its length, width and depth and use the following equation:

$L \times W \times D \times 6.25$ (in feet) = volume in imperial gallons
($\times 4.54$ = volume in litres)

The measurements are more precise in a regularly shaped, formal pond. In an informal pond with irregular shapes and varying depth, you need to average out measurements and estimate the dimensions as best you can. Once you have established the volume of your pond, make a note of it, as you'll need to refer to it throughout the pond's life.

Pond surface area relative to depth
Ponds A and B have the same volume, but are not equal in terms of the number of fish they can support.

Pond A
The relatively small surface area in this pond will limit how many fish you can keep in it. It will also be much cooler than pond B.

Pond B
This pond will perform better than A. It will receive more sunlight, exchange gases more effectively and sustain more fish. Ensure that your pond's depth is at least 1m (3 feet).

Pond styles

The shape of your garden will help you to decide which pond style to choose – either formal or informal. The choice of pond shape will also be determined by the current or planned shapes in your garden, especially any hard landscaping.

Formal ponds

Formal ponds are geometric in shape, taking the form of a square, rectangle, circle or oval, for example. They suit a garden that has been designed using similar angles and shapes. A formal pond is more likely to be raised above the ground and be sparsely planted (with the exception of a few lilies), and it may have a central fountain or statue.

Circular ponds
Formal ponds can easily be raised either partly or fully above the ground. This is quite common for circular ponds and can be a solution where excavation or the disposal of soil is difficult.

Rectangular ponds
A rectangular pond is ideal for a formal setting where the existing lawn, hedging, or hard landscape has already created a rectangular "space" for a pond. The mirror-like reflective surface of such a pond can add further dimensions to the garden by reflecting the sky and plants in the garden.

Raised ponds
It is quite common for a formal pond to be raised. Whatever the regular shape or size of the pond, using a different form of construction that involves building up rather than digging down, a raised pond can prove to be a stunning water feature. A raised pond is ideal if the site is covered in an existing substantial hard surface, where digging through it may prove too destructive and very hard work.

Hexagonal/octagonal ponds
A hexagonal or octagonal pond makes an ideal focal point for a patio, as it is encircled by a stone path. Where a pond can be viewed from any angle, symmetry in planting is essential, as is the careful choice of pond-building materials to achieve complete symmetry.

PRACTICAL IMPLICATIONS FOR FORMAL PONDS

A formal pond may contain many tight corners and symmetrical shapes and is best constructed using a preformed fibreglass structure (or, for the more adventurous, concrete). If a flexible liner is used, the corners and circular shapes will require a lot of careful folding, leaving creases in the pond liner. The rigid self-supporting structure provided by a fibreglass pond also allows you to install a raised pond easily, with minimal support. In a formal pond, the hardware, such as filters, can be a challenge to conceal.

Informal ponds

Informal ponds blend with existing styles in a garden's landscaping and planting scheme, becoming an integral part of the planting. The design is set by you, and the object is to create the illusion that the pond has occurred naturally, making it difficult for the observer to see where the garden ends and the pond starts. An informal pond does not contain a straight edge or angle anywhere. Such ponds lend themselves very well to the installation of an adjacent bog garden or a complementary waterfall. If you want lots of space for aquatic plants, this is the type of pond for you.

Lobe-shaped ponds

Resembling a bloated cloverleaf, a lobed pond is a good way of enabling a pond to encroach in different directions. One of the lobes could be made into a beached area and one could contain a waterfall, while decking could be shaped around another.

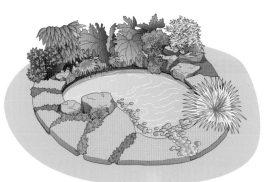

Kidney-shaped ponds

This is perhaps the classic informal shape. The gently sweeping sides and curves allow good water circulation, with the lobed side positioned toward the focal point. There is generally more opportunity for planting with this shape, with taller marginal plants best suited to the rear of the pond.

Bog gardens

A pond generally has a shallow, shelved area for the positioning of marginal plants. These are the plants that prefer just their feet to be wet, with their flowers and foliage proudly displayed above the water. At times, this shelf may be only 23cm (9 inches) wide (leaving more water for the fish). Avoid falling into the trap of lining your plants in a tight, regimented row along a narrow ledge. This is hardly appropriate or in keeping with the overall informal shape and design of your pond.

Wildlife ponds

The addition of a pond (even a raised formal pond) will encourage wildlife into your garden. A wildlife pond is best suited to an area of garden set aside as a conservation or "back-to-nature" area. It may be a part of the garden where you choose not to mow the grass but allow it to grow up to provide cover, perhaps even planting a wildflower mix in it. A wildlife pond should be regarded as an electricity and chemical-free zone, where, through your provision of an aquatic oasis, Mother Nature's creative hand will be encouraged to work. Pondkeepers simply act as the aquatic host to any wildlife "guests" that are so attracted to the hospitality offered that they feel inclined to visit and perhaps even take up full-time residence and – if you're fortunate – raise a family.

Flexible liner

A flexible liner will mould itself to a pond's sweeping contours under the weight of water.

PRACTICAL IMPLICATIONS FOR INFORMAL PONDS

Informal ponds put you in charge of the design and can therefore drift outside the realms of preformed ponds. Once you have designed and completed your excavation, a flexible pond liner is the best material to create a watertight pond. Under the weight of the water, it will mould itself perfectly to the contours and shape of the pond.

Materials and features

Just as a pond may have been planned and designed to complement existing features of the garden, the materials used in and around a pond must also fit in with the overall hard landscaping scheme.

Edging materials

You will notice from natural lakes and ponds that there is typically a defined edge between land and water. At times, this may blend with the land in the form of a bog garden, but more often than not it will be well defined by rock or stone. You should follow this natural precedent in your own pond for several practical reasons.

Bank stability: A pond must be edged to give the bank stability. Heavy edging laid in a bed of mortar provides an immovable barrier, indicating where the water ends and the rest of the garden starts. The edge of the pond should be constructed with large pieces of rock or paving, as they must support a weight safely.

Concealment: Position edging to conceal the liner. Any electrical cables or hoses must be covered by the edging material to maintain the illusion that your pond is natural.

Garden maintenance: If a substantial, immovable edge is not made around a pond, soil or grass will start to encroach into the pond. An effective boundary means that garden maintenance can be carried out without disturbing or affecting the pond.

Metal
Metalwork features have become popular, especially if they incorporate or feature moving water. Avoid copper or zinc (galvanized) items, as there is a risk that these will leach toxic heavy metals into the pond. (This is not a problem if the metal features don't come into contact with the pond water.)

Appropriate design

Inappropriate edging material around a pond can make it look contrived and unnatural. Be guided by the materials already present in your garden. For example, if there is a predominantly sandstone finish in the existing features, then sandstone should be used in and around the pond. Before you add a stonework edge to your pond, consider making other rockwork features in the garden from the same stone to tie the style of the garden and pond together.

Natural stone
There are many different types and sizes of natural stone available. Both sandstone and limestone are popular; they weather well and are easy to work with. Sandstone is available as large rocks or paving slabs. Limestone is not available in flat slabs, which does not make it a practical choice for waterfalls. However, it is naturally alkaline, helping to buffer the pond water against changes in pH.

Cobbles and pebbles
Cobbles and pebbles can be used with formal or informal ponds. They can be set in concrete or laid out loose to create a beach. To give a smooth, solid stone appearance to a pond bottom, pebbles can also be set in cement.

Wood
Wood near a pond should be treated with a preservative, but make sure that any preservative is fish-safe. Wood rounds can be an effective edge to a formal pond. Use them at ground height to form a border between the soil and pond or in a sweeping formation, rising out of the ground to retain a bank of soil. Wooden decking covers large areas adjacent to the pond quickly and economically.

Features

Three common pond features use materials imaginatively to add a new dimension to a pond.

Stepping stones

Stepping stones offer an irresistible challenge. When confronted with the opportunity to walk on water and partake in what appears to be a risky passage over a water body, people feel compelled to do so. Position stepping stones as an alternative route through a garden, offering a shortcut across the pond, as opposed to the more natural journey around it. Placed sufficiently close to each other to allow easy movement from one to the next, they should offer a safe route or vantage point from which to view the pond. Stepping stones cannot be an afterthought but must be built at the same time as the pond, as they must be placed on a firm foundation, ensuring that they are structurally sound and safe to walk on. Be sure to choose a stone with a rough finish that will afford a good grip to those using them. Natural flat (sedimentary) stone or "natural" concrete cast flags are ideal. Choose a shape of stone to complement the shape of the pond and surrounding rockwork.

Bridges

A bridge offers a means of crossing a pond. It can be built in situ or bought ready-made. A number of different designs are available, from simple flat bridges to elaborate hump-backed versions. A bridge may be purely ornamental or built to carry people who would like to view a pond from above. It must have good, level foundations on which to sit, and it may be excavated without interfering with the pond. It should be an integral part of the pond; try to keep handrails low and the width in keeping with the scale of the pond. A useful trick to give the impression that the bridge has been there forever is to continue it into the borders at either side of the pond. Soften both ends of the bridge with planting.

Beach

A beach arguably looks like one of the most natural edges to a pond and is relatively easy to construct. A pebble beach leads the eye down into a pond, with the same material used outside and within the pond itself. A pebble beach also allows birds and amphibians to access the water's edge, especially throughout the various fluctuations of water level in summer and winter. Use a mix of different-sized cobbles and pebbles (as would occur naturally). A concealed mortar retaining wall below the waterline will keep the pebble beach in place. As the beach matures, marginal and bog plants will soon colonize areas of the beach naturally – a superb finishing touch.

Fountains

A pond or water garden brings water into the garden,
and moving water brings that pond to life.

Incorporating movement into a pond
exploits the many facets of water,
adding sparkle, sound and reflection.
Moving water is also an effective way
of adding oxygen to a pond, which is
vital in the warmer summer months,
especially during hot, muggy nights
(see page 163).

Fountains are the simplest way of
introducing moving water but do not
look appropriate in every pond. They
suit more formal ponds that have a
regular shape, giving a classically shaped
pond a real sparkle. The huge array of
different fountainheads, statues and
ornaments means that an appropriate
display for the size and shape of your
pond is achievable. There are even
flood-lit fountainheads that will give any
evening garden party a touch of
glamour. As a fountain is not a natural
structure, it can look out of place in an
informal or "natural" garden pond.

Fountain types

A fountain consists very simply of a
pump connected to a fountainhead that
creates a shower of pressurized water,
transforming the nature of your pond.
The simplest form of fountainhead will
often be supplied with a fountain pump.
Similar in appearance to the rose of a
watering can, a simple push-fit onto the
pump is all that is required to install it.
Variations on this theme can be
achieved by adding different fountainheads, such as those that form a jet,
produce a foam, or even create a
hemispherical dome.

A fountain pump can also feed
statues and ornaments that issue water
into the pond (which acts as a
reservoir). These can range from a
piece of drilled stone that simply
dribbles or bubbles water to more
impressive statuary that might combine
several different fountain types.

Simple fountain
Even a simple fountain brings energy and life
to a pond – and adds vital oxygen, too.

Fountains and water features

Standard fountain
A range of interchangeable
push-fit fountainheads is usually
supplied with the small fountain
pump attached directly to the
fountainhead, and will come with
an adjustable T-piece to regulate
the flow through the fountain.

Larger pump
Capable of creating a
more impressive fountain
or feeding a waterfall.

Pump and separate fountain
Flexible hose attaches the pump to
the self-supported fountain. One
pump could feed several fountains.

Ornamental fountain
A spouting dolphin is connected
to the pump through pipe work
in its base via flexible hose.

Cascading saucer
A small pump connects
directly to the saucer,
filling it gently with little
splashing. A larger pump
could be used to make
the water "babble".

Installation

When choosing a fountain, you will need to establish which effect will work best in your pond and the size of pump required. You could install a dedicated fountain pump whose sole purpose is to produce the fountain. This means that if you wish to turn it off at night, no other pond appliances will be affected. In the most simple fountain installations, a sturdy submersible pump sits directly beneath the fountainhead which fits onto the pump body (see Larger pump, below left). Depending on the depth of the pond, you may need a rigid extension pipe between the pump and the fountainhead. It is advisable to place a fountain pump on or between several bricks, lifting it clear of the pond bottom. There will be a standard adjustable T-piece so that the flow can be regulated through the fountain. This kind of inexpensive fountain installation is ideal in a small pond where the fountain and pump can be reached from the pond side for maintenance. In a larger pond, for easier access, the pump is best positioned near the perimeter with a flexible hose leading to a fixed fountainhead or ornament.

If your pond incorporates a waterfall or external filter that needs to be fed continuously via a large submersible pump, a feed for the fountain could be taken via a T-piece to run both fountain and waterfall. If the pump becomes blocked, the reduction in flow through the fountain would be a useful indicator to show that the pump needs cleaning. If your fountain is a large statue sitting well above the pond's surface, you will need a larger pump than if you were simply operating a fountainhead at the water's surface.

Possible problems

Through splashing, a fountain can cause a pond to lose gallons of water every day in windy conditions. Choose a fountain whose spray is no greater than half the diameter of a pond. If the pond is in a windy location, choose a fountain that produces larger, heavier drops or one in which water simply runs down the surface of a statue or ornament.

Fountains can spoil an informal pond, as they would never be found in a naturally occurring pond. Furthermore, water that is constantly splashing onto the pond's surface will obscure the view into the depths of the pond, making it difficult to see the fish and spoiling the sense of tranquillity. Lilies

Formal fountain
This formal pond has a suitably sized fountain – and the design means that there is no danger of losing water from the pond on a windy day.

or other pond plants will not thrive if their foliage is permanently showered by water from a fountain – a good reason for choosing a less flamboyant water feature.

If you choose a fountainhead with fine holes, you are likely to experience frequent blockages caused by minute pieces of debris being circulated by the pump (even with the finest of prefilters fitted to the pump). If you live in a hard-water area, you may also find that dipping the fountainhead regularly in vinegar is required to clear the jets of limescale.

Self-contained water features
The following are quick and easy water features that can be installed inexpensively to add the effects of moving water, without having a pond.

Pebble fountains
The pebble display can vary. In each case, the water returns to the reservoir through a perforated false bottom. The larger the reservoir, the better. Monitor the flow and top up when it drops. Maintenance and removal of blockages can prove to be a difficult and lengthy job.

Spouting urns
Working on a similar basis to the pebble fountains, a submersible pump feeds a horizontal urn via a flexible hose, and water is returned to the concealed reservoir. It may be worth considering fitting an adjustable T-piece above the ground to allow you to adjust the flow rate easily.

Waterfalls and streams

An informal pond can be greatly enhanced by the addition of a waterfall or stream.

A waterfall is best constructed at the same time as the pond and, compared to a fountain, requires a much bigger pump to achieve a credible effect. A waterfall pump is required to lift water to great heights through a large-bore pipe, and you should choose one that will satisfy your waterfall's specific requirements.

Avoiding water loss

Although a sizable pond represents the reservoir for a large waterfall, even minor splashes will have an impact on the pond's level, causing it to drop by several centimetres in a day. Water loss from a waterfall can also cause subsidence, leading to greater leaks in the waterfall at a later date. Waterfalls cause ponds to lose water through splashing, leaking or evaporation, but the loss can be reduced by following a few simple rules during construction. Waterfalls can be constructed from preformed units (which interlink) or from natural stone. The same measures against water loss should be taken whatever the construction method.

Integrate the waterfall lining: Having excavated the site for your pond and the course for the waterfall (see page 30), purchase a piece of pond liner sufficient to line the pond and waterfall without having to cut the liner between the waterfall and pond.

PUMP SPECIFICATIONS AND FLOW RATE

The greater the vertical distance a pump has to reach, the lower the flow rate, resulting in a trickle rather than a torrent. A useful rule of thumb is that for a 15-cm (6-inch) wide waterfall to be covered with a realistic layer of water, a pump should deliver a minimum of 2,270 litres (500 gallons) per hour at that height. Check the pump's specifications before purchasing. (See pages 32 to 35 for more on pond pumps.)

To check that it will supply the required flow rate at the given head, a useful guide is that a mains tap will run at approximately 900 litres (200 gallons) per hour. If in doubt, always choose a larger pump than you think you may require, as these can be adjusted down. It is better to do that than to be disappointed with a small trickle over the waterfall and having to purchase a larger pump.

Waterfall construction
Waterfalls are notorious for leaking and losing water. Ensure that yours is constructed with a number of key design features to help prevent this.

Fix the tubing in rock work and conceal it from view.

Position the submersible pump at the opposite end of the pond from the waterfall, ensuring good water circulation. Choose a big enough pump to deliver sufficient water to make the waterfall look effective.

Lay an integral piece of liner beneath the waterfall. If the rock work does leak, any water will run back into the pond.

Make all the sills the same width, and fine-tune the cascades with loose stones to reduce splashing.

When the waterfall is an integral part of the pond, any leaking or splashing water will naturally return to the pond.

Lay a sand and cement bed:
Having positioned the liner, lay a bed of mixed sand and cement, on which you can place the preformed cascade or stream units or into which your natural stone can be embedded to form a natural stepped pattern. Add a lime-neutralizing compound to the mix to avoid water-quality problems during the waterfall's life, or paint a clear waterproof sealant onto the waterfall once the cement mixture has set.

Make sills the same width:
Make all the sills down the length of the waterfall the same width, otherwise wider falls will look less impressive than narrower ones. Try to add a curve to the waterfall to make it look natural, and, once running, use loose but heavy stones to fine-tune how the water runs over each cascade.

Using preformed units

Preformed waterfall units can range from semi-rigid plastic units to rigid fibreglass and even reconstituted "stone" shapes, ready to be laid down in an order and sequence of your choice. Even though these will not leak, water loss can still occur between units through splashing. This should not lead to a drop in water level if the cascade is laid on a foundation lined with the same piece of liner that makes the pond.

Using natural stone

The easiest stone to work with when making waterfalls is sandstone. This easily forms flat surfaces and can be chipped and broken into the desired size and shape. The stone can be embedded into a foundation of mortar that sits on the waterproof liner, returning any leaks or splashes to the pond. Construct the waterfall from the bottom up so that at each level, the lip of the upper cascade can overlap the pool below it. Only trim off any excess liner along the sides of the waterfall after a satisfactory test run. This will show you where water is likely to splash or spill over, allowing you to catch it in the liner. The path that the water takes can also be trained by the strategic placing of stones in the waterfall channel. Once trimmed, the liner can be buried out of sight. With this form of construction, the finished waterfall can be sealed as an extra precaution against leaks with a suitable waterproof sealant.

Aeration pumps

Aeration pumps are specifically designed to aerate the depths of a pond. This is essential in deep ponds. Diaphragm air compressors run silently, and will work tirelessly for many years between diaphragm replacements.

The air delivered by an aeration pump should be diffused to improve its oxygenating performance. One diffuser used by pondkeepers is the airstone. Versatile, inexpensive and durable, it can be placed in the pond or into biological chambers to aid the filtration process. More recent innovations include porous pipe that can be installed on the pond bottom or a flexible membrane diffuser which consists of a circular, perforated membrane mounted on a rigid backing plate connected to an air supply. The membrane forms a dome as pressure builds, releasing tiny bubbles from each pore.

Air diffuser
When an air diffuser is attached to an air pump and fixed to the bottom of the pond, it diffuses tiny bubbles through the pond – aerating it vigorously.

WATERFALL BOX

Rather than simply feeding the top of the cascade with tubing directly from the pump, install a waterfall box to give you better control over how the water feeds the waterfall. It also feeds the waterfall across the width of the cascade, creating an evenly distributed flow as soon as the water starts to cascade down the waterfall or rocky face. If you use a waterfall box, you must allocate some space behind the top of the waterfall during the pond's construction.

Pond liners

With an artificial liner, you can site your pond anywhere in your garden, even above ground. To achieve your goal, you must choose your pond-building method wisely.

All natural water bodies occur where they do because of the geological conditions (usually due to an abundance of clay). However, if you bring water into your garden, it may never form a pond naturally; the underlying soil may be too permeable, or the lie of the land may not collect water naturally. If you want a pond in your garden, it will probably be necessary to create an artificial lining for it.

Clay is the perfect pond-building material. It is impermeable, easy to work with (but difficult to dig), and the

soil type of choice for koi and goldfish farms. A natural clay pond lining provides fish with many environmental benefits that produce fish in tip-top condition. However, it will also make a pond very murky, making it less than ideal for viewing beautiful fish. Clay may still be an option if you want to install a conservation or wildlife pond. But one of the benefits of choosing a liner (rather than clay) is that you can achieve crystal-clear water and make a watertight pond in any soil type, whether clay, loam or sand.

POND-LINER OPTIONS

There are several options for lining your pond.
Preformed pool: an off-the-shelf, instant pond approach
Concrete: a heavier, handmade method of construction
Flexible liner: the no-holds-barred method for the more creative water gardener

There is obviously a market for all three approaches, but which will be the best one for you? Your choice will depend on your budget, the ease of installation and guarantee. A flexible liner is probably the most cost-effective. A preformed pond is more expensive than a liner but can be installed in a day. A concrete pond, however, can take weeks to construct and is also back-breaking work.

Preformed pools

A preformed pool is ideal for creating a symmetrical formal pond where sides that are exactly geometrical are required (and yet you do not have to dig a hole to the correct geometric shape or dimensions). Just make a hole large enough to take the preformed pond and backfill accordingly, and you will have created a perfect formal pond without using a set square or compass.

Types of preformed pools
There are two or three different types of preformed pools available, offering you differing degrees of rigidity, lifetime expectancy and size.

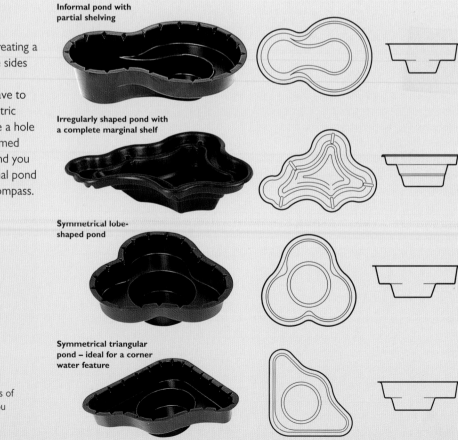

Informal pond with partial shelving

Irregularly shaped pond with a complete marginal shelf

Symmetrical lobe-shaped pond

Symmetrical triangular pond – ideal for a corner water feature

You will hand over the creativity of designing a pond to the manufacturer if you buy a ready-made pond, with the shelving, depth and contours already determined on your behalf. Choose one that has sections at least 60 to 100cm (2 to 3 feet) deep (or deeper) for overwintering. You will need to find a large pond retailer to view a good selection, with the range being limited on-site due to their sheer size (ask to see the full range available in the catalogue). Be aware that at the height of the season, there may be supply difficulties or increased waiting time for delivery from the manufacturer. If you choose a pond over 1,360 litres (300 gallons) – and it is best to do so – you will not be able to get it home in the boot of your car, so make sure the retailer will deliver it to you.

The most basic preformed pools are made from a very flexible plastic material that is moulded into various shapes. High-density polyethylene pools offer improved strength and puncture resistance and, although they are semi-rigid, they are capable of holding over 760 litres (166 gallons) when buried. The most durable, and popular, preformed pools are the rigid fibreglass types. Available in a range of volumes from under 190 litres (42 gallons) to well over 3,800 litres (833 gallons), these strong and durable ponds are built to last a lifetime.

Focus your choice

You need to have a good idea of the area of the garden that you want to give over to water. This will immediately allow you to focus on the preformed ponds that are the most appropriate for your plot. The models in your size range will offer different depths and shelving arrangements for marginal plants, some of which may be more to your liking than others.

INSTALLING A PREFORMED POOL

Installing a rigid pond is relatively straightforward. Levelling the pond can be the greatest challenge (and the biggest frustration). It's wise to level the pond as you fill it with water and backfill it with soil at several intervals.

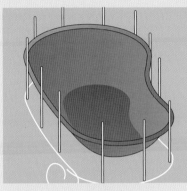

1 Mark out the perimeter of the pond with a length of rope, using the rigid pond liner as a guide.

2 Dig a hole a little bigger than the shape and depth of the pond. Place a loose covering of moist sand in the hole.

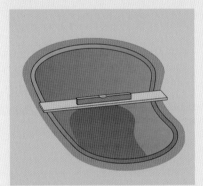

3 Place the pond in the hole. Check to see if it is level by using a plank of wood and a spirit level.

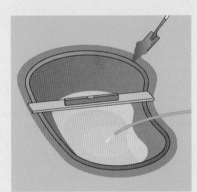

4 Begin filling the pond with a garden hose. As it fills, backfill the hole with soil or sand, checking regularly that the pond is level.

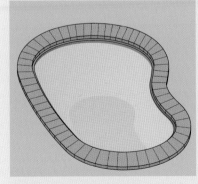

5 Add your chosen pond edging.

6 Start stocking the pond with plants and fish. (See pages 90 to 155.)

Concrete ponds

Concrete used to be the most common material for constructing a pond, but due to the ever-improving performance and guarantee of liners, it is rarely used nowadays.

It requires a great deal of skill and hard labour to construct a concrete pond. To allow for foundations and the concrete itself, you will need to excavate at least an extra 130cm (12 inches) in depth. You will need shuttering during the construction of the walls, and you will require several days of good weather to lay the concrete (and then several good weeks for it to set hard). The pond is finished with a smooth surface coat and a paint-on sealant to make it waterproof and prevent lime from leaching into the water, causing an extreme and unhealthy rise in pH. Concrete can be

brittle once set. Well-laid ponds can last a lifetime, but any hint of subsidence can lead to the formation of damaging cracks (which you wouldn't experience with a liner).

Deep ponds made specifically with koi in mind will have vertical sides. These are best made from concrete blocks placed on a concrete base and then sealed professionally by an application of several layers of fibreglass, topped with a final gel coat. This gives a pond a very professional finish that will last a lifetime, but the cost can be double that of a standard concrete pond.

Permanent feature
A concrete pond is hard to construct but can last a lifetime if done well.

INSTALLING A CONCRETE POND

Installing a concrete pond involves a lot of heavy work, but the end result can be robust and long lasting. A concrete pond requires a deeper excavation than other ponds (to allow for the foundations and thick concrete base and walls), and it will take several weeks before the pond is ready for plants or fish.

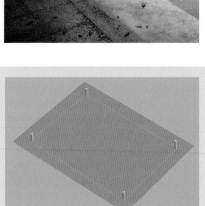

1 Remove any grass, and mark out the perimeter of the pond with pegs. Check that you are happy with the size and position.

2 Dig a hole a little bigger than the shape and depth of the pond. This is to allow for the depth of the concrete construction.

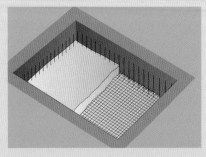

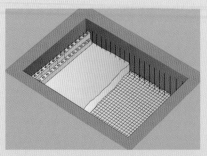

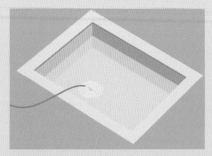

3 Line the bottom of the pond with compacted rubble, add reinforcing steel or mesh, and pour the concrete in one go. Level and smooth it out.

4 For vertical sides, use either concrete blocks or shuttering to support the concrete. Steel reinforcement will give the pond wall strength and rigidity, tying the walls to the base.

5 Having left the concrete and surface coat to cure for at least 3 weeks, you can fill the pond with water. Flush the pond through several times and monitor the pH.

Flexible pond liners

Pond liners offer flexibility in both the material used and the extent to which you can design a pond. Long gone are the days when a heavy-duty polyethylene sheet was the method for lining a pond. Today's pond liners have gone the way of pond pumps in that they have been re-engineered to meet expectations. They are made from materials such as pond-grade rubber and high-tech composites. Many are sold with a lifetime guarantee (in excess of 25 years) as long as they are installed correctly. Buy the best that you can afford, as generally, you do get what you pay for.

A liner should be installed over a protective underlay (so don't forget to figure this into your budget). If your liner does spring a leak, you can repair it with a patch and adhesive.

Liners are sold either pre-cut and packed or off the roll, depending on the size of the liner required. If your pond is bigger than the off-the-roll dimensions, a liner can also be spliced prior to delivery. Take your pond measurements to the store so that the staff can verify the area of liner you require.

The liner should fit into the boot of your car. Take extra care when preparing the excavation to protect against protruding stones or invasive roots. If you want the liner to last more than 25 years, you cannot expect it to do so if it is pressed down hard against a sharp object. For detailed instructions on installing a pond using a flexible liner, see page 30.

INSTALLING A BOG GARDEN

One excellent use for a flexible pond liner is to install a bog garden, providing a habitat for a range of marginal and bog plants and wildlife including amphibians such as frogs and newts. The pond liner keeps the soil moist and waterlogged.

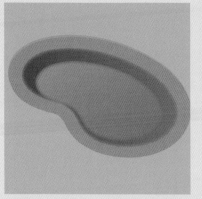

1 Dig a hole to the required size and shape for your bog garden. It should be between 45 to 60cm (1.5 and 2 ft) deep, and have sloping sides.

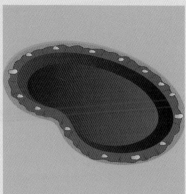

2 Cover the hole with a sheet of your chosen liner. Work the liner down into the hole, folding it to fit where necessary. Hold the edges in place with smooth stones.

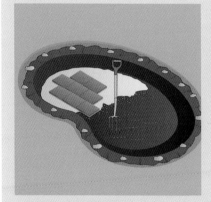

3 Puncture the liner with a fork around once every square yard. Place a layer of chippings on the bottom and then lay turf, grass-side down, on top.

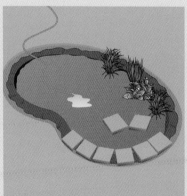

4 Fill in the hole with compost. Soak the compost thoroughly with a hosepipe. The bog garden is now ready for planting.

CALCULATING THE AMOUNT OF LINER YOU NEED

Measure the dimensions of your pond or bog garden: its length, width and maximum depth. You will need to add the depth measurement to the area measurement all around. For example, to line a pond 2.5 x 1.8 x 1m (8 x 6 x 3 feet) deep you will need a liner 4.5m/14 feet (2.5 + 1 + 1/8 + 3 + 3) by 3.8m/12 feet (1.8 + 1 + 1/6 + 3 + 3) in size. You then need to add 30cm (1 foot) to the width and length to allow overlap. In total, you will need a liner measuring 4.8 x 4.1m (15 by 13 feet).

Constructing a pond with flexible liner

Constructing a pond and waterfall using a flexible liner is the most popular way of creating a uniquely shaped pond. You can design the pond to any shape suitable for your garden, and then construct it using a few easy steps.

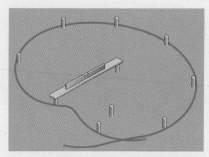

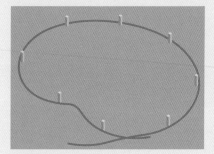

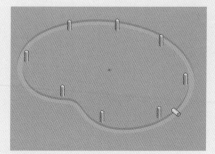

1 OUTLINE THE POND SHAPE

Once you have chosen the best location for your pond and settled on its size, finalize the shape by outlining it with a rope or garden hose. Remember to create an open shape that allows good water circulation (see page 16 for further discussion on pond shapes). Move and adjust the outline until you are completely happy with it from every direction. Include the waterfall in the outline to ensure that you can fit it in the plot as well as for measuring the liner.

2 LEVEL THE SITE

Levelling the site will create an attractive pond and make the whole installation process easier. It will also ensure that once filled, there will not be any unsightly exposed areas of liner around the perimeter. Knock in levelling pegs 1.2 to 1.8m (4 to 6 feet) apart along the pond outline. Make the first peg (the datum) level with the intended water level of the finished pond and adjust all pegs accordingly, using a straight-edged piece of wood and a spirit level, adding or removing topsoil until the tops of all the pegs are level.

3 CONSTRUCT A CONCRETE COLLAR

Dig a trench outside the outline, 15 to 23cm (6 to 8 inches) deep and as wide as the edging paving. Lay a pipe across the trench opposite the waterfall end, which is wide enough to carry the pump hose and any electrical cables. Lay the concrete collar in one go, levelling it off as you go, using the levelling pegs as a guide. Allow for the thickness of the paving so that it will sit level with the adjacent ground on top of the concrete. The liner will eventually run on top of this, sandwiched between the collar and the paving. Allow 48 hours for the collar to set.

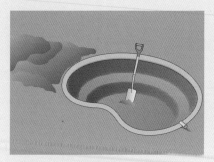

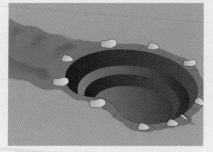

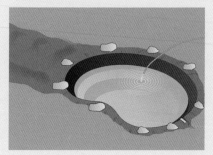

4 EXCAVATE THE POND

Mark the ground inside the collar where you intend to make a shelf for marginal plants. Do likewise for mid-level and deep-water areas. Shelves should be at least 30cm (12 inches) wide and 25cm (10 inches) deep below the top surface of the collar. Mid-level areas should go down to 37.5cm (15 inches) and the deepest areas should be at least 40 to 60cm (18 to 24 inches) deep. Near-vertical sides will give the pond a greater volume, which is desirable. Use the excavated soil to construct the waterfall, compacting every 30cm (12 inches) to give it a good foundation and forming the stepped cascade out of the compacted soil.

5 INSTALL THE LINER

Measure the maximum length, width and depth of the pond (to the outer edge of the collar and waterfall) to determine the area of the liner required (see page 29). You will also need the same area of protective underlay. Clean any loose soil from the hole, and check for stones and roots. Line the hole with underlay, and spray gently with water to help keep it in place. With the help of someone at each corner, walk the liner over the hole. Once it is in place, anchor the liner with stones or bricks placed around the edge. If you do this on a warm, sunny day, the liner will be supple and easy to work with.

6 FILL THE POND

Fill the pond with 15cm (6 inches) of water. This will start to mould the liner into the hole. As the liner starts to find its shape, gather any small creases into larger folds, making the liner as crease-free as possible. Make sure there is sufficient liner for covering the waterfall. Continue to fill the pond to the top. It may be necessary to get into the pond (be sure to remove your shoes) so that you can work out all the creases effectively. If you are able to fill the pond through a water meter, you will know the exact volume of your pond, which will then tell you what size pump and filter will be required.

ADAPTING THE POND EDGING

A beach makes an ideal edging for an informal pond. It also provides an easy means for wildlife to enter the pond. No concrete collar is required to create a beach, just a gently sloping bank that's closest to the preferred viewing point. A small retaining wall (out of sight and below the waterline) made from large cobbles or a preformed wall dug from the soil with the liner laid on top will prevent the beach from slipping into the pond. For the best effect, different-sized cobbles, pebbles and gravel should be used, with larger rocks randomly placed throughout (take your inspiration from nature). The liner beneath the cobbles must come up higher than the other banks, stretching 5cm (2 inches) past the waterline to prevent water loss by capillary action. Cover this excess in pebbles, cobbles and gravel. For an extra measure of safety, place a protective offcut of liner beneath the cobbles to protect the main liner from punctures. Over time, the beach will become colonized by plants, and you may even choose to insert a few into the gravel itself to help speed things along.

The finished pond

The use of natural stone around the perimeter and in the waterfall gives the pond a believable, natural appearance. Further creative planting in and around the pond finishes the effect. This pond has not long been finished, and the plants will spread over the coming months.

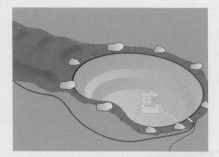

7 INSTALL THE PUMP AND FILTER

Place a submersible pump in the end opposite to the waterfall. Run the cable to the nearest power point and the hose around to the back of the waterfall, burying both. The location of the filter will be determined by its type. A pump-fed trickle filter should be placed above the waterfall and concealed in rockwork. A pressurized filter can be buried anywhere convenient. A skimmer filter will be adjacent to the pond. Ensure that all power is connected through a circuit breaker (RCD).

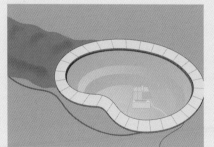

8 POSITION THE PAVING STONES

Depending on what material you choose for edging, position natural free-form rock or paving around the edge. If paving stones are your choice, place these on a bed of mortar on top of the concrete collar. The liner must come up behind the rock or paving to enable the pond to be filled all the way to the brim. If this is done correctly, you will avoid an unsightly border of liner being visible just above the surface of the water. If you use natural stone around the edge, remember to leave a gap for the electrical cord and hose.

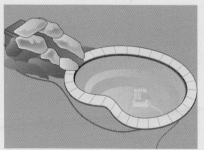

9 CONSTRUCT THE WATERFALL

Make a natural-looking waterfall from the same stone that was used around the pond. Place flat pieces of stone onto a bed of mortar, on steps you formed in the compacted mound of soil. Make the waterfall's path as irregular as possible. At the top of the waterfall, incorporate a waterfall box or a hose feeding from the pump via the pond's filter. You can now trim any excess liner from around the pond and waterfall. Once the waterfall has set and is running with water, position additional rocks to fine-tune the flow of water down the waterfall.

Pond pumps

If you're considering building a pond that features a fountain or waterfall or are looking to install an ultraviolet clarifier and filter, then you'll also need a pump.

A good pump is quiet and reliable and can almost be forgotten once installed. But if the pond pump fails, you stand to lose far more than the soothing effects of the fountain or waterfall.

Functional roles

A pump's lifesaving role is to circulate water through the pond filter. Without a pump, there is no filtration, which will lead to the deterioration of the water quality and health of the fish. The beneficial filter bacteria require a steady flow of aerated water to supply them with food and oxygen. If your pump malfunctions or its performance is reduced, then the colony of bacteria will deteriorate, leading to a similar deterioration in the water quality. If a pond experiences pump and filter problems, fish may be seen sulking or gasping at the surface as a result.

A pump may also circulate water through an ultraviolet clarifier (UV clarifier) to control green water (see page 39). Even though a UV clarifier is not 100 per cent efficient in flocculating all single-celled algae into filterable clumps in their first pass, its long-term relationship with a pump is essential for maintaining a clear pond.

Pumps can be installed with a dual role of water circulation and aeration, through the operation of a venturi device. This is most applicable in a gravity-fed filtration system, where the filter chambers are installed alongside the pond, running at the same level as the pond. In the final chamber, where the water is at its cleanest, a submersible pump can return the water to the pond through the pond wall via a venturi. The pressure provided by the pump causes air to be drawn into the flow through the venturi, leading to a jacuzzi-like aeration of the upper layers of the pond. If you want a venturi, check that your pump has the necessary power to drive one.

Aesthetic roles

A pump also has aesthetic functions. Fountains add another dimension to the life of a pond (see pages 22 to 23). With many different types of jet and fountainheads to choose from, you should find a fountain to your taste.

A pump may also power a waterfall. Waterfalls are more common than fountains in planted ponds because of the need to use some of the soil from the excavation as a feature or to incorporate a pump-fed filter (which will in turn feed a waterfall). Either way, a waterfall requires a larger pump than if a waterfall had not been installed.

Choosing the right pump for your pond

PUMP TYPE	SUITABLE POND SIZE	POSITION OF PUMP	TYPICAL TURNOVER RATE	COMPATIBLE WITH
SUBMERSIBLE FOUNTAIN PUMP	Any size – but only suited for running a fountain or ornament	Submersible, close to the fountain	Up to 1,800 litres (400 gallons) per hour for typical fountains	A pond containing a fountain or ornament
SUBMERSIBLE PUMP, CLOSE TO THE FOUNTAIN	Various sizes available to suit a range of ponds	Submersible, close to the fountain	1,800–3,200 litres (400–700 gallons) per hour	Small to medium ponds where pipe work and the filter can be concealed
SUBMERSIBLE FILTER/ WATERFALL PUMP	Up to 5,000 gallons – various sizes available to suit a range of ponds	Installed within the filter adjacent to the pond through the pond wall	3,200–7,000 litres (700–1,550) gallons per hour	External filter and/or waterfall
EXTERNAL PUMP	Larger ponds of several thousand gallons	External to a pond or external gravity-fed filter (not submersible)	8,100 litres (1,800) gallons or more per hour	External filter where it is used to return clean and filtered water back to the pond

Types of pumps

Two main types of pond pumps are available to the pondkeeper – the external or surface-mounted pump and the submersible pump.

External pumps are sited outside the pond. They should not get wet and ideally are installed in a small protective pump house. Water is sucked from the pond (or filter) through a rigid suction pipe or fed by gravity to a pump that sits below the waterline. These pumps are often referred to as swimming-pool pumps and are better suited to larger, more specialized situations where an above-average turnover of pond water is required. They are essential if a sand pressure filter is required as part of the filter system, as they are capable of pumping to high pressures.

Submersible pumps are by far the most popular. They are extremely versatile, being available in a range of sizes to suit most garden pond applications. They are very straightforward to install, and, having been developed in a very demanding market, are sold with lengthy guarantees.

Pump safety

When submersible pumps became mainstream in the trade, there was a degree of customer cynicism and aversion to dropping a standard voltage pump directly into a pond full of water (and expensive fish). There was a thriving alternative market for low-voltage pumps that represented less of a risk should water and electricity come into contact. However, as a consequence of their rugged design, submersible pumps have an excellent safety record; low-voltage pumps now occupy only a tiny part of the market. The pump casing that houses the electric motor is filled with liquid epoxy resin, which encases all electrical parts. The liquid epoxy resin sets, so the guts of the motor are sealed completely within the pump housing. To ensure complete safety, submersible pumps should be plugged into an outlet that is equipped with a circuit breaker (RCD). The only moving part is the impeller, which is located outside the motor casing, lubricated and cooled by the water.

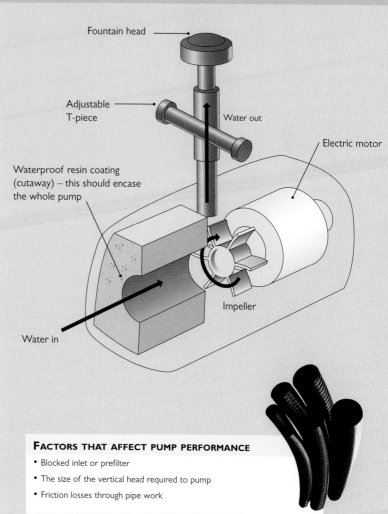

Submersible pump
The illustration shows the internal workings of a typical submersible pump, suitable for many kinds of ponds.

Fountain head

Adjustable T-piece

Water out

Electric motor

Waterproof resin coating (cutaway) – this should encase the whole pump

Impeller

Water in

FACTORS THAT AFFECT PUMP PERFORMANCE
- Blocked inlet or prefilter
- The size of the vertical head required to pump
- Friction losses through pipe work

Pipe work

Variations in pipe work between different systems can affect pump performance (including in-line items such as UV clarifiers and heaters.) When piping water from a pump to a filter, use sweeping bends in flexible tubing, if possible, and avoid "elbows". This will reduce the friction of the water in the pipe work. Always use the pipe diameter recommended by the pump manufacturer.

Turnover rate

A pond's volume should be turned over at least once every 2 hours. If your pond has a volume of 9,120 litres (2,000 gallons), you would need a pump capable of pumping 4,560 litres (1,000 gallons) per hour. Most data provided by pump manufacturers will relate to an ideal, weed-free pond with no restrictive pipe work. The work that a pump has to achieve in pumping water outside the pond – to a filter and waterfall – will also affect its performance.

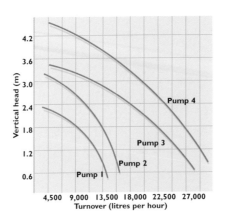

Pump performance curves

Let's say you have a 36,480-litre (8,000-gallon) pond and you need to pump 2.4m (8 feet) high. That means you need a pump with a turnover of at least 18,240 litres (4,000 gallons). Immediately, pumps 1 and 2 can be discounted, as they will not turn over your pond's volume every 2 hours (even at zero head). This leaves either pumps 3 or 4. As pump 3 will only just deliver 18,240 litres (4,000 gallons) at a head of 2.4 m (8 feet), it may underperform when it experiences the additional burdens of friction loss in the pipe work. Therefore, pump 4 should be the preferred choice.

Moving water vertically

If a pump has to move water vertically, its flow rate is reduced. The vertical distance between the water's surface and the delivery height of the pipe is known as the head. The greater the head, the lower the pump turnover. For example, if a pond has a volume of 9,120 litres (2,000 gallons) and requires a turnover of 4,560 litres (1,000 gallons) per hour, and it also has a waterfall that is 3 feet high, then a suitable pump would be one that provides a turnover of 4,560 litres (1,000 gallons) per hour at 1m (3 feet) of head.

For a waterfall to look realistic, with the full channel width covered in flowing water, sufficient water must be delivered by the pump to the top. A flow of at least 2,280 litres (500 gallons) per hour is required for a waterfall 15cm (6 inches) wide, and if a pump is not able to deliver this flow to the top of a waterfall, the effect will be a trickle rather than a cascading flow. Besides ensuring that the pump is sufficient for your pond and waterfall's demands, you will need to choose a filter that will be able to handle the flow rate required to make a waterfall look realistic.

When choosing a pump, opt for the largest one possible, as it will provide your fish with a superior environment in the long run. A greater flow rate can easily be reduced, but if the pump is too small, you'll have to buy a new one – an expensive mistake.

Vertical head

The vertical head is the distance between the surface of the pond and the top of the waterfall. Here, the head is approx. 1 metre (3 feet). Check that your pump will deliver sufficient volume to the vertical head required. (The output of most pumps is rated at a very flattering zero-m vertical head.)

1m (3 feet approx.)

Maintenance

Some pumps may be fitted with foam or perforated plastic prefilters to prevent the impeller from becoming blocked. These can reduce pump performance even when they are only partially blocked.

Garden ponds present some of the most demanding environments in which pumps are expected to perform. In response to pondkeepers' reluctance to get their hands wet for the sake of pump maintenance, manufacturers have re-engineered some of their models to handle solids. This means that, rather than clogging up with debris as they may have done before, pumps simply pass it through to the filter. Before buying a pump, check that it will handle solids. Where a pump is situated in the clear and filtered water of the final pump chamber of a gravity-fed filter system, pump blockages should not be a problem.

Buying the pump

Once you have calculated the volume of your pond, head requirements, and so on, you will have established your pump's required theoretical output. You then need to visit a pond specialist with a range of different pumps so that you can compare performance, power consumption and warranties. Handle each pump to see how rugged it feels and how easy it will be to clean or install into your system. Buy on value (over at least a 3-year period), rather than ticket price. Mail-order or Internet-based retailers may offer a good price, but check what service they offer in the event of a breakdown. Remember that a pump is synonymous with the pond's heart, and, if it fails, a speedy replacement is essential.

When choosing a pump, it can be very daunting to be presented with a vast array of different pump makes and models, each with its own features and performance claims. On the positive side, by virtue of the choice available, it is far more likely that you will find the pump that is just right for your pond.

Warranty

Most pumps are sold with a free extended warranty of anything up to 5 years. With standard maintenance and the use of correct pipe work that will not produce high back pressures, even these lengthy guarantees should be exceeded. Pumps are less likely to be temperamental if they are used continuously. Problems can occur if a pump becomes blocked with debris or blanketweed, choking the impeller and leading to burnout.

POWER CONSUMPTION

The running cost is a significant consideration when pricing a pump. Power consumption is measured in watts. Wattage will not always relate to the performance of a pump, as efficient designs enable some lower-wattage pumps to outperform pumps with larger motors. The difference in running costs over the guaranteed life span of two pumps could amount to the price of a new pump. Take pump running costs into account when considering which to buy.

For example, for every 100 watt difference between two pumps with the same output, the difference in running cost per year will be:

**1 year = 8,760 hours @ 100 watts =
876 KWh
if 1 KWh costs 10 pence.**

Total difference in running costs between two pumps over 1 year:

10 pence x 876 = £87.60

Over a 5-year life, this will cost £438.00, which might be the cost of a new pump.

Pump checklist

Your pond's requirements:
- Submersible or external pump?
- Pond volume (litres/gallons)
- Turnover required (relative to the pond's volume, the filter and a waterfall)
- Maximum head required
- Will it involve pumping up to a waterfall?
- If you're buying a replacement pump, what's the diameter of your existing pipe work?

Facts to compare when choosing between pumps:
- Turnover at your required head
- Reliability/reputation (i.e. what brand the retailer uses/recommends?)
- Maintenance/solids handling issues
- Power consumption (watts) and how that will affect running costs and overall cost of purchase
- Length and terms of guarantee
- Likely support in the event of a pump failure?
- Cost
- Length of electrical cable

Pump shopping list:
- Pump
- Tubing (correct diameter and length)
- Clips (stainless steel) for connecting tubing to pump
- Power cord plus outlet with circuit breaker (RCD).
- Spare prefilter
- T-piece and tubing fittings

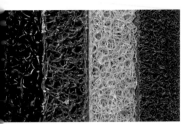

Pond filters

Admirers of a beautiful pond will be captivated by the tranquillity of cascading water and shoals of colourful fish gliding through the depths. Little do they know that the water's clarity and health are largely due to the pond filter.

If your objective when installing a pond is to re-create a slice of nature and to attract wildlife to your garden, then your pond will not require a filter. Such wildlife ponds are not heavily stocked with fish and can rely on dense planting to create and maintain the pond's balance. A pond filter is also optional if you want to make your pond a half-way house between a still-water wildlife pond and an ornamental fish pond, with a pump installed merely to add a little moving water "on demand".

Is a filter necessary?

Pond fish are just like any other animal in that they excrete waste that would be toxic if it accumulated in their bodies. The link between poor

sanitation and disease in humans has long been recognized. In the same way, fish are also threatened if they are exposed to a build-up of toxic waste; such risks can be reduced by installing a pond filter.

In natural water bodies, such as oceans, rivers or lakes, fish are in balance with their environment. These are so lightly stocked in relation to the water volume that there is no build-up of fish waste. This is not true in most garden ponds, however. Ponds are typically stocked with fish in all shapes, colours and sizes, well above the stocking density that is found in the wild. The fish require additional food to sustain them (as the pond will not provide sufficient food naturally). In a

similar way, there is insufficient natural bacterial action in ponds to break down the waste produced. In most cases, if there is no pond filter, there can be no fish.

Fortunately, you can buy effective garden pond filters, complete and ready to go, with many types of units fitting in the boot of a car. Note that adequate filtration cannot be achieved by the small foam prefilter placed on the intake of a pump (which is there mainly to protect the pump).

Supply of fresh water
A natural water body keeps clean by the constant flow of fresh water through it. In a garden pond, a filter is required to keep the recirculating water clean and healthy.

Filter choices

There are many different types of filter to choose from, each with its specific benefits and locations in and around the pond.

A. Internal filter – push-fits directly onto the pump, excellent for concealing a filter in a formal pond

B. External trickle filter – filter is pump-fed, and the clean water returns to the pond under gravity (often via a waterfall)
C. Pressurized filter – a pump-fed filter that is completely sealed and can be buried out of sight
D. Skimmer filter – positioned through the wall of the pond

E. External multi-chamber filter – gravity-fed via a bottom drain in the base of the pond; must be sited at the same level as the pond. Water returns to the pond via a pump in the final chamber.

The filter's roles

A filter performs several roles that help to maintain a suitable condition for the fish in the pond. Besides removing solid debris from the pond (material from fish, food and the garden), a filter matures to provide a supportive environment for beneficial bacteria that break down soluble waste. A biofilter gives a pond far more capacity for holding fish than an unfiltered pond. A filter also allows you to feed your fish more intensively, with a reduced risk of polluting your pond.

A submersible pump placed near the pond bottom will continually dump solid matter into the filter, keeping the pond clean and sediment free. Regular maintenance of the filter will mean that the need to clean out a silted-up pond will be put off for years, if not forever.

Filter options

Internal filters sit inside the pond and are only really suitable for smaller ponds. Internal pond filters generally consist of large foam blocks that replace the pump's strainer. They are easy to fit but have a tendency to block, reducing the output of the pump. Cleaning them can also disturb life within the pond.

External trickle filters consist of an external chamber (or chambers) placed outside the pond. They are either pump-fed or gravity-fed where the filter is buried and runs at the same level as the pond. The water from a gravity-fed filter is returned to the pond from the final chamber via a pump, whereas the water returning from a pump-fed filter, depending on the design, may return under gravity or under pressure from the pump.

Pump-fed single-chamber filter units (trickle or pressurized) are the most widely used. They can be installed in minutes (even on an existing pond), and, because the largest units can filter a 7,600-litre (1,670-gallon) pond, it is easy to find an off-the-shelf filter for most ponds.

One of the challenges when installing a pump-fed trickle filter is figuring out how to conceal it. Often, it might be hidden behind rock work, feeding a waterfall.

Pressurized filters are totally sealed and can be buried, with the return consisting of tubing feeding directly into the pond or via a waterfall. This makes pressure filters sympathetic to the natural look – with no visual clues given as to how the pond is sustained. Because of their relatively small size, they tend to block quickly and need regular maintenance. They are suited to smaller ponds.

Skimmer filters are gravity-fed from the surface of the pond, "skimming" it of any debris, and creating a clean, glassy surface. Installed (and concealed) adjacent to the pond through the pond wall, a skimmer filter houses the filter media, UV clarifier and pump, which returns the filtered water via a waterfall.

External multichamber filters are tailored to ponds containing several thousand gallons, usually heavily stocked with koi. Gravity-fed filters need to be planned as part of the pond's design and consist of a series of chambers, divided into mechanical and

FILTER TYPE	SUITABLE FOR POND SIZE (RANGE)	POSITION	HOW IT IS FED	TYPE OF POND FOR WHICH IT IS SUITABLE
INTERNAL	Up to 1,900 litres (420 gallons)	Hidden out of sight within the pond, attached directly to the pump	Water drawn through it by the pump	Small ponds – especially raised ponds, as no pipe work is required
EXTERNAL TRICKLE	Up to 7,600 litres (1,700 gallons) – various sizes available to suit	Positioned outside the pond, where it can be concealed at the head of a waterfall	Via tubing from a submersible pump	Small to medium ponds where pipe work and the filter can be concealed
SKIMMER	Up to 19,000 litres (4,200 gallons) – various sizes available to suit	Installed adjacent to the pond through the pond wall	Via gravity, taking water from the surface	Medium to large ponds
PRESSURIZED	Up to 5,700 litres (1,300 gallons) – various sizes available to suit	Buried out of sight – anywhere between the submersible pump and return to the pond	Via a submersible pump	Small garden ponds
GRAVITY-FED EXTERNAL MULTICHAMBER	From 3,800 litres (850 gallons) upwards	Adjacent to a pond, set at the same level as the pond	Via gravity, from a bottom drain constructed in the pond's bottom	Large koi ponds

biological functions. These units can be bought off the shelf or constructed in situ with the pond out of concrete blocks and fibreglass – something for the serious koi keeper with a handsome budget to spend.

How filters work

The guts of a filter are made up of inert, washable filter media – usually a porous biofoam (in several grades), used in conjunction with ceramic media or broken pipe work. The media will take months to fully mature. Rinse it carefully during any maintenance, trying not to disrupt the beneficial bacteria.

A filter has two complementary functions. The first is to remove solid matter pumped from the pond. This varies in size from fallen leaf matter to microscopic particles that make the water slightly cloudy. Solids removal enhances the subsequent biological filtration processes. Most filter space should be designated for solids

removal, as debris will soon collect (especially if a UV clarifier is installed) and be passed through to the other filter media.

Entrapment is the method used in standard external black box biofilters, where two or three grades of foam, from coarse to fine, trap solids as they pass through. Acting in a similar way to a sieve, the first filter media that the pumped dirty water encounters is quite coarse in structure, trapping and removing suspended solids from the water.

Once the solids are removed, the clear water passes through the part of the filter designed for biofiltration. The biofilter is colonized by millions of beneficial bacteria whose role is to consume and break down the toxic ammonia that is constantly excreted by the fish and other organisms.

The beneficial bacteria will colonize any hard surfaces (including the pond liner, pipe work and rock work),

Hidden filtration
The sturdy casting allows a pressurized filter to be buried out of sight.

making them feel slippery and slimy. A biofilter is designed to provide a vast surface area that these bacteria can colonize, equivalent to many square yards of a natural pond or lake bottom.

Keeping a filter alive

The steady turnover of water through the filter provides the bacteria with a constant source of "food" in the form of ammonia, as well as an essential supply of dissolved oxygen.

As this vital part of filtration is "living", unlike mechanical filtration, the bacterial colony takes time to become established, and a filter must be broken in gently over the first months of its life. Add fish a few at a time, so that the bacteria can adjust and catch up with the rate of ammonia being produced by the fish. (For more about the nitrogen cycle, ammonia, and maturing a filter, see page 174.)

Filter maintenance

Filters must be treated like the living entities they are. If they are not provided with oxygen, water and food, they will deteriorate and die. For this reason, a biofilter must be run continuously, ensuring that the bacteria are provided with the materials for life.

There are times when the filter must be cleaned and maintained. In the summer especially, waste will build up rapidly within filter media, and these should be cleaned out before they clog or restrict the filter. This can be done without disturbing the more sensitive biofilter.

In a box filter, where the foam layers may act as both mechanical and biological media, take care when rinsing out the foams. Bacteria are very sensitive to changes in their environment and any adverse action could set the filter's maturity and efficiency back months. For this reason, when rinsing out the foams or cleaning any biological media, buckets of pond water should be used. If unfiltered tap water is used, chlorine and other variations in the water quality can have a detrimental effect on the bacteria.

External multi-chamber filter

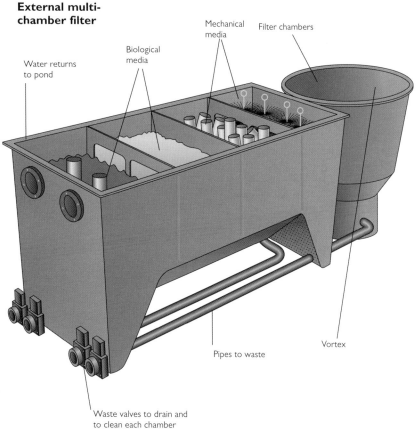

Water returns to pond

Biological media

Mechanical media

Filter chambers

Pipes to waste

Vortex

Waste valves to drain and to clean each chamber

ANATOMY OF A UV CLARIFIER

A filter also provides the opportunity to install an ultraviolet clarifier between the pump and the filter. The size of the UV clarifier required is determined by the volume of the pond and is a guaranteed method of creating a pond with crystal-clear water. A UV clarifier causes the algal cells to clump together, but unless a filter is installed to remove these clumps of dying algae, they will simply recirculate around the pond.

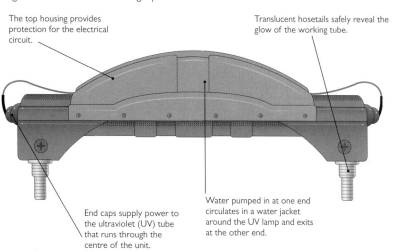

The top housing provides protection for the electrical circuit.

Translucent hosetails safely reveal the glow of the working tube.

End caps supply power to the ultraviolet (UV) tube that runs through the centre of the unit.

Water pumped in at one end circulates in a water jacket around the UV lamp and exits at the other end.

Pond lighting

Lighting is not essential, but it can be used creatively in and around a pond to convey different moods and effects.

Lighting does not assist the health or well-being of fish or plants, and most ponds manage beautifully without it. But underwater lighting can extend the entertainment from a pond into the night, creating a focal point of sight and sound, while subtle lighting can be used to delineate a path or give a lit backdrop to your pond.

Benefits of lighting

Artificial lighting allows you to beam light upwards out of a pond, bounce it off the underside of a bridge or shine it from beneath stepping stones. It also allows you to see your fish illuminated from below, so you can watch their silhouettes moving about in the twilight.

Simple underwater spotlights can be used to cast shadows in crystal-clear water. They can also be used outside a pond; their low-wattage bulbs will not overheat, and they are weatherproof.

Power options

Standard voltage underwater lighting consists of single spotlights supplied on their own bases. Like other underwater lights, interchangeable colored lenses may be available.

The vast majority of underwater lights are low voltage, as they pose less risk than standard-voltage lights. Unlike submersible pumps, lights cannot be encased in resin to make them watertight but must be accessible for maintenance and bulb changes.

A low-voltage light system requires a transformer to drop the current down to 12 or 24 volts. The transformer is usually housed indoors in a well-ventilated site. Some (resin-encased) transformers can be sited within the

Night-time feature
Pond lighting can combine very effectively with garden lighting to form a beautiful night-time display – furthering your enjoyment from the pond and garden.

Lighting options

Submerged lights:
- May be single spotlights
- Multiple lights may be fixed to the pump
- Choice of white or coloured lenses.

Fountain lights:
- Illuminate the water as it is ejected through a fountain head
- Ejected water picks up the light "fibre-optic-style" as it cascades onto the pond

Floating lights:
- Solar and low-voltage options
- Available in various shapes and sizes, including a floating Plexiglass ball

Fibre-optic lights:
- Have the benefit that many lights can be generated and controlled from a single remote light source

pond, which eliminates the risk of overheating. A benefit of low-voltage lighting is that the wiring installation may be tool-free, using clamping systems that pinch through the cable to make contact – inconceivable for standard-voltage lighting.

Solar-powered lights have an integral battery that is charged by a solar panel during the day. At night, a photocell in the light switches the light on (a feature also found in many low-voltage systems). To be most effective, these lights must be installed in direct sunlight, as their night-time output is directly related to the power stored during the day. They are not as bright as low-voltage lights, providing more of a glow, and do have limitations in the winter months.

Choosing lights

Unlike the choice of other pond hardware, the lighting you choose comes down to personal taste. The biggest considerations will be the light output, number of lights, desired effect and length of electrical cord required. If you choose low-voltage lighting, you need to decide where to locate the transformer, as this will determine the length of cable needed. Add 20 per cent extra to the planned length when purchasing cable.

Running costs: Solar-powered units have no electrical running costs; the only expense is replacement bulbs. Low-voltage running costs will amount to several pence each day (or night) for an average pond. The wattage displayed on your transformer will give you the best indication for power consumption of your lights. Standard-voltage lights are the brightest and most powerful of the three options and so will consume more power.

Other essentials: A circuit breaker (RCD) is required for safety purposes with underwater lighting. A circuit breaker should be fitted as standard to the electrical supply of any pond. Put the lighting on its own dedicated supply so that if the circuit trips, it doesn't affect the pump.

Additional cable and waterproof connectors will be necessary when standard lights are used.

Lighting controls: Lights can be controlled using a simple switch (ideally located inside the house). Or a simple light-sensor may be used to switch the lighting on automatically as dusk falls. Some lighting units are now supplied with a remote-control that can be used to operate or dim the lights.

Maintenance: The most common and regular maintenance carried out on underwater lighting is cleaning the light/lens to remove algae and slime. Be sure to do this when the light is turned off.

Guarantees: Many light units are available with guarantees longer than 12 months. Replacement bulbs are usually standard halogen-type and are available at most hardware stores.

Fibre-optic lighting

Fibre-optic based lighting systems offer many benefits over conventional pond lighting systems. Fibre-optic technology allows up to 16 different light fixtures to be driven off just one lightbulb. This means that the light box can be remote from the pond, with the fibre-optic cables transmitting the light risk-free into the garden and pond. Should it need replacing, only one bulb is required rather than 16 – and all that without getting your hands wet or disturbing your pond!

There is no heat or electricity in the pond, and the inconspicuous light apertures at the end of each fibre-optic cable means that they are easy to hide and position in and around the pond – waterfalls are a speciality.

Furthermore, colourwheel technology means that with just the flick of a (remote-control) switch, white light can be transformed into a rainbow of colours that moves throughout your pond and garden. This dynamic lighting effect is something that cannot be achieved with standard pond lighting.

Lighting choices
Fibre optic lights (left) are small and easy to conceal in the pond. Low-voltage halogen lights (right) look more conventional and give out more light.

Accent lighting
A tiny, well-concealed, underwater fibre-optic light illuminates the planted margins of a pond.

STOCKING PLANTS AND FISH

Having carefully planned and constructed your pond, it's time to bring it to life with plants and fish. These will be the players on the stage that you have created – putting on a show in your water garden. The plants must be chosen wisely to create the effect you are seeking, as well as to help to mature and balance your pond – ready for the fish. These too need to be introduced with care and you will benefit from some practical information on how to spot and treat any health issues, should they arise. If all goes to plan, the fish may eventually breed. Your pond will also continue to mature courtesy of the developing diversity of wildlife that sees it as a suitable environment to inhabit – what a compliment!

Planting basics

Once you have designed and constructed your pond, and thus determined the space that you can allocate for plants, you need to set about selecting and installing the various types of plants.

It will soon become apparent that, compared with garden plants, pond plants are more prolific and rampant, so you will need to give your pond frequent maintenance to keep the planting in balance and proportion.

The more conventional method of installing plants in a pond is to plant them into baskets. (In a natural, clay-bottomed pond, you may plant specimens directly into the pond bottom.) Planting baskets are the pond's equivalent to garden pots and are ideally suited to the plants' needs as well as the pondkeeper's.

SEE ALSO
Plant directory,
page 96

A typical planted basket

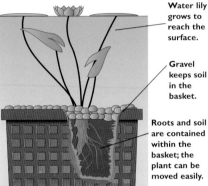

Water lily grows to reach the surface.

Gravel keeps soil in the basket.

Roots and soil are contained within the basket; the plant can be moved easily.

A variety of planting types
This pond contains: submerged plants – water lilies emerge from planted baskets located on the pond bottom; marginals – variegated iris breaks up the straight pond edging; and floating and submerged oxygenating plants beneath the surface. A formal, hard-edged pond like this is not suitable for bog plants.

TIP: HEALTHY PLANTS

To avoid introducing rogue pests, such as snails, pondweed or diseases into your pond, check all new plants for signs of ailments.

Choosing baskets

Planting baskets are made from dark plastic (to remain unobtrusive) and come in different sizes and shapes (square, round, kidney-shaped and so on) to suit different areas of the pond. Baskets give you control over some plants' rampant nature by retaining their roots in a confined space and curtailing their growth to some degree.

Because an artificially lined pond will not be lined with a soft-rooting media (in fact, it is desirable for it to be relatively sediment-free), plants will thrive only if they are rooted into a basket containing soil. The porous nature of the basket enables water to move through the soil, allowing easier uptake of nutrients and the roots to breathe. Individually basketed plants are also easier to maintain. They can be removed from the pond (but don't strain your back – even in a basket, plants can grow into a heavy mass), be thinned, rebasketed and returned to the pond. Solid plastic pots are an acceptable alternative to baskets and contain the soil securely to prevent it from ending up on the pond bottom.

A collection of baskets or pots also enables you to grow a diverse selection of plants, preventing the more vigorous plants from overrunning and outcompeting more delicate varieties – something that is virtually impossible in a natural clay-bottomed pond.

Installing the finished baskets

Place the finished baskets directly into their final positions by lowering them gently, saturating the soil until it sits comfortably under its own weight in position. See pages 46 to 55 for more details on how to install each type of plant.

Preparing the plant and potting: Once the plant has been prepared, fill the lined basket with soil, add the plant, and add more soil to 2.5cm (1 inch) below the rim, making sure the soil is pressed down. If planting a marginal plant that is likely to grow tall and catch the wind, insert some stones in the bottom of the basket, for stability. If you are potting a plant that requires a lot of feed, place a slow-release fertilizer tablet in the centre of the basket on top of the infill soil before you add the plant and remaining soil to prevent the tablet from making direct contact with the plant roots. Specimen plants in very large containers will require several fertilizer tablets.

Basket and lining: You will need to line the basket with a piece of hessian, pond liner underlay, or foam, unless it has a suitable microfine mesh that will retain the soil. Do not allow soil to leach into the pond because this will encourage algae and may even discolour the water.

Soil: A heavy loam soil is best for baskets. If your own garden soil is suitable, ensure that it does not contain too much organic matter (which will start to rot and "sour" the water) or fertilizer, which may encourage algae. Select soil that is labelled for aquatic use, since other bagged mixes may contain ingredients that can be detrimental in the water.

Top with gravel: Finish off the basket with a 2.5-cm (1-inch) deep layer of fine gravel on top of the soil. This will retain the soil within the basket and give the basket added weight and stability, as well as preventing instinctively inquisitive pond fish from rooting into the soil in search of a tasty morsel.

Floating plants

Floating plants are able to thrive without being rooted into the soil. They will either float on the pond surface or be slightly submerged, and they range in size and complexity from a tiny single leaf and rootlet (*Azolla*) up to a flowering plant several feet wide (*Stratiotes aloides*).

SEE ALSO
Plant directory, page 96
Invasive plants, page 66

The obvious benefit of having floating plants in a pond is their ease of planting and, conversely, their ease of removal (except for *Azolla* and *Lemna*). They will drift around your pond, absorbing the nutrients they need directly from the water. They give a new pond instant cover, which will help to shade against nuisance algae, and provide an excellent habitat for fish and their fry.

Floating plants in winter

Several of the larger and more ornamental floating plants will not overwinter well, dying back at below 10°C (50°F). Such plants are best viewed as aquatic bedding plants that can be replaced each year. Remove them completely prior to frost to prevent the decaying matter from remaining in the pond.

Water lettuce
Water lettuce is a delicate floating plant that will not survive a frost.

Bright green foliage is covered with microscopic hairs that cause water droplets to run off.

Fine roots take up nutrients directly from the pond water.

Fine hairs on the long roots act as a haven for fish fry and aquatic invertebrates.

Water hyacinth
Water hyacinth floats on the pond surface, courtesy of its bulbous stems. In the height of summer, water hyacinth will produce violet flowers (see page 96).

Thriving water hyacinth will produce daughter plants.

Very delicate black roots enable the plant to thrive without being rooted in soil.

Top floating plants

Frog's bit
(*Hydrocharis morsus-ranae*)

Water hyacinth
(*Eichhornia crassipes*)

Water chestnut
(*Trapa natans*)

Water lettuce
(*Pistia stratiotes*)

Water soldier
(*Stratiotes aloides*)

Spreading plants

The smaller, less complex floating plants (for example, *Azolla* or *Lemna*) will overwinter in a temperate zone and also have a reputation for spreading rapidly. What may have seemed a good idea initially for instant cover may actually result in an ever-present plague that you cannot completely eradicate. If your pond becomes covered, the water will suffer from reduced light and oxygen. Many ponds have become overrun by floating plants unintentionally, where the first few fragments may have been introduced on other plants or having been carried by birds – that's why *Lemna minor* is called duckweed. (See also Invasive plants, page 56.)

Choosing floating plants

If you need some instant summer cover and colour, choose larger floating plants. If you are contemplating adding a small leafed floater such as *Lemna* or *Azolla*, think carefully, as it could invade your pond and be impossible to remove later. However, bear in mind that neither of these floating plants establish heavily in ponds with large ornamental fish, who consider it a natural delicacy.

Water soldier

One floater that is to be encouraged is the water soldier, *Stratiotes aloides*. This plant floats beneath the surface, trailing its roots speculatively down to the pond bottom. It acts as an oxygenator, and its structure is so tough that it resists grazing by fish and snails. It will produce smaller whole plants that can be broken off the parent plant. Water soldiers rise to the surface to flower in the summer and sink to the bottom to survive the winter.

Removing duckweed

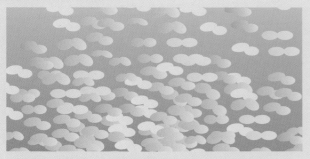

1 Duckweed can soon cover the surface of a pond, starving it of light and oxygen.

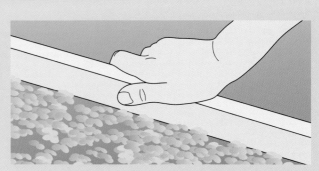

2 Using a length of wood, push the duckweed to one end, where it can be netted out. Alternatively, cause the pond to overflow by running a hose into it. The water will take the floating duckweed with it.

Marginal plants

As their name suggests, marginal plants are found around the pond's margin. To differentiate them from bog plants (see page 52), marginals are planted in baskets or containers within the boundary of the pond. However, some bog plants and marginals can be planted interchangeably.

SEE ALSO

Bog plants, page 52
Plant directory, page 96

The key attribute for marginal plants is that their roots are likely to be permanently submerged in water and are adapted to variations in water levels, such is the unpredictable and ever-changing life on the water's edge. In a natural pond or stream, marginal plants will help to stabilize the bank and, depending on the species, will tend to show a preference for either spreading into the water or onto the land. Consequently, although not essential for their survival in your pond, it is prudent to see at what depth specific marginals that you choose for your pond prefer to be planted at, bearing in mind that your marginal shelf will be approximately 23 to 30cm (9 to12 inches) deep, and deeper for areas intended to hold tall, bold-foliaged plants.

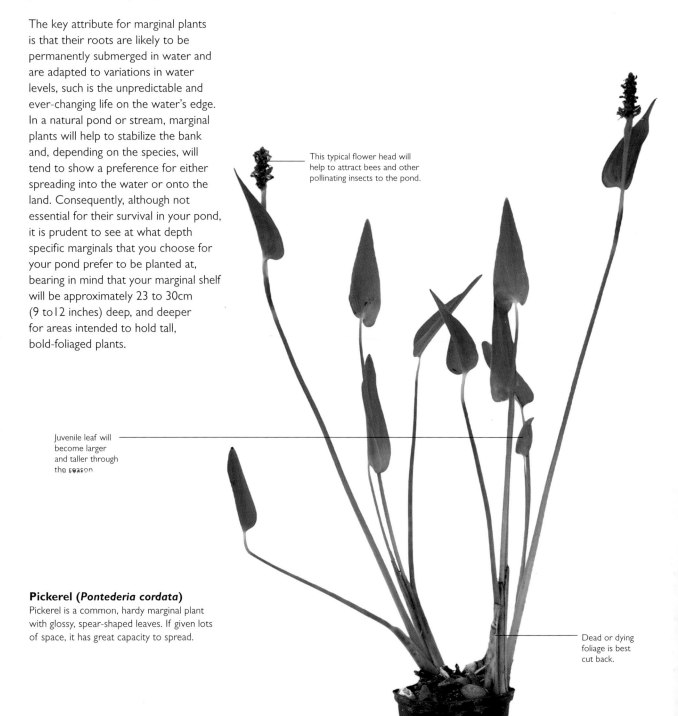

This typical flower head will help to attract bees and other pollinating insects to the pond.

Juvenile leaf will become larger and taller through the season

Dead or dying foliage is best cut back.

Pickerel (*Pontederia cordata*)
Pickerel is a common, hardy marginal plant with glossy, spear-shaped leaves. If given lots of space, it has great capacity to spread.

Choosing marginals

Choose marginal plants on the basis of what your pond needs to make it look natural. They are ideal for breaking up any harsh lines created by an artificial pond edge or for masking any exposed liner or pipework. A well-planted margin helps the pond to merge with the rest of the garden and is an open invitation for wildlife. In garden terms, the marginals are the pond's equivalent of an herbaceous border.

Marginal categories

Marginals can be categorized into four types as an aid for deciding how each plant is best used in your pond. Continuing with the gardening principle, shorter plants work best in the foreground, taller plants at the rear. Your choice of plants and their positions should be determined by the pond's viewing point.

Creepers and ground-covering marginals
Creepers and ground covers are ideal at covering the "feet" (and baskets) of all other marginals, introducing real informality.

Marsh marigold
(*Caltha palustris*)

Water mint
(*Mentha aquatica*)

Blue flag iris
(*Iris versicolor*)

Sweet flag
(*Acorus calamus*)

Cardinal flower
(*Lobelia cardinalis*)

Intermediate marginals
Intermediate marginals like this water forget-me-not (*Myosotis palustris*) grow to a moderate height, and some will flower vigorously.

Strong vertical marginals
Strong verticals, such as iris, provide height at the back of the pond. These structural plants set off the plants in the foreground.

Specimen marginals
Individual feature plants like these variegated irises, create a natural focus and talking point for the pond due to their size and display.

DIVISION OF A MARGINAL POND PLANT

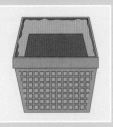

1 Remove the established plant from its basket.

2 Divide the plant and roots in two.

3 Prepare and line new baskets for replanting.

4 Replant the divided plant in separate containers.

5 Place the baskets back in the pond.

Submerged plants

Plants will inhabit a pond at all levels, from those whose roots sit on the bottom to those that emerge from the pond, getting only their feet wet.

SEE ALSO
Plant care, page 44
Plants, page 88
Plant directory, page 96

In a natural pond, plants will colonize at all levels over successive years, rooting in the soft sediment that accumulates at the bottom and then directly into the clay. The artificially constructed pond using an impregnable liner will prevent plants from rooting naturally, so you need to step in and provide the planting substrate yourself. You should do this in a way that confines it, so that soil will not discolour the water, encourage the growth of algae, and prevent fish from foraging into the soft aquatic soil – something they will do naturally and ever so eagerly.

Installation

Pond plants purchased from a garden centre are usually already potted up. However, there will come a time when plants will become too big for a basket (and perhaps even your pond) and will need repotting. An increasing number of plants are now available loose via mail order and also need to be planted up. This is particularly true for water lilies. Spring (or shortly after you have installed a new pond) is the best time to pot up plants. You can also pot them in the summer, when certain plants become rampant and need thinning out.

YOUNG LILY SPECIMEN

Don't cut back the young unfurled leaves.

Tuber full of energy

Healthy-looking roots; trim back stragglers.

Trim back open, brown, or damaged leaves.

TOP SUBMERGED PLANTS

Water hawthorn (*Aponogeton distachyos*)

Pond lily (*Nuphar* species)

Golden club (*Orontium aqauticum*)

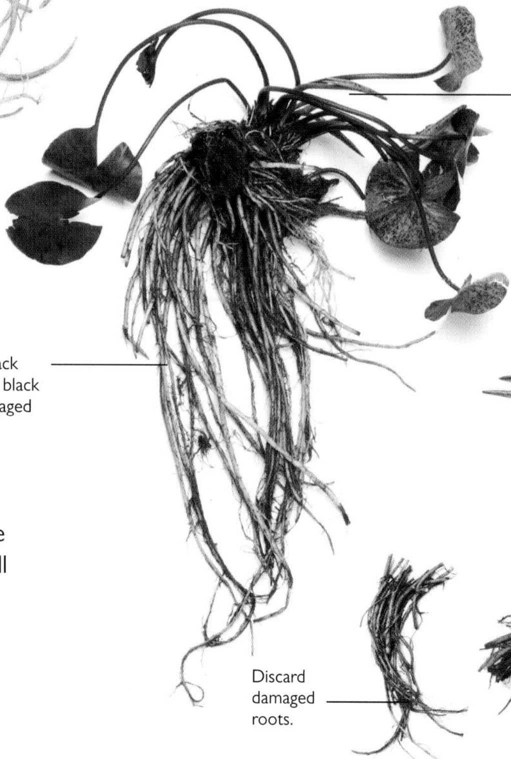

OLDER LILY SPECIMEN

Spear-like leaves ready to emerge; retain these.

Snail damage

LILY READY FOR POTTING UP

Young flower buds

Discard damaged leaves.

Use secateurs to make clean cuts.

Trim away old fibrous roots.

Trim back brown, black or damaged roots.

Examine the plant

Lily plants, especially those supplied via mail order, will consist of an "eye" that has been removed from the starch-rich parent rootstock. Check for the points shown here.

Discard damaged roots.

Keeping the ecosystem in balance

The combination of good coverage by water lilies and other plants will help keep the pond balanced and free from nuisance algae. A planted pond also provides fish and pond life with a diversity of niches to exploit.

TIP: HEALTHY PLANTS

To avoid introducing rogue pests, such as snails, pondweed or diseases into your pond, check all new plants for signs of ailments. Always remove new plants from their containers, and wash them in cold running water.

POTTING UP A WATER LILY

1 Using pruners or a sharp knife, cut back to within about 5cm (2 inches) of the crown any older roots or ones that are damaged or too long. Leave only spear-like foliage close to the crown, and any flower buds.

2 Line the basket with burlap or thin foam squares. Both liners retain the soil within the basket and allow the soil and plant to breathe.

3 Fill the basket half full with aquatic soil. Add a slow-release fertilizer tablet beneath where the plant will be positioned. Put the prepared lily into position. Add further soil and tamp it down.

4 Carefully add a 2.5-cm (1-inch) deep layer of fine, smooth gravel to just below the rim and firm down. The gravel will help to retain the soil and prevent fish from uprooting plants. Trim off excess liner.

5 Place on a stack of bricks in the position where the lily will be sited, so that the top of the planted basket is no more than 3cm (1 inch) below the surface. As the leaves start to extend, remove the bricks until the basket is on the pond bottom.

Bog plants

Bog plants are not true pond plants but, rather, normal garden plants that prefer wet or very moist soil.

Bog plants can either make a stand-alone bog feature or form part of the planting in and around a pond. Bog plants give you the opportunity to spread the water garden's boundaries until they blend with your other garden plants.

SEE ALSO

Pond shapes, page 16
How to install a bog garden, page 29

Astilbe

Astilbe is a slow-growing bog plant capable of stunning floral displays. It is very hardy and grows best in damp rather than wet soils.

Characteristic "feathery" flowers last a long time relative to other flowering bog plants.

Hosta

Hosta is a very popular, easy-growing bog plant. It's available in a range of foliage and flower types and dies back completely in the winter.

Hosta is available in different flowering varieties.

Rich, moist soil will encourage the hosta to spread and thrive.

Planting in a bog area, unbounded by a pot or basket, will greatly encourage growth.

Bog conditions

Bog plants are adapted to exploit the potentially highly fertile and moist soil that is created by the water table being just beneath the soil's surface. Such a feature in a garden is usually created artificially (see page 29), but damp, shady spots can also occur naturally in many north-facing gardens.

Being land plants, bog plants are not grown in baskets but are planted directly into the soil. Do not allow a bog garden to become waterlogged or dry out. As the bog matures, it will develop into an area of lush, deep greens and will evolve as the plants enjoy their free-range existence.

Feature bog plant
Zantedeschia aethiopica is a is a striking, perennial marginal plant that produces stunning funnel-like spathes high above the water's surface.

TOP BOG PLANTS

Plantain lily
(*Hosta fortunei*)

Astilbe
(*Astilbe arendsii*)

Royal fern
(*Osmunda regalis*)

Lady's mantle
(*Alchemilla mollis*)

Primula
(*Primula* spp. eg *Primula japonica*)

Vulnerable to attack
Slugs thrive in damp, shady, boggy areas and will decimate the soft foliage of a hosta. Fortunately, frogs will not be far away as a natural control for these pests.

Locating bog plants

The larger the area you can dedicate to the bog garden the better, giving you greater display options and transforming a pond quite literally into a water garden. You will find that each bog plant will have a preferred position along the moisture spectrum, with iris and lobelia preferring wetter conditions closer to the pond, and astilbe and hosta preferring a drained but moist soil, adjacent to the other garden plants.

You will find bog plants in garden centres among marginal pond plants, but you will also discover them intermixed with garden plants, requiring you to hunt them out and check their suitability and preferred location.

Oxygenating plants

As their name suggests, the main function of this group of submerged, lush green and fast-growing plants is to release oxygen into the pond.

SEE ALSO
Recycling nutrients, page 162
The web of life, page 164
Pond chemistry, page 166

Oxygenator functions

Oxygenators are essential for any pond and should be among the first plants you buy. Besides being net producers of oxygen, these very functional plants also provide shelter for aquatic invertebrates, your own home-grown fry and other tiny pond life. A good spread of oxygenating plants also provides cover for your fish to hide away from the hungry heron, and helps to guard against a bloom of green water in a new pond.

The spiny foliage is resistant to snail or fish damage.

Ceratophyllum (hornwort)
Ceratophyllum will grow well without being planted. It does not produce roots but absorbs all its nutrients directly from the water.

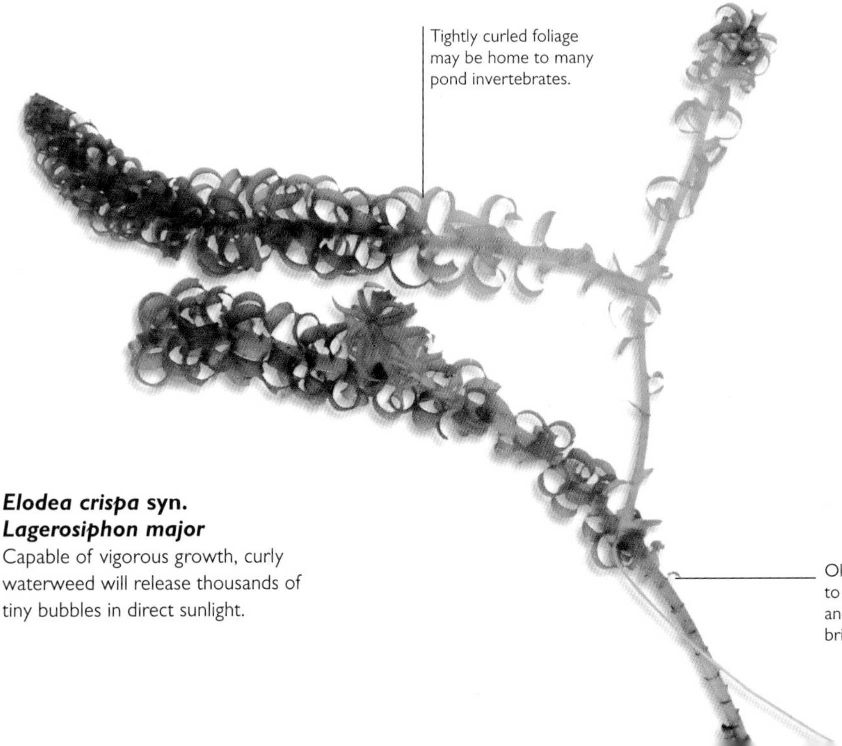

Small fragments will soon grow into a larger mass of oxygenating plant.

Tightly curled foliage may be home to many pond invertebrates.

Choosing oxygenators

Not only are oxygenators the least ornamental of plants, they are also the least expensive. A new pond will benefit from having the oxygenators spaced regularly across the bottom to stimulate growth toward the light. A pond will benefit from a diversity of different types of oxygenators to encourage a diversity of wildlife, with each behaving differently in a pond. Hornwort, for example, is much tougher than the lush *Anacharis* and resists being eaten by snails and fish.

Elodea crispa syn.
Lagerosiphon major
Capable of vigorous growth, curly waterweed will release thousands of tiny bubbles in direct sunlight.

Older stems will start to lose their foliage and become more brittle with age.

Excessive growth

Collectively referred to as pondweed, oxygenators spread quickly. This is ideal for a new pond, but they should not be released into the wild as they are mostly invasive. They can be cut back very easily in the knowledge that if even a small amount remains, it will have the capacity to grow back. A sign that pondweed needs to be thinned out is when the stems that grow up vertically from the pond bottom reach the surface and start to creep horizontally just below the water's surface. Excessive oxygenator growth can paradoxically lead to a dawn depletion of oxygen after warm, muggy summer nights and will soon make your fish gasp for oxygen.

Negative effect

Hornwort is an effective oxygenator that will give out oxygen in the day but, like other oxygenators, will also remove it from the pond at night.

TOP OXYGENATING PLANTS

Goldfish weed
(*Lagarosiphon major*)

Hornwort
(*Ceratophyllum demersum*)

Water soldier
(*Stratiotes aloides*)

Water milfoil
(*Myriophyllum aquaticum*)

Water violet
(*Hottonia palustris*)

PLANTING OXYGENATORS

Usually sold in bunches held together with a heavy metal weight, oxygenators are best planted right at the bottom of the pond, in a mesh basked (see page 45 for more on choosing baskets). Hornwort does not require a basket and can be weighted to the bottom of the pond.

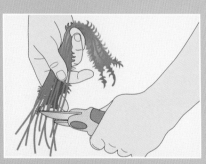

1 Trim off old "woody" stems. This will help to stimulate root growth.

2 If required, use a metal strip to bind the trimmed bunches.

3 Insert the bunches into a basket of aquatic soil.

4 Top the basket off with gravel to help retain the soil.

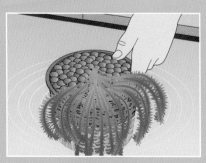

5 Slowly immerse the basket and guide it onto the pond bottom.

Invasive plants

The pond industry is a global business. Ornamental plants and fish are flown thousands of miles around the globe to make it to your pond – and this can lead to problems.

SEE ALSO
Plant care, page 44
Algae, page 86
Plant directory, page 96

The problem with ponds

Ponds are no different from gardens in that a good proportion of plants available are non-native species. The particular problem specific to pond plants is that if they find their way into the wild, they can prove to be invasive and more difficult to control in the water environment than non-aquatic plants, outcompeting wild native species and taking over their natural habitats.

Many pond plants (especially oxygenators and small floating plants) are sold as "vigorous" or "fast growing" – which, in other words, means that they are potentially invasive if they are let loose into the wild. Once they find their way into a suitable wild environment, such as a natural pond or waterway, they are almost impossible to eradicate. These invasive plants are not subject to the pests and diseases that would control them in their native habitat.

Azolla

Azolla is a floating water fern that is capable of rapid division, covering a pond rapidly. It can change colour through the seasons, from a lush green to a deep, crimson red.

Parrot feather
(Myriophyllum aquaticum)

Parrot feather is an effective oxygenating plant that will creep from the pond's margins into the open water, choking up free space.

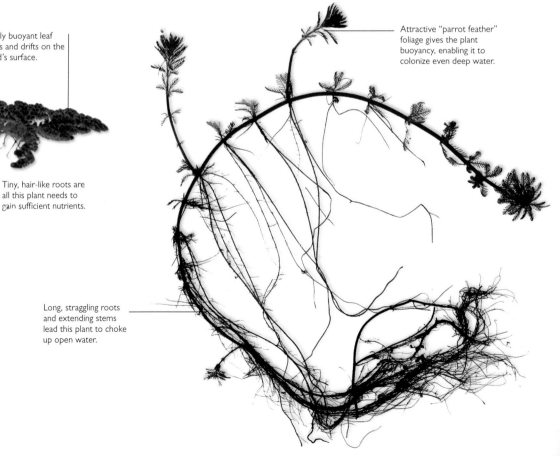

Highly buoyant leaf floats and drifts on the pond's surface.

Tiny, hair-like roots are all this plant needs to gain sufficient nutrients.

Long, straggling roots and extending stems lead this plant to choke up open water.

Attractive "parrot feather" foliage gives the plant buoyancy, enabling it to colonize even deep water.

Preventing spread

All pond owners have a responsibility to prevent their potentially invasive plants from escaping into the wild. It's impossible to know how invasive pond plants have escaped in the past – whether by accident (carried by birds, windblown seed, flooding and so on) or intentionally – but there are several things you can do to prevent your pond plants from blighting any more native environments.

• **Buy native plants.** Ask your plant supplier for a choice of native alternatives and, hopefully, as the demand for the non-native invasives declines, they will be replaced with more suitable varieties.

• **Choose knowledgeable, reputable suppliers, and buy properly labelled plants.** This way, you will know exactly what you are buying and will not put yourself in danger of spreading an invasive plant.

• **Dispose of all pond plants in your own garden by composting.** This retains the risk within your garden and is ecologically sound recycling.

• **Beware of frogspawn.** If your pond becomes overrun with spawn or tadpoles, do not move it to your local pond. The nature of invasive aquatic plants means that only a tiny fragment of stem or leaf is required for them to gain a foothold. So keep all spawn and pond water in your garden.

• **Educate yourself, prior to planting, about the plants that are considered invasive exotics in your area.** Climate is the biggest contributing factor to the subdued or excessive growth of some plants. Not all invasive plants exhibit invasive tendencies in alternate climates.

REMOVING BLANKETWEED

1 Although not classed as an alien or non-native plant, blanketweed is a pest in many garden ponds and should be removed to prevent it from choking submerged plants and your pump.

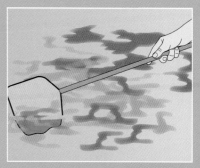

2 Use a net or rough stick to remove the blanketweed.

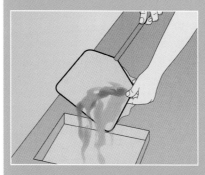

3 Place all the blanketweed you have removed adjacent to the pond.

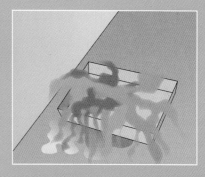

4 Leave the weed in place to allow the water to drain and any valuable pond life to return to the pond.

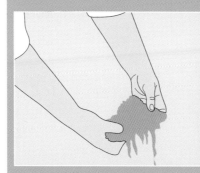

5 Finally, place the blanketweed into your compost heap to prevent its introduction to the wild.

MOST INVASIVE PLANTS

Australian swamp stonecrop
(Crassula helmsii)

Duckweed
(Lemna sp)

Fairy moss
(Azolla caroliniana)

Eichhornia

Fish basics

Keeping fish in a pond certainly does add another dimension to "gardening" and allows you to interact with your garden in a completely new way.

SEE ALSO
Stocking your pond, page 62
Breeding pond fish, page 72

By stocking your pond with fish, not only will you develop from a horticulturist to a zoologist, but you will also understand how to create a suitable pond environment for your fish and help maintain good water quality. But if you choose not to keep fish and prefer to tend your aquatic plants, then you will not need to understand water quality, and your level of achievement and fulfilment in the water garden will probably be far less.

Once stocked, fish are the ideal barometer of your pond's well-being. Certainly, they may be the cause of most pond imbalances, but their behaviour is also a good window on your pond's performance. That's why time spent "fish watching" and simply enjoying your pond is time well spent.

Bristol shubunkin

Ornamental pond fish characteristics

Genetically unstable

Any offspring of ornamental pond fish are unlikely to resemble their parents, as they are genetic mutants whose genes are very unstable. Because of this, to be able to achieve a good proportion of well-coloured ornamental offspring, commercial fish farmers need to cross closely related fish. But in your own pond, as soon as fish are able to breed randomly in an uncontrolled way, the offspring are usually less brightly coloured than their parents.

Interactive

Fish perform aesthetic and functional roles in a pond. There are far fewer fish to choose from compared to plants, but the range of shapes, colours and sizes, and the fact that they move and interact with you soon makes up for that.

Tame

Carp, the most widely cultured fish in the world, prefer still or slow-moving water and are tolerant of a wide range of water qualities. They soon become tame and domesticated and will even eat out of your hand. Most ornamental pond fish (such as koi, goldfish and shubunkins) are members of the carp family.

Easy to breed

One female can release hundreds of thousands of eggs, making it a real probability that most pondkeepers will find home-grown fish in their own ponds.

Adaptable

These adaptable fish are naturally mid- to bottom water feeders (except orfe, which prefer to feed on the surface) yet will soon rise to the surface to compete for a floating food in a feeding frenzy.

Seasonal

Pond fish are like any other fish in that they are cold-blooded, with their activity and behaviour following the pond's temperature. In spring and summer, when the water is warm, fish have a ravenous appetite, grow quickly, and are capable of swimming at high speeds (which makes them difficult to catch). In the autumn and winter, when the water temperature is consistently below 8°C (45°F), fish will stop feeding, become inactive, and spend their time on the bottom of the pond, sheltering themselves in the warmer layers.

Ryukin goldfish

Koi kin showa

Pond fish origins

The majority of pond fish (goldfish, koi, shubunkins and so on) are related to carp (cyprinids). Ornamental carp are ideally suited to life in a garden pond because they still retain many of the characteristics of their wild ancestors.

An environment for fish

It's important to understand and control the fishes' environment because they adversely affect the pond's water simply by living in it.

DEVIATING FROM NATURE

Unless your aim is a sparsely (yet naturally) stocked wildlife pond, as soon as you add fish to your pond, you will be inadvertently deviating from the natural model in several ways, increasing the risk of pond problems.

Number of fish

Most garden ponds are stocked at levels greater than could be sustained naturally. Most pondkeepers are not content with a couple of fish in their ponds, so they add them in higher numbers to achieve an eye-catching and ornamental display. You must add a pump and filter so that your artificial pond can sustain them.

Long-lived

Some koi are believed to be over 200 years old. Because ornamental fish are inherently weak, you must provide them with a good, stable environment. If you do, you will be rewarded by fish that look stunning but will also go on to grow to a large size and breed.

Opportunistic feeders

Ornamental carp found in ponds are omnivorous scavengers, which means they will coexist and not prey or fight. This opportunistic feeder is easily satisfied and readily takes an artificial food (which makes carp very easy to feed).

Tolerant

Carp are tolerant of a wide range of temperatures, overwintering in a pond as cold as 1°C (34°F) to the heady summer pond temperatures of 30°C (86°F) and above. They also breed relatively easily, with most pondkeepers observing the boisterous spawning activity at some time.

Inbred

One problem associated with intensive inbreeding of ornamental pond fish to achieve good pattern and colours is that their vigour and resistance to disease declines, making them less hardy than their wild ancestors. You may see this in fish that are bred in your own pond. First, they will be less ornamental (for example, black/brown goldfish which are hard to see, or monochrome koi); second, the drabber fish show more vigour than their ornamental relatives, growing faster and to a bigger size.

Artificial food

Because a new artificial pond will not have established its own self-sustaining food chain by the time you come to stock it, your fish must rely on you for food. To be able to feed them reliably throughout the year, you will depend on an artificial dry food.

Type and appearance of fish

Naturally, pond fish are visually unappealing and camouflaged from view to avoid predation. What could be less desirable than to have fish in your pond that you cannot see? Most pond fish are selectively bred, ornamental variants of wild-type fish. Generations of fish have been crossed to create the visually stunning varieties that are available today – from the classic goldfish to the seemingly endless varieties of koi.

Black moor goldfish

Koi gin risi asagi

Choosing and buying fish

You have designed, purchased and put in a landscaped garden pond. It has been planted for a couple of weeks, the pump and filter are installed, and your back is still aching from digging and carting the soil from the excavation. Now for the finishing touch – a selection of colourful pond fish to inhabit, thrive and perhaps breed in your own aquatic creation.

You have researched how many fish can be stocked in a pond your size, and you've still got some money left to go out and buy them. Being confronted by an aquatic store's tanks full of lively and colourful fish waiting for a new home can be one of the most tempting times for a pond owner. But if you don't follow a few golden rules, the stocking of your pond with fish may prove to be a costly exercise that turns your freshly installed slice of aquatic paradise into a watery nightmare.

SEE ALSO
Stocking your pond, page 62
Fish diseases, page 69

CHARACTERISTICS OF A HEALTHY FISH

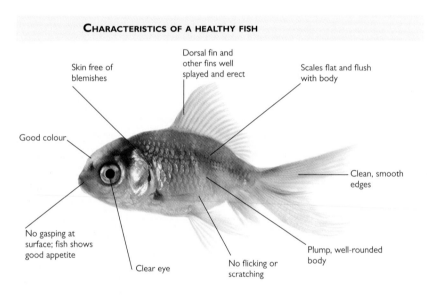

Skin free of blemishes

Dorsal fin and other fins well splayed and erect

Scales flat and flush with body

Good colour

Clean, smooth edges

No gasping at surface; fish shows good appetite

Clear eye

No flicking or scratching

Plump, well-rounded body

BUYING FISH FOR A NEW POND

- **Find a local shop offering a good variety and selection of dry goods and fish.**
  This means less travel for you and your fish. Look for someone who puts giving good advice ahead of making a sale.

- **Buy from a reliable store, rather than various different sources.**
  If you do have a problem, you know where to go back to get the best advice.

- **Provide fish with a stable environment where any changes are gradual.**
  Anything that deviates from this will cause stress, which may lead to disease. The move and purchase of fish is a significantly stressful and vulnerable time for your new fish.

- **Ask retailers if they quarantine or acclimatize their fish before they are displayed for sale.**
  By giving fish a rest period after delivery into their store, the retailer offers a healthier, less stressed fish, which reduces the risk of problems once you've stocked them in your own pond.

- **Prepare your pond for fish.**
  Before buying any fish for your pond, you should consider whether a new pond is ready to receive its first fish, or if an existing pond is ready for some extra fish (see the checklist opposite).

HEALTHY FISH:

- Swim actively in the tank
- React and even swim towards you in response to your shadow or silhouette
- Have been quarantined/acclimatized prior to sale
- Live in clear, colourless and odourless water
- Have an erect and well-distended dorsal fin
- Are vibrantly and deeply coloured
- Have a good appetite and feed readily; have a full body shape

UNHEALTHY FISH:

- Hang at sides of the tank, sulk on the bottom or at the surface, or hang in the water flow
- Visibly flick and flash
- Remain motionless when you walk by the tank
- Have skin, scales and fins that are ragged or raised, or have off-colour protrusions of tissue from the body
- May have been put on sale on arrival at the store
- Swim in water that has a blue tinge (a sign of medication) or is milky

Getting your fish home

Once the fish have been netted and bagged by the retailer, view your choices again from underneath for any blemishes or ulcers that may be present on their undersides. There is no need to rush home with your fish, but on the other hand, don't return after a 3-hour shopping trip when the fish are left in a hot car. The retailer will fill the bag with one-third water and two-thirds air (or oxygen), allowing your fish to last for several hours. They are likely to have already experienced 24 hours in a bag, flying into the country from their overseas breeder.

Start inexpensively

Once your pond is ready to receive new fish, select them wisely. In a new pond, it is wise to choose half a dozen of the cheapest fish as a means of testing the water for its suitability for fish. If there is a water-quality problem that has not been detected and the fish show signs of stress, you are less likely to suffer considerable financial loss.

Consider compatibility

Choose fish that will be compatible and are the right size for your pond. For example, varieties of goldfish will be suitable for most ponds, whereas faster-growing and voracious feeders such as koi are best kept in a large and well-filtered pond. Fortunately, most pond fish are not aggressive to each other and live easily together. If a wide variety of sizes is selected, then competition at feeding time may be an issue. Also, it is good to choose smaller fish that grow into the size of the pond rather than buy large fish that may be too large for it. If you buy small fish, you will have the pleasure of watching them grow. This is not only more satisfying but also less expensive.

Minimize risk

No fish are disease free because it's natural for them to be in balance with their pathogens. In fact, the only fish that are pathogen free are dead fish! By buying wisely and moving your fish in a way that minimizes any stress, you can manage the risk accordingly, ensuring that they reach your pond in a healthy state, free from the risk of a disease outbreak.

Preparing the pond for the fish

✓ Plant the pond and let the pump run for at least a week – ideally a fortnight – before you stock a new pond. Raw tap water and the new pond materials used in construction create a very hygienic and unnatural environment for the fish.

✓ Check for leaks, and allow the water to "age" and be turned over through a filter for as long as possible before stocking with fish.

✓ If possible, "seed" the biological filter and pond with media from a friend's mature filter (see page 174 to 175).

✓ Test the pH of your pond water to confirm that it is within the acceptable 7.0 to 8.5 range before your first fish-buying trip. There is no need to check for ammonia or nitrite – these will be zero, as there are no fish in the pond.

✓ If you are considering buying fish to replace some recent losses in an existing pond, make sure you have established the reason for losing the fish (disease, poor water quality, old age or predation, for example) before you introduce any replacements, or you may experience similar problems again.

✓ Ensure a clear 2-week period after losing any fish through disease, and only restock once you are happy with the behaviour and health of the remaining fish in your pond.

✓ You must be absolutely certain that any new additions will not cause the pond to become overstocked. Adding too many fish will tip the balance unfavourably in a well-managed pond, increasing the likelihood of water quality and disease problems, as well as a reduction in growth rates.

Stocking your pond

The stocking levels in a typical garden pond are greater than a natural pond, but they still have an upper limit.

SEE ALSO
> Choosing and buying fish, page 60
> Understanding pond, page 158
> Pond chemistry, page 166

When you see how densely fish can be stocked in display vats in a garden centre, where the water "boils" with activity at feeding time, you may be tempted to reproduce a similar effect in your own pond.

Stock the pond gradually

A golden rule when introducing fish to a new pond is "proceed with caution". Do not be afraid of introducing fish over a long period, but make the ongoing quality of your water your priority and the welfare of your fish should follow automatically.

In a new pond, it takes time for the biofilter to react to an increase in waste produced by your new fish, and if too many fish are added too quickly, the waste builds up faster than it can be broken down. As a result, the pond becomes toxic, which will cause stress to your new purchases, leading to disease or even death.

It is important to add the fish gradually over a number of weeks, and monitor the water quality at every stage.

Quarantine and acclimatization

Even if your retailer quarantines his stock before they go on sale, they will still be carrying disease. If practical, it may be wise to create a holding system where newly purchased fish can acclimatize for 2 weeks before they are introduced into your pond. This will allow them to gain confidence, start feeding and become accustomed to your specific water chemistry. Whether you provide an acclimatization system will be determined by the cost and benefit involved, as well as whether you are confident that your proposed system will be large enough and stable enough to provide your new fish with a stress-free resting period.

STOCKING LEVELS

There are no hard and fast rules about stocking levels, and seeing the garden centre display vats shows what levels can be achieved with the right filtration system. A rule of thumb for a garden pond is 7.5cm (3 inches) of fish (ignoring tails) per 30cm (1 foot) square of water. This should be achieved over several months of stocking gradually, allowing space for your fish to continue to grow.

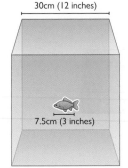

30cm (12 inches)

7.5cm (3 inches)

INTRODUCING FISH TO YOUR POND

Your objective when introducing fish into your new pond is to keep stress to a minimum. Introducing fish is about striking a balance between giving the fish long enough to acclimate before they are released and holding them for too long in the bag, which will cause them stress and anxiety.

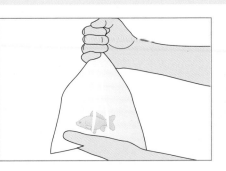

1 When you return home with your new fish, you will be carrying them in a sealed polyethylene bag.

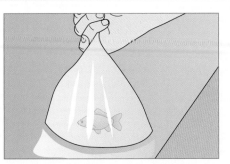

2 Allow the sealed bag to float in the pond for at least 30 minutes. This will help the water in the bag reach the same temperature as that of the pond. Be sure to keep the bag shaded from direct sunlight.

Testing the water

If you are in the process of stocking and are returning to a shop for a second or third instalment of fish, it is essential that the filter is maturing and keeping pace with the expanding collection of fish. Most retailers offer a water-testing service and will be able to tell you whether it is safe to continue stocking or if you should wait a week for the filter to catch up. However, to avoid a wasted journey, you can buy a test kit and test the water yourself at home. Ammonia and nitrite tests are essential at this stage. There is more detail about the types and frequency of tests that you need to do on pages 168 to 171.

Testing pH
Use a pH test kit to confirm that the water is in the correct range for pond fish. A pH of between 7.0 (neutral) and 8.5 is ideal. Watch out for a pH below 7, because acid water conditions must be avoided in a pond. With a test kit, reagent is added to the water sample, which then changes colour according to its acidity or alkalinity.

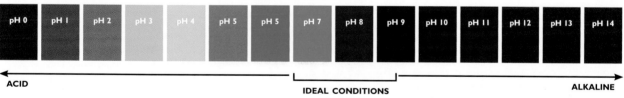

THE pH SCALE

The pH of a liquid is measured on a scale from 0 to 14. The scale below shows the typical colours associated with different pH readings.

| pH 0 | pH 1 | pH 2 | pH 3 | pH 4 | pH 5 | pH 5 | pH 7 | pH 8 | pH 9 | pH 10 | pH 11 | pH 12 | pH 13 | pH 14 |

ACID ← → ALKALINE

IDEAL CONDITIONS
FOR FISH

NEW FISH TIPS

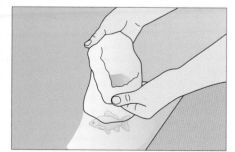

3 Untie the bag, roll down the neck and double the amount of water in the bag by adding pond water. Leave for a further 30 minutes. This will equalize the temperatures and also start to acclimatize the fish to the pond's own particular water chemistry.

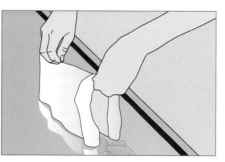

4 Tilt the neck of the bag below the surface and let the fish swim out. Don't pour the water and fish out of the bag from above the surface. Keep the bag intact – it will come in handy for other pond-related jobs.

- Don't be concerned if your new fish are uninterested in food for several days – they won't starve. The biggest threat at this stage is adding food that they are not going to eat, potentially polluting the water.
- Your newly introduced fish are likely to hide for several days as they settle into their new environment. It will take them time to adjust to the fact that there are so few fish in such a large pond.

Pond fish food

SEE ALSO
Fish basics, page 58
Fish health, page 84

Just like any other fish or animal, ornamental carp such as goldfish, shubunkins and koi have particular nutritional requirements. After water quality, nutrition has the greatest influence on the health and appearance of pond fish.

A fish's diet will affect its growth, coloration, resistance to disease, and breeding performance. Because pond fish are traditionally kept in a densely stocked pond, they rely on the pondkeeper to provide a complete and balanced artificial diet. The food you give your fish can also have a significant impact on your pond's water quality.

The natural diet

Because ornamental pond fish are not naturally occurring, but are ornamental variants of carp, their diets are largely based on the nutritional requirements of that species. If you look at a carp from the side, you'll notice that its mouth protrudes in a downward direction. This is a typical feature of a bottom-feeding fish. Using the sensitive barbels positioned on each side of its mouth, a carp roots around in the soft sediment of lakes and ponds in search of food.

BUYING FOOD

When buying pond food, the range of options can be daunting. There are several useful guidelines to follow.

Although many diets may look the same, formulations and performance vary greatly. Not only will they vary between brands, but brands will also produce a number of diets in their range, from low to high protein, from staple to colour-enhancing.

Read the packaging carefully to identify which foods offer the characteristics you want. Things to look out for include protein level, colour-enhancing properties and vitamin C content. It is also useful to ask the aquatic outlets what food they use to feed their valuable stock on the premises.

"Best before" date

Vitamins deteriorate quickly over time. Check the "best before" date on a pack before buying it to ensure that it will be fresh until the end of the season.

Packaging

A pond food that is available in a robust or resealable container will remain fresh once opened. Food that cannot be kept airtight will deteriorate quickly.

Value

As floating pellets are expanded with air to make them float, it is wise to check what weight of food is in the package. Larger-volume packs may give the impression of offering good value, but check and compare weights and prices of the contents.

Food specification

Ensure that you are purchasing a pellet size that all your fish can consume. Check that the protein content is suitable for the time of year (see page 67), and whether the food offers any additional features such as a guaranteed vitamin content, an immuno-stimulant, or a range of colour enhancers.

ASIAKOI

GROWTH
net weight 2.5kg

Food types

Choose from different types of food to suit the range of fish in your pond.

PELLETS AND STICKS

Pellets make up the bulk of the pond food market on account of their versatility. They are available in a wide range of sizes, from tiny pellets for 5-cm (2-inch) fish to jumbo pellets for much larger fish. As the vast majority of pelleted diets float, fish are encouraged to feed at the surface (so you can inspect them at close quarters). You can easily judge how much to feed, and remove any uneaten pellets.

Food sticks are produced in a similar fashion to pellets but are longer and generally less dense. They will usually soften up quite quickly, enabling even the smaller fish to nibble away at them.

Fish food

The different types of commercially available foods come in fairly standard resealable containers and boxes.

SINKING PELLETS

More recently, sinking pellets have become available for bottom-dwelling fish such as tench. These must be used with great care and only when you can safely judge how much food those fish will easily consume. With a sinking pellet, any uneaten food will drop to the pond bottom and break down, polluting the pond water.

FLAKES

An assortment of coloured flakes is blended to offer a complete and balanced diet. Although they are more popular in the indoor market (where they don't get blown away), some pondkeepers use flakes to feed smaller pond fish. In addition, they have a tendency to sink, which also enables deeper-water fish such as tench (and other shy varieties) to gain their daily food.

LIVE FOOD

Live or fresh food is appreciated by pond fish. Live food may range from an earthworm dug from your own garden to bags of live daphnia or bloodworm purchased from your pond store. There is a small risk of introducing disease with aquatic live foods, but this is outweighed by the enjoyment with which pond fish investigate and devour a live food treat.

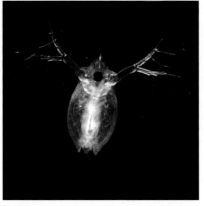

Daphnia

Bloodworm

Feeding pond fish

Pond fish such as koi, goldfish and shubunkins are all related to the carp, which is naturally a grazing fish, constantly feeding as it picks its way through the silt and debris in a pond. They do not have stomachs and do not digest single large amounts of food effectively but, rather, digest many small mouthfuls throughout the day.

Automatic fish feeder

An autofeeder is useful for dispensing a regular, fixed amount of food, should you be away for a few days. Ensure that the level of food is correct to avoid overfeeding.

Regulated feeding

An autofeeder can regulate the amount of food and frequency of feeding.

More fish are harmed by overfeeding than through starvation – because too much food leads to poor water quality rather than the fish becoming overweight. Fish are so much more efficient at using food than other creatures that they can safely go for several weeks without food.

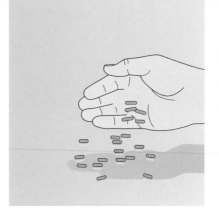
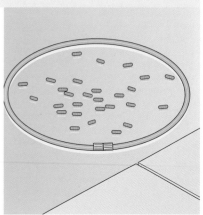

1 Feed your fish frequently; three times a day is the recommended. Fish growth is better if they are fed on a basis of "little and often". This is how carp feed naturally, constantly scavenging food items, and their digestion is optimized when they get a few small meals rather than one feed per day.

2 Consider using a feeding ring to contain the food in one part of the pond. The fish can feed from underneath it, and it stops food from drifting amongst plants, where it may go uneaten.

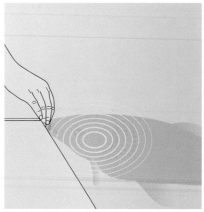

3 After five minutes, remove any uneaten food with a net.

4 Through a regular feeding routine, pond fish can be become very tame and may grow to recognize the sound of your footsteps as you approach the pond or even the opening of your back door.

Feeding in spring and autumn

When water temperatures rise or fall to around 10°C (50°F), you should give your fish a low-protein diet. They will not have a high-protein requirement at these temperatures, nor will their digestive enzymes be working optimally. Diets typically offered at these times are vegetable-based, in which the protein content is provided in the form of highly digestible wheatgerm.

Feeding in summer

When water temperatures are at their highest, your fish will be at their most active, with great potential for growth. High-protein diets should be fed during these periods to maximize growth. It is during this peak in activity that your fish will also be feeding for their winter reserves. A good-quality diet fed at this time will ensure the healthy growth of your fish, while sufficient energy is being stored for winter. Your fish will respond well to a colour-enhancing diet during the summer months.

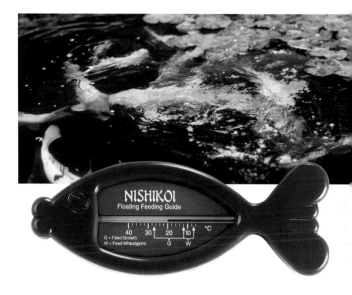

Pond thermometer

A pond thermometer will show you when to start (and stop) feeding your fish and when to change to a different food through the seasons.

Treat foods

It can be tempting to feed your fish a range of treat foods such as brown bread, sweetcorn, peas, lettuce or even mussels and prawns. Take care with such foods though, as they do not represent a balanced diet and may be less digestible than you imagine.

Treats may lead to the production of excessive waste or cause the water to cloud. Many treats are very high in protein and if your fish are fed excessive amounts of protein, they will either use some as a source of energy or excrete the excess. Either way, the overall effect will be a rise in ammonia excreted by your fish, risking a rapid decline in water quality. If the pond is suitably stocked and they are fed a balanced diet, such problems should not arise if the pond is adequately filtered.

Carry out a partial water change every 2 weeks when your fish are actively feeding – this will keep the water fresh and sweet.

Fish treats

Pond fish enjoy occasional treats, eagerly taking them from you.

Keeping fish healthy

It's not uncommon for goldfish to live for 20 to 30 years in a garden pond. Pondkeepers who have achieved this have grasped the few basic principles of fish care. Fish are susceptible to some diseases though, caused by four different types of pathogen: viruses, bacteria, fungi and parasites.

The importance of fish watching

The first indication that all is not well will be a change in the fishes' behaviour, which is only noticeable if you are confident of identifying "normal" behaviour. You can get a good understanding of your fishes' behaviour by watching them regularly and becoming accustomed to their typical performance. Feeding time is an excellent opportunity for a spot check. Watch out for how long they take to come up to feed, how they respond to your shadow, and whether certain fish in the pond are always more reluctant to feed than others. It is important to note whether the changes apply to individual fish or if all the fish in the pond are affected.

SEE ALSO
Stocking your pond, page 62
New Pond Syndrome, page 174
Pond chemistry, page 166

SINGLE FISH AFFECTED

If only one or a couple of fish in a pond appear to be affected, this points to an isolated incident, such as localized damage caused by a collision or abrasion. It may be a weak fish succumbing to an ailment such as an internal problem or genetic disorder. A single affected fish may also indicate the start of a larger problem.

Netting the fish
Single fish must be netted and inspected for any obvious damage or causative symptoms. If it is clear that the fish is unhealthy or damaged, it may have to be isolated and treated separately. However, there are cases where there is no external evidence of a cause for a change in behaviour.

What action is needed?
Treatment may be counterproductive, and it may be wise to return the affected fish to the pond and closely monitor its progress over the next few days. Check that its condition does not deteriorate or that other fish begin to show similar symptoms. If, after testing, the water quality is shown to be fine, then the provision of a healthy pond environment and food (if the fish has an appetite) may be enough to bring the fish back to full health.

ALL FISH AFFECTED

If all the fish are less inclined to feed or are hanging and gasping at the surface, it is likely that the problem has a straightforward cause (not necessarily a disease). First, check the water quality. A pH test will indicate whether the water is within the safe band of 7 to 8.5, with anything outside these levels (particularly less than 7) likely to cause stress and a change in behaviour. The ammonia and nitrite readings should be zero, and any positive reading is a likely indication that this is the cause of the problems (for more on testing the water, see page 168). Other possible causes of stress in fish that may not be detected by pH and nitrite test kits, include:

Low dissolved oxygen
If dissolved oxygen is decreasing, the fish can become sluggish and may be seen gasping at the surface. This is easily remedied by the addition of extra aeration or by increasing the water turnover. Diseased fish can also be seen gasping at the surface.

Intoxication
Toxic substances may accidentally be added to a pond, and will cause the fish great discomfort. Take care when using insecticides or weed-killers, as they can easily find their way into the water.

Runoff from untreated lime in brickwork or patios
This can cause pH to soar above the safe limits of 8.5, again causing the fish to suffer.

Disease
The fish may have succumbed to a disease such as white spot, gill flukes, or other parasites, causing them to flick and flash. Other diseases are evident to the naked eye (such as the ragged fins associated with "fin rot") and may not lead to a change in behaviour. Depending upon the symptoms, most diseases can be treated effectively with the correct medications. However, be careful to identify the disease accurately and dose correctly, as overdosing will cause the fish additional unnecessary stress.

Fish diseases

Except for fungi and larger external parasites, it is not possible to identify individual fish pathogens by eye, so individual symptoms that are very specific to each type of pathogen must be identified. These symptoms will include a lesion on the fish or a change in behaviour – sometimes both. Viral diseases cannot be treated and may lead to secondary infections, which must be treated.

SEE ALSO

Choosing and buying fish, page 60
Fish health, page 84

VIRAL DISEASES

Viral diseases cannot be treated with any medication and are usually highly infectious. Fish health and behaviour may remain unaffected, or a virus may lead to mortalities directly or through secondary diseases.

CARP POX

Symptoms: Whitish or opaque, wax-like lumps on the fish's body. May be localized or cover the entire body. It is unsightly but not life-threatening. Caused by a herpes-type virus, carp pox emerges in spring and autumn when the fish's immune system becomes depressed due to the cool temperature. Symptoms may re-emerge every season, with fish continuing to behave normally.
Treatment: No treatment, but candle-wax lumps will disappear as the temperature rises and the immune response becomes more effective.

The wax-like lumps of carp pox look unpleasant, but they are harmless and will disappear over time.

SPRING VIRAEMIA OF CARP (SVC)

Symptoms: Affects the carp family only, with external haemorrhaging from the skin and vent. The body may also become bloated. Carp are affected when the water temperature starts to rise in spring, leading to very high mortalities. It is also highly infectious and is a "notifiable" disease in most countries, meaning any incidents must be reported to the relevant animal health authority, which will try to control the spread of the disease.
Treatment: There is no known treatment. Any surviving fish will have become resistant to the disease.

KOI HERPES VIRUS (KHV)

Symptoms: Affects koi only. This virus incapacitates a koi's immune system, leading to over 90 per cent mortality rate, with symptoms such as body ulceration and rot, gill rot, and haemorrhaging. KHV becomes active once temperatures rise above 21°C (70°F). At these temperatures, outbreaks typically occur 14 days after newly infected koi have been introduced to an existing pond. KHV is a relatively new disease, first discovered in the mid-1990s.
Treatment: There is no treatment. Quarantine all koi at above 21°C (70°F) for 14 days before you introduce them to your pond.

BACTERIAL INFECTIONS

Like viruses, bacterial infections are too small to be seen by the naked eye. You will be alerted first to a bacterial disease by noticing clearly infected tissue or a change in the fish's behaviour. Bacterial diseases can spread rapidly but usually respond well to commonly available pond treatments.

FIN ROT/TAIL ROT

Symptoms: Split fins or edges of the translucent fin tissue have a white edge. Fin rays can appear reddened or bloodshot. This is caused by rough handling or poor water quality. Fancy long-finned fish are particularly prone to this disease, especially in the spring, having lost blood circulation to the fin's extremities during the preceding winter.
Treatment: Fin rot responds well to antibacterial pond treatments, which work best in warm temperatures.

Fin rot is easy to identify – look for ragged fins.

MOUTH FUNGUS

Symptoms: Whitish fungal-like growths around the mouth. In extreme cases, the mouth tissue is eroded completely, exposing the jawbone. It is usually caused by fish "mouthing" at or on sharp objects and even rough stones.
Treatment: Use a broad-spectrum antibacterial pond treatment, which also works for fin rot.

>

BACTERIAL INFECTIONS CONTINUED

ULCERS

Ulcers are very easy to diagnose but not so easy to treat. Bacteria that cause ulcers in fish can prove to be virulent and aggressive. They are caused by a bruise or a knock becoming infected or are brought on by stress.

Symptoms: Ulcers rarely cause a change in fish behaviour, but they can soon become life threatening. An ulcer starts as a small red raised area that then breaks out to form a symmetrical ulcer with a red-raw centre and white perimeter.

Treatment: Ulcers can be very difficult to treat. Dose the pond with a broad-spectrum antibacterial treatment, and regularly apply the same treatment in concentrated form topically onto the wound while holding the fish in a net. Due to the virulent and systemic nature of ulcer infections, it is not uncommon for affected fish to require antibiotics. Fish suffering from ulcers can die very quickly through kidney failure as a result of the constant, unabated ingress of water into the fish through the ulcer.

DROPSY

There are many different suspected causes of dropsy, which makes it difficult to treat. It is, however, one of the easiest diseases to recognize.

Symptoms: The fish swells, causing its scales to protrude, so that it resembles a pinecone. Eyes can also start to protrude, caused by the accumulation of fluid within the fish.

Treatment: Dropsy is difficult to treat because of the various likely causes and internal nature of the disease. It is best to quarantine any affected fish to prevent them from spreading the disease to other fish. Fish suffering from dropsy usually die, and it is sometimes best to euthanize them.

FUNGAL DISEASE

A fungal disease is easy to identify and treat – and it will not necesarily affect all the fish in your pond.

COTTON WOOL DISEASE

Symptoms: Localized areas of a fish's body become covered in white, "furry", cottonwool-like growths. Cottonwool is regarded as a secondary disease because fungal spores will only germinate in an existing open wound. Consequently, the fungus usually affects single fish and is not contagious to other "healthy" and intact fish. It is common in spring and autumn.

Treatment: Standard proprietary antifungal pond treatments are effective.

A fish showing a heavy fungal infection that has also started to play host to algae, giving it a green tinge.

MICROSCOPIC PARASITES

External parasites irritate fish, causing them to scratch against hard objects in the pond. This flicking or flashing behaviour is typical of a parasite problem. Many external parasites are single-celled protozoan parasites that are not visible to the naked eye.

GILL FLUKES/SKIN FLUKES (DACTYLOGYRUS/GYRODACTYLUS)

Although these are metazoan parasites (multicellular), they are still too small to see. These tiny worms attach to skin or gill tissue by sharp hooks, causing severe irritation.

Symptoms: Besides scratching, fish will respond to infestation by secreting excess mucus (thus losing colour). This can lead to breathing difficulties and rapid gill movements. Fish may also regularly jump clear of the surface.

Treatment: As the parasites get larger, they become more difficult to treat. Standard anti-parasite pond treatments may be effective, but concentrated short-term bath treatments in a separate tank may also be required.

COSTIA /TRICHODINA/CHILODONELLA

These three microscopic parasites are often found together in the mucus layer that covers the fish's skin.

Symptoms: Thickening of the mucus causes colours to look dull under a whitish cast. Fish vigour becomes depressed, and the mild irritation can cause fish to show the typical scratching behaviour. The fish's fins will also tend to be clamped toward the body. The disease may also affect gill function, causing the fish to hang at the pond surface or near moving water.

Treatment: Standard antiparasite treatments applied directly to the pond generally prove very effective.

Visible parasites

These parasites are visible, but they may go unnoticed unless you closely inspect individual fish. The irritation they cause will result in changed behaviour.

WHITE SPOT OR "ICH" (ICHTHYOPHTHIRIUS)

Even though this disease is caused by a microscopic parasite, it forms visible cysts under the skin of host fish, causing the characteristic white spots.

Symptoms: The entire body is covered in a scattering of tiny white spots that resemble sugar grains. Affected fish will become lethargic several days before the spots appear. It is highly contagious, infecting most fish in the pond. Outbreaks are associated with the stress of a rapid change in water temperature. White spot can cause irritation, causing infected fish to scratch or show rapid gill movements.

Treatment: General white spot pond treatment that is dosed 5 days apart will prove to be effective.

LEECHES (PISCICOLA)

These are rare in artificial ponds, but incidents will increase in a pond that wildfowl visit.

Symptoms: Leeches are 5-cm (2-inch) long, dark, worm-like parasites with suckers at each end. A leech attaches itself to fish via its mouth end. Leeches generally become attached to weaker fish while they sit on the pond bottom in the cooler months. Reddened areas of previous attachments can become infected with fungus.

Treatment: Leeches are difficult to eradicate. The pond can be dosed with salt and the affected fish given a more concentrated salt bath, causing the leeches to drop off. As a last resort, you may have to drain the pond completely and discard the plants, which naturally harbour leech eggs.

A bloodsucking leech is easy to spot on a brightly coloured ornamental pond fish.

FISH LOUSE (ARGULUS)

Symptoms: A jelly-covered, translucent, disc-shaped louse (½ inch in diameter) that attaches itself to the fish's body and causes much irritation. It can be difficult to spot as it crawls around the body, relocating itself to feed. Fish lice are typically a summer problem in ponds that are visited by wildfowl.

Treatment: Remove the lice with tweezers, then dab the areas of attachment with neat antibacterial treatment to prevent infection of the attachment sites.

ANCHOR WORM (LERNEA)

Symptoms: This long, thin, worm-like parasite resembles a fine rice grain. Two white egg sacs hang off each side of its posterior. Only females attach and feed off fish. The fish suffer similar irritation caused by a fish louse.

Treatment: Anchor worm rarely responds to pond treatments. It needs to be physically removed with tweezers, or the fish will require a prolonged concentrated salt bath.

The translucent fish louse will cause irritation and can be difficult to spot on a fish.

A carp showing an extreme case of white spot. Tiny, sugar-like spots clearly identify the parasitic disease.

Changes in behaviour

Unwell fish will show changed behaviour.

Fish sulking
Fish stay on the pond bottom or hang just under the water's surface. They are sluggish in their escape response when approached at close hand.

Loss of appetite
Fish do not respond at feeding time. Feeding fish with a floating food is an ideal way of assessing the health of all of your fish. You should make a mental note of their numbers at feeding time to see if any are abnormally reluctant to come to the surface.

Fins clamped close to the body
The fins on a healthy fish should be well splayed, tight and erect. Erect fins can be compared to the glossy coat of a cat – both indicate a state of good health.

Breeding pond fish

For a pondkeeper whose aim has been to re-create a natural pond in the back garden, there can be no greater compliment of his or her efforts than to have fish breeding in their pond.

SEE ALSO

Fish basics, page 58
Seasonal pond maintenance, page 178

The breeding pattern of carp is controlled by the complex interaction of environmental factors that will stimulate them to spawn between June and August in a temperate climate – or even sooner in a warmer climate.

In a temperate climate, the eggs that are spawned in, say, June are formed in the ovaries of the female some 11 months earlier. They are retained through the winter period and begin to mature within the ovaries through spring as the spawning period approaches.

Just as a carp's metabolism and growth rate are affected by temperature, so is the maturation of eggs and the bringing into condition of the mature broodfish.

Another important factor is the lengthening of the day (photoperiod), which stimulates the fish's sensory systems, causing the release of hormones that control the spawning process (see right).

Spawning time

In a larger pond with a good spread of submerged oxygenating plants acting both as a soft spawning media and a protective nursery for the vulnerable newly hatched fry, it will be possible to produce your own homebred fish.

When your fish are ready to spawn, the activity of the males increases, and they may be seen shoaling around the perimeter of the pond at the surface. The pond

surface may start to froth from the proteins released by the fish before they spawn.

Mature goldfish and koi can be triggered to spawn by carrying out a rapid water change to reduce water temperature. This will stimulate spawning activity, and the fish will deposit their adhesive eggs in the pondweed, which can then be either removed to a separate pond or kept in the main pond. Fertilization and hatching rates can be quite low, with hatching taking 3 to 6 days, depending on the temperature.

Ornamental carp do not make good parents, and they will readily consume their own eggs (as will other fish in the pond). Those that find sanctuary within the weed will survive.

A GAME OF CHANCE

A chance spawning in a garden pond where different varieties of fish from different breeders and origins are found is not likely to produce many brightly-coloured ornamental offspring but rather dull variants that a commercial breeder would usually cull. However, it will provide valuable experience required to nurture fry that are produced, and it can still be fulfilling to know that your pond and attention to detail played a part in creating new homegrown fish.

Male and female carp

Carp become sexually mature in their second or third year and are difficult to sex before that time. Males remain slender and will generally mature a season sooner than females. Female carp ultimately grow to become larger fish with plump, rounded abdomens that swell considerably towards spawning time.

The female fish is plumper and rounder than the male. As spawning approaches, the female's abdomen will become very swollen.

In male and female fish of the same age, the female will tend to be larger.

The male fish is more slender than the female.

As the spawning period approaches, male fish develop rough tubercles on their opercula.

Prolonged periods of warm weather are likely to precede spawning behaviour. Mature females will swell up as they approach spawning time. Males start to show over-amorous behavior, cruising alongside any fish as prospective mates.

Often, first thing in the morning, boisterous, physical spawning behaviour will be seen and heard. For up to an hour, fish will appear to be fighting. So frenetic is the behaviour that water will be splashed as males chase females into the weeds.

If you miss the spawning event, a proteinaceous froth and scum on the pond's surface may indicate your fish have spawned. Thousands of tiny, adhesive translucent eggs will be released into the weed where they will remain attached for the next few days until they are either eaten, or hatch. Try running your hand over the smooth sides of the pond or along pipework to feel for tiny bumps.

Spawned females may become stressed through continued attention of males. Consider removing them to recover. Check all fish for lost scales or tissue damage.

Other pond fish may root through the weed, eating the eggs as soon as they are released by the female.

CONDITIONS FOR SPAWNING

• It is vital that females undergo the right breeding conditions to lead to a predictable spawn. The males do not require such specific conditions to stimulate sperm production but do so generally when temperatures exceed 15°C (59°F).

• A useful guide for determining when broodfish may be ready to spawn is by calculating how many degree-days they have experienced since winter. To do so, multiply the temperature (in °C) by the number of days for which the fish experience that temperature – for example 4 days at 17°C (63°F) = 68 degree-days. Once a total of 1,000 degree-days has been reached, the fish are likely to spawn.

• Generally, it is accepted that only those days spent above 15°C (59°F) are recorded, and when a running total of 1,000 degree-days has elapsed, it is safe to expect a spawn at any time. It is useful to keep a diary of pond temperatures so that you can predict a spawn.

Upon hatching, the fry are translucent and barely visible to the naked eye. They will absorb their yolk sacs over the next couple of days, and only then will they require a first food, grazing on microscopic particles retained within submerged pondweed.

Raising the fry

Raising fry is probably the biggest challenge in a pond, and many pond-keepers are unaware that they have been successful until they are surprised to notice 5-cm-long fish emerging from the weed the following spring. An artificially constructed pond that is well filtered will by its very nature be clear, with little natural food. Fry require a constant supply of microscopic food that can be easily digested. Prepared foods such as powdered diets, hard-boiled eggs or commercial fry food can be used but may have a tendency to rapidly pollute the water. Professional koi farmers improve their chances by providing a separate clay-based, fry-rearing pond into which the egg-laden weed can be placed.

SIGNS OF SPAWNING

It is difficult to predict when spawning will occur, but watch for the following:

• Females begin to swell and regularly feed more eagerly than males.
• The opercula and head on the males become quite rough, like sandpaper.
• Males start cruising around the pond edges in groups at the surface.
• Koi and goldfish will generally spawn just after or during an isolated warm spell.

• Spawning will occur in the shallows and around the pond edges, so place spawning rope in the corners.

Spawning may only last for 20 to 30 minutes and can easily be missed. Keep checking for translucent eggs, as all pond fish will eagerly eat them. A good indicator that spawning is imminent or has just finished is the presence of a froth or scum on the water's surface, with venturis or waterfalls creating bubbles.

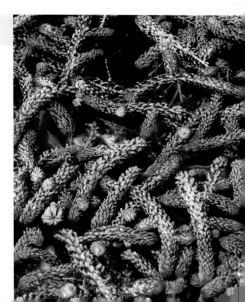

Spawning goldfish will head for densely planted shallow areas to lay their eggs.

Pond wildlife

One of the many benefits of building a pond in your back garden is bringing the sound and sight of water nearby so you can enjoy it. A pond also provides a much-needed haven for wildlife, attracting many different types of animals into your back garden.

SEE ALSO
Pond shapes, page 16
Understanding the pond, page 158

Mosquito larvae

Attracting wildlife to your back garden is a real bonus to building a pond. You will have invested a sizable sum on pond materials, hardware, plants and fish. You now stand to enjoy – free of charge – all the wildlife that your creation attracts! Even if your pond is in a small urban garden surrounded by a concrete and steel jungle, a pond magnetically attracts all sorts of wildlife.

Besides being free, the arrival of pond wildlife seems to give your pond a stamp of approval. An intriguing diversity of pond organisms will take up residence for many years or simply visit for a few seconds and move on, adding real interest and dynamism to the life of your pond.

As a pond ages, the diversity and complexity of webs and relationships within the pond will help to mature and stabilize it further. Very rarely (unlike with plants or fish) does any pond wildlife that arrives as a guest get out of control, with predator–prey chains helping to maintain a balance.

A pond provides wildlife with plenty of niches to inhabit. The more diverse the design and planting, the wider the diversity of pond organisms that will be attracted. This is why it is never a good idea to completely empty and clean out a pond, as you will lose the beneficial diversity that has taken years to establish.

Ram's horn snail

Common pond wildlife

Different types of organisms are able to exploit compatible yet different niches within your pond. A pond can quite literally teem with life. Even a filtered, re-circulating garden pond is likely to enjoy a diversity of pond organisms in and around it, exploiting various niches within it. Many are insect larvae that later spend their adult life as flies above the pond.

INVERTEBRATES BELOW THE SURFACE

Water fleas (*Daphnia*)
Water fleas are tiny planktonic crustaceans that appear to tread water in a jerky motion, often gathering in dense clouds in the pond. They are filter feeders, sieving tiny suspended particles (such as algae) from the pond. Fish find water fleas irresistible, so they tend to be found more abundantly in still, sparsely stocked wildlife ponds.

Pond snails
Pond snails will generally find their way into a pond via plants.

Ram's horn snails (*Planorbis*)
Ram's horn snails are the pond snail of choice, as they graze off hard surfaces without damaging the foliage on submerged aquatic plants.

Great pond snail (*Lymnaea*)
Great pond snails resemble land snails, with twisted conical shells, and will consume the leaves on pond plants, eroding lily pads from underneath (where they also deposit their gelatinous egg capsules). These snails should be removed whenever your find them, giving preference to ram's horn snails.

Mosquito larvae (*Culex*)
Mosquitoes are one of the many insects whose larvae develop in a pond. Like water fleas, they are more common in still-water ponds and are equally irresistible to fish. If you are ever concerned about your pond playing host to mosquitoes, simply add a few more fish. Other fly larvae found in a pond include Chironomidae (midges), whose worm-like larvae are called bloodworm due to their blood-red pigmentation.

Great diving beetle (*Dytiscus*)
Great diving beetles can be unwelcome in a pond if it contains fry or small fish. A beetle will fly to a pond and then dive, taking down a bubble of air, which it uses until it has to surface for more. These beetles are carnivorous and will take small fish – they may even give you a nip. If you find one in your pond (and can catch it), remove it.

Dragonfly larvae
Dragonflies are also carnivorous and adapted for a more permanent life underwater. Depending on the species, the larvae will remain underwater for several years, consuming other insects and fry. Once fully developed, the larva will crawl out onto a reed and emerge out of its case to become a dragonfly.

Great diving beetle

AMPHIBIANS

Amphibians are usually only found in the water during their breeding season. At other times, they live outside the pond in damp areas. They all produce tadpoles but will court and spawn slightly differently.

Newts

Resembling slimy aquatic lizards, newts are less mobile than other amphibians, staying loyal to a pond. They usually have a strong pairing bond, with the males being more brightly coloured underneath. Eggs are laid singly rather than in masses, as laid by frogs.

Frogs

Frogs soon find a new pond. However, if you don't want to wait, introduce some spawn or tadpoles from a neighbour's pond. Frogs will produce copious quantities of spawn, making a pond overrun with tadpoles in spring. These start vegetarian and then develop into carnivores, often preying on each other. Frogs prefer to inhabit a well-planted bog garden where they take insects, worms and slugs at night.

Toads

Toads are differentiated from frogs by their shorter legs, warty skin and preference for walking rather than hopping. They also produce strings of spawn rather than a single large mass and prefer to spend more time outside the pond itself, sheltering under rocks.

Frog

Whirligig beetles

INVERTEBRATES ON THE SURFACE

Many aquatic invertebrates exploit the pond's surface. They are able to breathe air and yet benefit from the sanctuary and protection of the pond, if necessary.

Pond skater (*Gerris*)

Pond skaters fly in and exploit the pond's surface tension to stay afloat. They will feed off stranded and drowning insects that are unable to master the art of skating on the surface. They pose no threat to fish but may be in danger of being eaten by fish, especially orfe.

Water boatman (*Corixidae*)

Water boatmen hang just below the surface at rest (a bit like a mirror image to pond skaters), swimming head down. Some get quite large and may become a threat to small fry and even nip human skin.

Whirligig beetles (*Gyrinidae*)

Whirligig beetles are often seen in groups, swimming rapidly in endless circles on the pond's surface. They can be mesmerizing, looking like downsized great diving beetles.

Heron

INVERTEBRATES ABOVE THE SURFACE

Damselflies

Damselflies are unmistakable, showing off their bright livery, particularly electric blue, as well as other colours. They lay eggs in the water and are attracted by tall marginal foliage. They are often seen flitting around a pond, coupled with a mate, joined and flying in tandem. They are a real delight in summer, but their presence is short-lived.

Dragonflies

Dragonflies are similar in form to damselflies but much bigger. They dart about and venture farther from the pond. They are also carnivorous and may seem to patrol a preferred route in search of prey.

Birds

Wild garden birds are a welcome sight, drinking from and bathing in your pond or waterfall. However, herons, ducks and other wildfowl are unwelcome visitors.

Herons

Herons are very patient predators, attracted to the easy pickings of brightly coloured fish stocked densely in a small crystal-clear pond. Preferring to hunt at dawn and dusk, a heron can decimate the fish in a pond and stress the remaining fish so much that they are too shy to surface, spoiling the whole character of your pond. There are novel suggestions each year on how to protect your pond from herons, ranging from decoy to infrared heron scarers. The only guaranteed way to protect your fish is to cover the pond with a fine mesh net at least 50cm (18 inches) above the surface. Unfortunately, this spoils the overall impression of your pond.

Ducks and wildfowl

Ducks and wildfowl are most unwelcome visitors to a garden pond. They will dig into planted baskets, uprooting lilies. They can turn a tranquil, clear-water pond into a muddy hole very quickly. Ducks also tend to be carriers of other pests and fish parasites from wild water sources and may even introduce impossible-to-control duckweed (*Lemna*).

COMMON PROBLEMS
AND SOLUTIONS

Whatever the size, location or type of pond you have, you are likely to encounter the same problems or seek answers to similar key questions as other water gardeners. Some issues can only be addressed as they happen; others can be prevented by advance planning – and there are questions that you may ask simply for the need to know why. Water gardening is a very practical and hands-on pastime, and everyone can benefit from the experience of other water gardeners. Common questions on water quality, food, fish health, algae, pond equipment, seasonal care and pond safety are answered to help you to get things right the first time in your own pond.

Water quality

Providing and maintaining good water quality in your pond is the key to successful pondkeeping. There are a number of common questions with practical solutions to help you achieve success.

 Q Do I need to do anything to the tap water that I have filled my pond with to make it safe for fish?

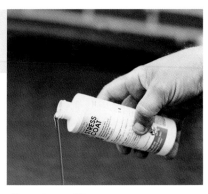

Tap-water conditioner
Add sufficient tap-water conditioner to your new pond to make it safe for fish.

A Most tap water is treated with a disinfectant such as chlorine or chloramine to make it safe for humans to drink, but these compounds are toxic to fish. Tap water may also contain traces of undesirable compounds such as heavy metals and pesticides. Consequently, water used to fill a new pond (or added as part of a partial water change) must be treated. A simple solution is to add a tap-water conditioner (relative to the volume of the pond). Any subsequent partial water changes should also be treated accordingly. Chlorine is a volatile gas that irritates the fish's delicate gill tissues. Chloramine (chlorine combined with ammonia) is a more stable and long-lasting disinfectant but can also prove to be difficult to neutralize. Take care to use a tap-water conditioner that is effective against both.

An alternative solution to a conditioner is an in-line water purifier. This treats tap water for a wide range of soluble contaminants, with each set of purifiers remaining effective for a given volume of water. Installing one is more expensive than adding a tap-water conditioner, but you know that every drop of water that enters your pond will be safe.

Q The fish in my 3-week-old pond have stopped feeding, and, after testing, the water shows a high nitrite reading. What does this mean, and what should I do?

A Every new pond must go through a maturation phase.
The bacteria that reprocess the soluble wastes produced by your fish must be given time to grow in response to the increasing workload. Toxic ammonia that is released by fish is broken down by beneficial bacteria into nitrites and then less toxic nitrates. But if too many fish or too much food is added relative to your new pond filter's ability to break it down, toxic nitrites will accumulate in the water. This is "new pond syndrome" and explains why your test has detected a high nitrite level – the desirable level is zero.

As nitrite has started to accumulate in your pond, it has had a negative effect on your fish, causing them to exhibit a classic change in behaviour: loss of appetite. You may also discover them gasping and scratching through irritation. If the high nitrite level persists, your fish will be susceptible to disease and may even die.

If you have a high nitrite level, stop feeding the fish, carry out a partial water change (20 per cent), and provide plenty of aeration and water circulation. Retest the water the next day and, if necessary, carry out daily partial water changes until the nitrite levels drop to near zero. It may take several weeks until the nitrite level stabilizes, at which stage you can start feeding again, but sparingly. Keep testing to make sure that your filter is coping until the pond stabilizes.

Q In a mature pond, why is it necessary to carry out partial water changes, especially if I have created a balanced pond?

A Compared to a naturally occurring pond or lake, the water in an artificial garden pond is not balanced. Due to the unnaturally high stocking density, the addition of artificial food is necessary, which leads to the accumulation of nutrients in the water. Even if there is a low stocking density or no addition of food (as in a wildlife pond), because of its insular and isolated nature, nutrients will still accumulate.

Consequently, as a pond ages, the water's appearance may deteriorate, becoming discoloured. Nutrient build-up will also lead to the risk of nuisance algae, which will thrive on any freely available nutrients, such as nitrates and phosphates. To maintain the balance, you will need to intervene with frequent partial water changes. When the fish are feeding and growing in the warmer months, a pond will benefit from a 10 to 20 per cent water change every 2 weeks (also use this as an opportunity to clean out part of the filter). To maintain a stable environment, it's better to carry out frequent, small water changes rather than fewer, larger ones. In the colder months, when the fish are not feeding and fewer nutrients enter the pond, water changes are less vital. A good measure to use is the nitrate reading.

Try to keep nitrates close to or less than 50 ppm. As soon as they rise above that level, keep them in check with a partial water change (remembering to use a tap-water conditioner as required).

A well-planted pond
Even a well-planted pond is not balanced and will require regular partial water changes.

Q Why is it best for a pond to be at least 1m (3 feet) deep?

Flexibility of design
If you choose to construct your pond using a flexible pond liner or concrete, you have complete control over the depth.

A The dimensions that you make your pond will have a significant impact on the environment it creates for your fish. If you use a preformed pond, the depth will be predetermined by the mould's design and, in most cases, will be less than 1m (3 feet). If you are using a liner (or concrete), then you have complete flexibility as to how deep you make your pond – the deeper the better. A deep pond protects overwintering fish from the extremes of winter, insulating them against the icy air temperatures that would chill them too quickly and could cause physiological problems. In their wild, natural setting, fish will overwinter under ice for weeks very satisfactorily if they are provided with sufficient depth. In addition, because a deep pond holds a greater volume of water, it is a more stable environment. It will also provide your fish with added protection against herons and other predatory birds.

Q I have seen an array of test kits in my local pond store. Do I need to buy them all, and what will they tell me?

A It can be quite daunting to face the vast selection of test kits available for different parameters. You can save money by buying just three – these will provide you with the essential information relating to your pond. The most useful test kits to choose are:

pH: Testing the water's pH will help you determine whether your pond is within the desired pH range of between 7 and 8.5. Anywhere within these limits is satisfactory, as long as it is stable between them.

Nitrite: A new pond is prone to accumulating nitrite, the toxic by-product of the breakdown of ammonia that fish excrete. It is lethal and can prove to be very persistent in a new pond. The only safe nitrite level is zero, so a positive reading, which will often coincide with an adverse change in fish behaviour, should always be addressed.

Nitrate: Eventually, nitrites are broken down by biofilter bacteria into relatively harmless nitrates. Nitrates are tolerated by fish, but if they are allowed to rise above 50 ppm, you will start to encounter problems with algae and notice the fish becoming lethargic. A test kit will show you when you need to carry out a partial water change and to reduce the nitrate level.

Q I recently lost a couple of orfe during an unusually warm, muggy summer night. My guess is that the problem was a low dissolved oxygen level. What can I do to ensure this doesn't happen again?

A It sounds as though your pond is heavily planted, especially with submerged plants. These are net oxygen producers during the day but oxygen consumers at night. In a heavily stocked pond, plants demand a lot of oxygen from the water at night. The water's capacity to hold oxygen in warm weather is also greatly reduced, so during a warm, muggy night, there are two factors that combine to cause a pond's dissolved oxygen level to drop dangerously low. Under such circumstances, it is quite normal for orfe, which have a higher dissolved oxygen requirement than other fish, to be the first in the pond to succumb. The steps you should take to prevent this from happening again are:

Thin out plants
Remove some submerged plants to provide more space for the fish.

Improve water circulation
Add a waterfall or fountain, and keep it running overnight.

Review your stocking level
Consider removing some fish from your pond.

Remove silt
Vacuum up silt on the pond bottom; the bacteria that break it down demand oxygen.

Improve water circulation
Add a fountain or waterfall to improve the circulation of water in your pond.

Thin out pondweed
Remove pondweed, and leave it piled next to the pond for a day or so to allow the invaluable resident pond life inside to return to the pond. Under no circumstances should you try to discard pond plants "benevolently" into your local pond or stream, as they will invade and outcompete other plants in your local aquatic habitat. They do, however, make excellent compost.

Food and feeding

Feeding is a very enjoyable part of pondkeeping. But there are a number of pitfalls to avoid to ensure your pond and fish remain healthy.

Q My fish have been feeding and growing well all summer, but recently, they have started to eat less. Even when I return to the pond after a couple of hours, food is still on the surface. Why might this be?

A As long as you haven't changed the type of food you have been offering, the cause is not likely to be food-related. There are four areas you should investigate.

Water quality: Feeding fish heavily over the summer will have several consequences. The filter will need cleaning more frequently, and the pond will benefit from more regular partial water changes. The drop in your fish's appetite could be due to deteriorating water quality. Check that pH, nitrite and nitrate levels are all acceptable. Keep the filter media clear so that it can perform its task efficiently.

Temperature: Because pond fish are cold-blooded, their metabolism and appetite are dependent on the pond's temperature. This is why your fish are more active in summer. It's useful to check the water temperature with a pond thermometer. If summer is turning into autumn, then you may simply be seeing your fish's appetite respond accordingly. If the temperature has dropped to around 12°C (54°F), you would expect a drop in their appetite.

Disease: Check that apart from loss of appetite, your fish are behaving normally. Are they hanging at the surface, sulking or flicking through irritation? Are there any signs of disease? The manner in which fish feed is a good barometer for checking their health. Do your fish still seem alert, or are they too easy to catch with a net?

Shy behaviour: Although perhaps not relevant to your situation, newly introduced fish in sparsely stocked ponds may exhibit shy behaviour – that is, until there is more competition at feeding time, when more fish are added to the pond.

Whatever the cause, be careful not to let food go uneaten for more than 5 minutes, as this can lead to further water-quality problems.

Floating pond sticks
Remove any uneaten food, such as sticks or pellets, after 5 minutes.

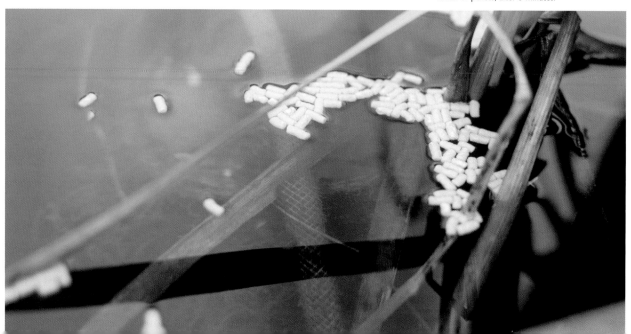

Q My fish seem to eat continuously. How often should I feed them?

A Pond fish (such as goldfish, koi and shubunkins) are members of the carp family and are often referred to as pigs of the pond because of how and what they eat. They are scavenging, opportunistic fish whose inquisitive nature leads them to root around in search of food. Feed them little and often – whatever they will eat in 5 minutes – and then remove any uneaten food. The fish will gain far more nutrition from their food when it spends more time in their relatively long guts. Feed them three or four times a day at the most, and you will strike the right balance. Frequent, smaller feedings give your fish a sufficient amount to grow, without putting undue pressure on the water quality in your pond.

Q I've been to my aquatic store to buy food for my pond fish and have been amazed at all the choices available. Why are there so many different types of food?

A Keeping pond fish is a seasonal hobby, and with every season, your fish will go through different phases, meaning that they will benefit from different foods.

Summer growth foods: When the pond is above 16°C (61°F), fish have the can grow at a fast rate, as long as they receive sufficient nutrition. At these temperatures, offer them a higher-protein (35 to 40 per cent) growth food, which will provide them with sufficient building blocks for growth.

Spring and autumn foods: When the pond is at an in-between temperature, and the fish are active but not necessarily growing, both the fish and the balance of the pond will benefit from a low-protein, easily digestible diet. Offer a 20 per cent protein food that is high in wheatgerm (a highly digestible protein source). If a higher-protein food is offered when your fish don't need it, the excess will pollute the pond and lead to water-quality problems.

Hand-feeding koi
Feeding your pond fish can become very interactive – but be careful not to overfeed.

Staple: A staple food is an all-around, no-frills food that provides sufficient nutrition for moderate growth and is priced accordingly. A staple food is not likely to contain ingredients to improve the colour of your fish and may also exclude other health-promoting ingredients.

Sinking: The vast majority of pond foods float so the feeding fish can be viewed close at hand. Sinking foods are less common and increase the risk of overfeeding, with uneaten food going unnoticed at the bottom of the pond. Sinking food is ideal for bottom-feeding fish such as green tench, however. Even so, offer it carefully so that bottom-feeders are not overfed.

Fish health

How your fish behave can tell you a great deal about your pond. You will need to know what to do (and what not to do) if things appear to go wrong.

Q I thought that koi and goldfish were compatible. However, I have been surprised at seeing lots of aggressive behaviour, with some fish chasing and bashing into others in the pond. At one stage, some fish actually jumped out of the water on top of some oxygenating plants. What can I do to stop them fighting?

A Your fish are not fighting but are in fact doing the opposite: breeding. Spawning behaviour is very boisterous and physical – it has to be for spawning to be successful. Plump females release their eggs when driven by the males, whose pressure causes them to expel the eggs. The male fish develop rough tubercles, which give them added purchase so they can exert physical pressure on the females' swollen abdomens. In response, a female swims toward the shallow water or areas that are thick with submerged vegetation, into which she releases her eggs. The adhesive eggs stick to the submerged weed until they hatch several days later. Females can become quite exhausted and even physically damaged, especially if they accidentally rub against hard or abrasive surfaces within the pond. Spawning behaviour may last for several hours; if necessary, you should isolate females once they have spawned to prevent them from becoming exhausted by the uninterrupted attention of the overamorous males.

Watching for signs of spawning
Monitor your pond for signs of spawning, and if necessary remove vulnerable females after they have spawned.

Q When watching my fish, every few seconds my eye is caught by a mirror-like glint. It's caused by my fish periodically scratching and rubbing against hard objects in the pond. What's going on?

A The behaviour you describe is often referred to as flicking or flashing and is caused by irritation to your fish. The most likely cause is an infestation of parasites on the fish's skin or in the gills, which causes them to "scratch". These external parasites feed off the skin or mucus, and their means of attachment (usually microscopic hooks) can cause irritation as well as a potential site for secondary infection. It's rare to see tiny parasites with the naked eye, but if the majority of your fish are flicking or flashing repeatedly, it is a strong indication of parasites. These can usually be treated effectively by a course of anti-parasite pond treatment, available at any pond store.

Before treating, you should discount poor water quality, particularly high nitrite, as the cause of flicking or flashing. Nitrites can also irritate the delicate gill tissue, causing a similar response in the fish. A simple water test will show whether nitrite is present, with zero being the only acceptable reading.

Q Some of my goldfish have started to change colour. Why does this occur, and how does it reflect on my pondkeeping skills?

A Goldfish are a genetically unstable ornamental variant of an olive-coloured wild carp. Many home-bred goldfish start out brown, and some will remain so all their lives, while others will turn into classic "gold" goldfish. This is purely a function of their particular genetic make-up. Similarly, goldfish that start off red or gold may develop other markings, such as areas of black or white. The same is true for koi, whose patterns will develop and change over time – as a result of genes.

Fish can change colour through environmental causes, too. The colour of ornamental fish will fade if they do not feed on sufficient, naturally occurring, colour-enhancing foods such as algae. It is possible to feed fish a colour-enhancing food that will improve their appearance – though such a food will not transform a brown goldfish into a "gold" goldfish.

Brown goldfish
Due to the genetic make-up of goldfish, natural spawnings in your pond will produce a range of different coloured offspring – including brown.

Algae

Algae is probably the biggest cause of frustration to the pondkeeper. How best can you control it, and why does it seem to be an ever-present threat?

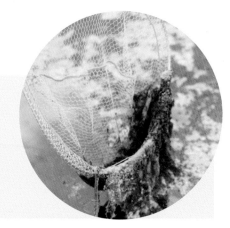

Q My new pond turned green after a few weeks of adding fish. I was advised to install an ultraviolet clarifier (UVC), which I did. After about 10 days, the water became crystal clear again, but my pond has since started to suffer from string algae, which is now choking the plants and blocks up my pump frequently. Having won the battle against green water, what can I do to get rid of string algae?

A Algae in its various forms can be a real nuisance in a pond. Green water is caused by uni-cellular algae that proliferates in an enclosed and nutrient-rich environment. The ultraviolet clarifier you installed soon controlled this by irradiating the waterborne algal cells as they passed through it. These clumped together and were removed by the filter (forming a green sludge). However, the ultraviolet clarifier simply addresses the symptoms of a nutrient-rich pond rather than addressing the cause. Consequently, the string algae, no longer shaded by green water, is able to thrive unhindered in your crystal-clear, nutrient-rich pond. Because string algae adheres to the hard surfaces within a pond, it does not pass through the UV clarifier, and its growth continues unchecked.

To control string algae, you need to address the cause – rising levels of nutrients (nitrates and phosphates) arriving through food and even in the tap water. Some string-algae treatments involve harsh herbicidal chemicals that, like the ultraviolet clarifier, address the symptoms, only for the algae to return later. The best approach is to use natural methods to keep the nutrient levels low, preventing the algae from thriving in the first place. There are various bacteria-based remedies that work very effectively, competing for the nutrients and causing the string algae to die back. There are other barley straw-based treatments that break down naturally to release various natural compounds that are effective against algae. Strategic planting also helps to outcompete algae for nutrients and light. As nutrients inevitably continue to enter the pond, the threat will remain, so you will have to continue treating against the threat of nuisance algae.

Blocked pump prefilter
Algae will soon block a foam prefilter, causing the pump's output to suffer.

Q My wildlife pond is 4 months old. It is well planted and has a few native fish that I don't feed. It is a still-water pond with no pump or filter. At times, the water clarity varies from almost clear to virtually opaque with green water, so that I can't see my fish. I'm encouraged, though, by the abundance and diversity of wildlife that my pond has already attracted, and I don't want to upset the developing ecosystem. So is green water in my pond a good or bad thing?

Green water
Fish will thrive in green water, but it can spoil a pond's appearance.

A Green water indicates an imbalance in your pond, but its mild presence in a wildlife pond will have some benefits. It provides a superb primary food for many micro-organisms and invertebrates and can fuel a really beneficial biodiversity in a pond. Green water is also full of colour-enhancing carotenoids, which, if your fish are ornamental, will help to produce stunning and vibrant colours. You should expect to see its occurrence decline as your pond matures and the plants start to outcompete it. Extreme cases of green water should be avoided because at night, it can cause severe dissolved oxygen depletion, which threatens the life of any fish and invertebrates. With some patience and continual creative planting, you should see the level of green water in your wildlife pond decline to acceptable levels.

Q I don't know how it happened, but duckweed has found its way into my pond. It has spread very quickly, and I have to net it out each week. How can I get rid of it completely?

A Duckweed is a very frustrating weed. It finds its way into your pond on other plants or via birds – that's why it's called duckweed. Only a single fragment is required, and under the right conditions it will rapidly divide and quickly cover the whole pond. This can then deprive beneficial submerged plants of light and even prevent gas exchange in still-water ponds, leading to anoxic conditions and the telltale "bad eggs" smell. As there are no safe chemical treatments, try leaving a hose running in your pond, causing it to overflow slightly and taking the floating duckweed with it. Even so, you will need to get rid of every last fragment. Larger koi and goldfish love to eat duckweed. A reduction in commercial feed will encourage the fish to consume the duckweed and eventually eradicate it, that is, as long as the duckweed population is reduced initially, which gives the fish an advantage.

Duckweed
Duckweed can soon spread to cover a pond completely, threatening the life within it.

Plants

Plants will transform your pond into a beautiful water garden. A few simple guiding principles will put you on the road to success.

Q What are the key considerations when comparing the planting in a wildlife pond and a standard garden pond?

A A wildlife pond will be planted with native plants directly into the pond's muddy substrate. There can be a risk of certain pond plants overgrowing other areas when planted in this way, but they can also give you the freedom to make a pond look quite natural.

When establishing a pond for the purpose of attracting wildlife, it is important to consider the threat of invasive plant species. Wildfowl and other visitors to the pond can carry plant parts and pieces on their feet and bodies. The ingested seeds will travel great distances, and some of them will be expelled with waste in other natural bodies of water. Keep an eye out for the arrival of any successful – yet unwanted – invasive plants.

In ornamental ponds that are in close proximity to natural ponds, there are the same considerations. Other, more secluded ornamental ponds in urban areas can be planted more liberally, as the plants will be retained in pots or baskets, so rampant growth is much less likely to present a problem. It is important to note that many native plants are extremely attractive when cultivated in all types of ponds, and they are generally easier to care for than non-native plants, so there will be a crossover between

Ornamental planting
It is possible to be adventurous with planting in an ornamental pond, but native plants will be easiest to care for.

plants found in ornamental and wildlife ponds. Native plants are already accustomed to the local climate and provide the necessary food, shelter and attraction for all kinds of wildlife.

Q When is the best time to thin out plants and carry out any other necessary plant maintenance?

A Any time is a good time for thinning excess plant growth. Plants consume nutrients from the water, so removing excess growth also permanently removes nutrients from the water body. Excessive plant growth detracts from the overall appearance of the pond by looking weedy and closing off the open areas that let sunlight penetrate to underwater plants, as well as limiting reflective space and open water for the fish.

Well-planted ponds are key to maintaining water quality because of their nutrient uptake, but removing decaying or rampant foliage growth in the autumn is critical to prevent those nutrients from being released back into the water during winter. Keeping decaying matter to a minimum is also important to prevent declining water quality because the process of decomposition requires high levels of oxygen. In fact, aquatic plants make excellent compost because few of the seeds generated by them will germinate in drier soils.

Dividing and repotting can generally be done anytime during the growing season, as long as sufficient time is allowed for the plants to establish a healthy root system prior to winter. If a substantial amount of the roots is removed when dividing, an equal amount of foliage should be removed to help the plants recover more quickly. Iris and lotus are the only exceptions to this rule. Iris prefers to be divided in the autumn, while lotus tubers should be collected in the early spring while dormant, prior to active growth.

Q Why don't my water lilies bloom as much as they used to?

A Water lilies are often sold in small planting containers that are suitable to the display area and easily handled. The container is usually sufficient to support healthy growth for a season or two, depending on the variety, and enables the retailer to display more lilies. As the plant matures, the area for new growth becomes limited and the available nutrients are consumed, resulting in smaller leaves and fewer flowers.

Water lilies require a sufficient surface area to perform at their best. Placing lilies in a broad, shallow container will give them the room they need to spread freely on the surface and provide enough open soil area to insert fertilizer to support that growth. Pots deeper than 15 to 25cm (6 to 10 inches) only make lifting them up more difficult, and the deeper soil isn't necessary to sustain growth. Since water lilies grow horizontally, placing the cut end of the tuber closest to the pot's edge increases the amount of space for new growth. Planting off centre takes a little getting used to, but the plants will quickly prosper and fill the pot. When the new growth reaches the other side, the leaf size will diminish, and flowering will slow down or halt entirely. Eventually, it becomes increasingly difficult for the plants to push new growth up between themselves and the sides of the pot, indicating that it is time to thin

Maintaining healthy water lilies
Water lilies need enough container space to allow them to perform at their best and will need regular repotting.

1 After a season or two, the water lily will probably have outgrown the pot it was supplied in. Remove it from the pot.

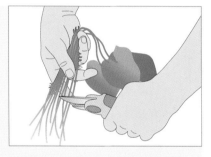

2 Trim back any old or dying leaves and do likewise with the roots.

3 Line the pot and fill it with heavy garden soil. Plant the lily in the pot, and top it off with gravel to keep the soil in place.

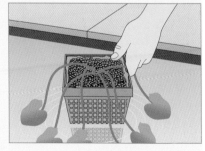

4 Lower the basket into the pond and position it at the correct depth, using bricks if necessary.

out and repot. Another sign that the plants need to be repotted is when buds rot off before they make it to the surface, indicating that the plant is running out of nutrients and energy.

Pond equipment

Pond equipment will keep your pond clear and healthy.
You will encounter some problems that need to be resolved
quickly – for the health of both your fish and your pond.

Q I am about to build my first pond, and I've seen both rigid preformed pools and rolls of flexible liner. Which should I choose?

A Flexible liners (available prepacked or off the roll) are by far the most popular means of creating a pond. They offer complete flexibility in design – you simply dig the hole to your dimensions, and buy sufficient liner for the job. This means you have complete control over the pond's shape and depth. Flexible liners are available in a range of different materials, with lengthy guarantees of over 20 years. A liner also makes it possible to fit the supplies for a pond containing several thousand gallons in the back of your vehicle, something you will simply not achieve with a rigid pond.

Flexible liners can prove a little harder to lay correctly, with creases and folds necessary to make a flat piece of material fit an irregular shape. It's important to lay a flexible liner properly, however, or it will be prone to leaks, with stones and roots a real threat; underlay is a good idea.

A rigid preformed pond gives greater confidence against leaks and will resist stones and other hard objects, but your design is limited to the shapes and sizes available. A rigid liner must be installed in a perfectly level excavation because it is difficult to level it once in place (unlike a flexible liner). Although more robust than a flexible liner, a rigid preformed pond will generally carry the same guarantee. It's perhaps the best way of creating a formal, geometrically shaped pond.

Q I've received mixed advice about whether I should turn off my biofilter during the winter. What should I do?

A Your biofilter is essential for maintaining a good, stable pond environment, as it is responsible for breaking down the waste produced by your fish in the warmer months. In the winter, when fish are not feeding and are less active, they will hardly excrete any waste, so there will be little need for a filter.

However, one of your pond's greatest assets is a mature biofilter, so even though the pond and your fish will not need it to sustain them over the winter, it is best to keep water moving through it (at a reduced rate) to keep the beneficial filter bacteria alive. There is a risk to your pond in doing so, because this can chill the water, which then makes the whole pond colder, risking the health of the fish during the winter.

A useful compromise is to put a reduced flow of water through the filter as well as insulate it so that the water is not chilled – but at all costs, keep your filter alive!

Informal pond shape – flexible liner.

Formal pond shape – rigid liner (or concrete).

Q I've noticed over the last few days that the level in my pond has dropped by several centimetres. If my pond is leaking, how do I locate the problem and then fix it?

Finding the leak
Once the pond level stops falling (above), you will have located the level of the puncture.

A When faced with a leaking pond, the hardest part is finding the actual leak. If you have a fountain or waterfall, turn it off, if possible, because it is the most likely area of water loss. Splashes or leaks from a waterfall and spray from a fountain will soon cause the level of a pond to drop. Fill up the pond and see what happens when the fountain or waterfall is turned off. Once you have isolated the cause of the leak, you can start to remedy it. For a fountain, you could choose a lower jet. If you suspect the waterfall, check for any splashes, and use some stones to redirect the flow. If the waterfall is still the cause, then you will need to reseal it with a clear sealant or even rebuild it.

If both the waterfall and fountain have been eliminated as causes of a leak, and you have checked any pipe work around the pond, you need to let the pond level drop until the seepage stops, indicating the level of the hole in the liner. Once you have found the hole (check any seams first), a standard pond-liner puncture-repair kit, available from pond stores, will soon solve the problem.

Patch
A simple patch can be used to seal a puncture in a flexible liner.

High fountain
Splashes from a fountain (below) can be the cause of water loss from a pond.

Seasonal care

Your pond changes through the seasons. So do the challenges in keeping it healthy and well maintained.

Q Spring is when my garden bursts into life. I presume the same is true for a pond. What jobs should I be doing in and around my pond in this season?

A A pond that has overwintered will be dormant, ready to start a new year, and it may well have been neglected a little. Springtime is a good time to make a few pre-season checks.

Test the water: Check that the pH, ammonia, nitrite and nitrate levels are acceptable before you start feeding the fish. If any levels are unacceptable, respond with a partial water change.

Check the pump: Ensure the pump is running properly and the prefilter or intake is free from any debris.

Clear silt: Use a pond vacuum to clear away any silt and leaf matter that settled over winter. This will also reduce the risk of the pump blocking.

Monitor the temperature: Keep track of the pond's temperature with a pond thermometer so you can determine when your fish will be ready to start feeding.

Check the filter: Confirm that the pond filter is clean and the media is unblocked; it is likely to be needed as the water temperature rises and your fish start to feed.

Feed cautiously: Feed the fish sparingly at first, with a low-protein food, and check the water accordingly.

Q How do I ensure that my pond and fish will overwinter safely?

A Winter can be a hazardous time for fish, which may be subjected to lengthy periods of below freezing temperatures. If the pond is at least 1m (3 feet) deep, the fish should be suitably protected from icy weather, sheltering in the warmer lower layers of the pond. There are several other steps you can take to help ensure their safety during the winter months.

Keep leaves out: Stretch a simple pond net tightly across the pond to prevent leaf matter from falling into the water. Although water quality is likely to be at its best (and clearest) in winter, it can soon deteriorate if leaf matter is allowed to settle.

Melt a hole in the ice: Do not break or crack the ice, but melt a hole with hot water and keep it open with a pond de-icer (a low-wattage heater). By itself ice is not a direct threat to fish, but it can cause problems indirectly by preventing gas from escaping.

Minimize water movement: Be sure to keep water movement to a minimum to help preserve the warmer layer in the deeper parts of the pond.

Filter spring-cleaning
Check that your filter media is clean and rinsed – ready for the spring.

Q What should I do about going on summer holiday?
Should I ask a neighbour to pond-sit, and will my fish need feeding?

A Prepare your pond for your holiday in a number of ways.

Clean the filter and prefilter:
Clean the filter, vacuum any silt and clean the pump prefilter, so you reduce the need for maintenance while you are away.

Remove string algae: Remove as much string algae as you can – it can grow to be a problem even over a 2-week period – and then apply your preferred and most effective method of string algae control.

Fit a temporary net: Cover the pond with a temporary net to ensure that you will return to a pond full of fish. A heron will find a quiet, unprotected pond irresistible.

Ration food portions: Package up individual daily rations for your neighbour if you are keen for your fish to feed while you are away (fish in a planted pond can manage without food for 2 weeks). This prevents them from overfeeding and from being killed with kindness, which is a real risk with a well-meaning neighbour.

Inspect the pond on returning:
When you are back home, carry out a quick visual inspection right away to see that your fish are all behaving normally. Clean out the pump and filter (it's probably been several weeks since they were cleaned), and don't forget a thank-you gift for the neighbour who looked after your pond while you were away.

Pond safety and security

Water can be a hazard in the garden for you and young children. Your fish can also be at risk from predation.

Q I'm planning a pond and would like some advice on how to ensure it poses no danger to my small children or those of my friends and neighbours.

Q Electricity and water do not mix and can prove to be a lethal combination. How can I make my pond safe, considering the equipment I am likely to have in and around my pond?

A Ponds do pose many dangers for children, with reports each year of tragic accidents. Children are attracted by the sound and sight of splashing water, so you must ensure that they are never left unattended near your pond; young, curious visitors are most at risk. It's wise not to build a pond if you have children younger than 5 years old. If your garden is likely to be visited by children, there are several ways to keep them safer.

Fence the pond: Build a fence or barrier around the pond. With a little creativity, a fence can actually become an integral feature, in keeping with the rest of the garden.

Build a raised pond: Consider a raised pond; a surface that's 60 to 90cm (2 to 3 feet) above the ground will make it harder for a child to fall in.

Fit a submerged grille: Fit a metal grille just below the water's surface, out of sight. Strong enough to hold the weight of a child, it will prevent a child who falls in from sinking to the bottom of the pond.

A A pond set-up might include an electrical pump, ultraviolet clarifier, lights and even a heater, all of which might come into direct contact with water. All electrical pond equipment is designed to be safe for use in a pond. However, it is still wise to take additional precautions, the best of which is to install a circuit breaker (RCD). If a manufactured seal breaks or an electrical cable corrodes, letting water in, the circuit will break as soon as there is a leakage to earth. This device costs just a few pounds but could potentially save a life.

Consult an electrician: All electrical work should be carried out by a registered electrician.

Go for low-voltage: If possible, consider low-voltage lights and even a pump to reduce the risk of electric shock, should a malfunction occur.

Use waterproof junction boxes: Use waterproof junction boxes or switching units, which will prevent the circuit breaker (RCD) from tripping unnecessarily and endangering your fish.

Q My friend's pond was decimated by a heron that took all but a few of his most beautiful and treasured fish. I am planning a pond, so how can I stop this from happening to my fish?

A Besides taking fish, a heron can be a carrier of disease. Its presence can also stress fish, causing them to become shy, reclusive creatures. If a heron is successful, even if disturbed midway through its visit, it will return later to get its catch. The only guaranteed method of preventing losses through heron predation is to cover the pond with tight netting fixed well above the pond. A major drawback to this is that anti-predator netting detracts from the attractiveness of an ornamental pond. A compromise is to erect a pergola above the pond that may be well covered with shading or climbing vegetation. However, this will not prevent a heron from landing and walking up to the pond edge to fish. Invisible lengths of fishing line stretched around the perimeter of a pond might startle an unsuspecting heron, causing it to fly off. The following devices have been designed to deter herons.

Protective drainpipe: Several sections of drainpipe placed on the pond bottom offer heron-proof cover for fish. This relies on the fish being quick enough and the heron not being patient enough to wait for the fish to leave their cover.

Heron scarer: This is a bamboo see-saw arrangement in which water gradually feeds into a hollow, open-ended section of bamboo, tipping the balance and causing a sudden movement and rush of water. It is also quite pleasing to look at and can make a nice water feature by itself.

Imitation heron: This is alleged to work on the principle that herons are territorial and will not fish together. However, as many as 14 herons have been seen sitting together in one corner of a field! Imitation herons have mixed reviews.

Heron scarer

Imitation heron

PLANT DIRECTORY

The addition of plants transforms a water feature into a
water garden and invites an abundance of wildlife and insects.
Bees, butterflies, dragonflies and damselflies will delight in the
flowers and foliage. Birds will bathe and drink on the surface,
while the fish move beneath the lilypads. Frogs will nestle in
the perimeter plantings in search of a meal. The surface water
will ripple in the breeze or capture the reflection of the sky.
A well-designed and thoughtfully planted water garden is the
foundation for the entire ecosystem that will develop within it.

Key to icons

Flowering season

Climate zones

Height

Spread/width

Floating plants

New lined ponds always benefit from the addition of floating plants. They provide quick access to shade and cover for fish while the more permanent plantings establish themselves. They require no soil or planting, so the dangling roots will immediately compete with algae for nutrients, taking all they require directly from the water. Fish love to graze on the roots and search through them for insect snacks. The roots also provide an excellent spawning area. All have very invasive tendencies and should be avoided in earth-bottomed ponds. Any large masses of growth that form during the growing season should be removed before the first frost. When excessive amounts of decaying matter remain in the pond, it upsets the balance of the entire ecosystem and can cause a fish kill.

Azolla caroliniana
Fairy moss
⬥ 7–11

A nitrogen-harbouring true fern, fairy moss can multiply its weight three times each week during the summer months. The emerald-green colour turns red during periods of cold or in the hot summer sun. The gentle shifts in colour create a mossy mosaic. Large koi and goldfish love to eat this tiny floater. If it establishes itself in the shallows beneath other marginal plants or in a decorative container full of water, a handful can be tossed into the water regularly as a fresh-food treat for the fish. Fairy moss is not recommended unless ornamental fish are present.

Eichhornia crassipes
Water hyacinth
⬥ 8–11

Eichhornia is useful in improving water quality and clarity. The dangling roots collect sediment and consume excess nutrients. Take indoors prior to the first frost to keep decaying matter from remaining in the pond during winter. It grows best in part shade and/or moving water, reaching heights of 30cm (12 inches) when crowded. The lavender-blue flowers have a pattern that resembles a peacock's tail feathers but they only appear during a warm summer.

Azolla caroliniana ▶

▼ Eichhornia crassipes

Hydrocharis ▶

Hydrocharis morsus-ranae
Frog's bit
🌿 4–11

The attractive, shiny, heart-shaped foliage of frog's bit is 2.5 to 5cm (1 to 2 inches) across. The flowers usually go unnoticed but generate a healthy seed crop that overwinters on the pond bottom. It reproduces very rapidly and often presents a problem in earth-bottomed ponds. It is ideally suited to container gardens and tolerates shade. Overwinter some in a jam jar indoors.

Lemna minor
Lesser duckweed
🌿 3–11

One of the smallest floating plants, duckweed measures only 0.5 to 1cm (⅛ to ¼ inch) across. It is a favourite food of koi and goldfish. It is notorious for taking over the entire surface of ponds that do not contain ornamental fish and is very difficult to control in their absence.

▲ *Stratiotes aloides*

Pistia stratiotes and P. stratiotes 'Rosette'
Water lettuce and rosette lettuce
🌿 9–11
↔ 25–50cm (10–20 inches)

Both of these floating lettuces prefer part shade and moving water. The larger standard water lettuce will reach diameters of 37 to 50cm (15 to 20 inches) when in a nutrient-rich environment. The rosette variety seldom exceeds 25cm (10 inches) and has a dense, ruffled appearance. The rosette lettuce is less attractive to aphids than the standard variety, which is a magnet for them. The plants should be removed prior to frost to prevent decaying matter from remaining in the pond during the winter months.

Stratiotes aloides
(Water soldier)
↔ 60cm (24 inches)
✳ Summer

A very handy plant that can be found completely submerged or floating at the surface, with its uniquely-shaped, pointed leaves emerging from the pond. This free-floating oxygenating plant will rise in the summer, flower, and then sink for the colder months. It enjoys a full-sun position, and will tolerate freezing winter temperatures. Plants will produce both male and female flowers, but they are easiest to propagate by removing daughter plants that are produced off the parent.

▲ *Lemna minor*

Pistia stratiotes ▶

◄ Calla palustris

Marginal plants

Planning for marginal plants should begin during the design phase. It is important to understand their preferences and growth habits. Many marginal plants are overlooked because they don't produce colourful flowers, but effective landscapes often rely on varying shapes and textures rather than colour. Marginal plants can be divided into four general categories: creepers and ground covers, intermediate, strong verticals and specimens. These can all co-exist comfortably. Broad planting shelves allow established plants to generate a necessary depth of field.

Selections can be made from any group to accomplish the same goals; for example, *Menyanthes* and *Cyperus* are specimen plants but may function as vertical background plantings in a large feature. Additionally, iris can be used as an intermediate plant in a large pond or as a vertical plant in a small pond.

Most aquatic plants are shallow-rooted and prefer wide, shallow containers. Wide planting containers provide adequate ballast from the wind. Allow sufficient soil mass for roots to penetrate, and reduce maintenance by preventing plants from becoming root-bound too quickly, which contributes to the health of the plants. Weak plants are more susceptible to pest and disease problems. To allow for generous containers, consider eliminating the foreground planting shelf and increasing the planting area in the background. The foreground can then be reserved for intimate fish interaction.

Whether the plants are in containers or planted direct on the bottom, a well-planned background adds a number of attractions. It creates a foraging area for the fish and allows complementary insect and amphibian populations to establish themselves, contributing to a better overall environment and ecosystem. It is best to select between three and seven varieties of marginal plants and plant flowing masses of each. Too many varieties spaced in individual containers causes the water feature to look weedy. If circulation is provided through the well-planted areas, it will result in increased nutrient uptake by the plants as well.

Creepers and ground covers

Creepers and ground covers are ideally suited to growing as understorey to more upright plants or in crevices between rocks. They disguise containers and create a natural-looking environment around the perimeter of the water garden. They provide shade and cover for fish and contribute to the transition from the surrounding area to the water's surface.

Calla palustris
Bog arum
◗ *3–6*
⬍ *15–25cm (6–10 inches)*
❋ *Early spring*

Glossy, heart-shaped foliage forms along the creeping rhizome. The white calla-like flowers form early in spring, signalling warmer weather ahead. This lily requires a cold climate and/or partial shade.

Houttuynia – houttuynia

Houttuynia is an East Asian herb used as a leaf vegetable or garnish, or for tea. Houttuynia has been used as an indoor natural air-freshener by growing it near an open window so the breeze carries its distinct, pungent scent through the home. Most people consider the aroma refreshing, but some find it too strong. Houttuynia is at home in very shallow water or moist soil. It can be invasive if not confined and will penetrate dense healthy turf and established gardens.

Houttuynia cordata

⬧ 6–11
⬍ 30cm (12 inches)
✳ Summer

Deep-green, heart-shaped leaves are outlined with red, and form spreading mounds of growth. Four delicate, evenly spaced white petals surround an upright yellow centre.

Houttuynia cordata 'Chameleon'
Chameleon plant

⬧ 6–11
⬍ 30cm (12 inches)
✳ Summer

Shades of yellow, green, blue and red grace the leaves of the beautiful chameleon plant, so named because it continually changes its foliage colour with varying amounts of sunlight. Mature foliage in full sun will emphasize the red colour, and shaded plantings will be marked more heavily with yellow. The full range of colours is the most dramatic with a half day of sun.

▲ **Houttuynia cordata 'Chameleon'**

▲ **Houttuynia cordata**

Butomus umbellatus
Flowering rush

⬍ 120cm (48 inches)
✳ Late summer

Originating from Northern Asia, this shallow water marginal is not a true rush. A good specimen is capable of producing an impressive display of rose-pink blooms in rounded heads. Young purple leaves emerge which gradually turn green. The Latin name describes the inverted umbrella-like display of the blooms which emerge in the late summer. Propagation is by dividing an overgrown clump.

Corex riparia

⬍ 50cm (20 inches)
✳ Spring

This "grass" will thrive either as a bog plant or by having its roots submerged in the water. It will benefit from being planted in full sun, where new growth will emerge in spring. The evergreen display makes it a good background marginal for a pond, with any old leaves being cut back just before the new ones emerge in spring. As a grass, it produces small inflorescences in spring, but its main feature is its golden leaves.

Butomus umbellatus ▶

Cotula coronopifolia
Brass buttons
- ⊟ *20cm (8 inches)*
- ⊡ *40cm (16 inches)*
- ✳ *Late spring to early fall*

Its profusion of brassy-yellow, button-like flowers gives this marginal plant its name. Its tender nature makes it an annual, which will easily seed, helping to ensure it continues in the pond. Under suitable conditions, it is capable of spreading and colonizing large areas around the edge of the pond. It will flower from late spring right through to early autumn, releasing copious amounts of seeds, then dying back in freezing conditions.

Eriophorum latifolium
Cotton grass
- ⊡ *60cm (24 inches)*
- ✳ *Spring*

A relatively slow-growing grass, in summer it exhibits cottonwool-like tufts. It thrives in acidic/peaty conditions. Small yellow blooms appear in spring, developing into brown pods which release the fibrous cotton tufts. If allowed to grow out of control it can be quite invasive.

Hypericum elodeoides
Marsh hypericum
- ⊡ *30cm (12 inches)*
- ✳ *Summer*

This creeping plant is ideal for concealing pond edges. It thrives in full sun, producing dense, green, rounded foliage with delicate yellow flowers. It will overwinter even the harshest of conditions. Propagation is simply achieved by dividing clumps and replanting.

▲ **Hypericum elodeoides**

◄ **Cotula coronopifolia**   ▲ **Eriophorum latifolium**

Mentha aquatica
Aquatic mint
- 🌢 5–11
- ↕ 30cm (12 inches)
- ✳ Summer

Like most mints, the aquatic mint also has a rampant, free-roaming habit. However, it is extremely useful in a new pond to establish shade and cover for fish very quickly. It is unfazed by a severe haircut to keep it in check and will rebound quickly. This mint produces dense clusters of lavender flowers. Bees and butterflies always flock to the blossoms.

Mentha aquatica var. crispa
Curly mint
- 🌢 5–11
- ↕ 30cm (12 inches)
- ✳ Summer

Curly mint is very similar to aquatic mint, except the leaves are heavily crinkled and ruffled. The lavender-pink flowers form on stiff upright stems around the leaf nodes and are slightly more showy than those of aquatic mint.

Menyanthes trifoliata
Bog bean
- 🌢 3–8
- ↕ 15 cm (6 inches)
- ✳ Early spring

Bog bean flowers in early spring, when pink buds on tiered stems unfold to display delicate white-fringed flowers. Menyanthes is ideal for softening hard rock edges around the pool. It will creep between the stones and establish itself in surrounding soil as long as the original planting remains in the water. Bog bean will persist for many years without fertilizer or attention and thrives in moving water. It is very tolerant and can be planted in full sun or part shade.

◀ *Menyanthes trifoliata*
▼ *Myosotis scorpioides*

▲ *Ranunculus lingua*

Phalaris arundinacea
⬍ *100cm (39 inches)*

A graceful, variegated grass that can be quite invasive if not retained in a basket. Its evergreen nature gives a pond a good variegated background that will also fill the senses with sound as the leaves rustle in the wind. It should be trimmed back each spring to allow for new growth, when it will produce brighter green leaves.

Ranunculus lingua
Water buttercup/greater spearwort
✳ *Summer*

This invasive waterside plant works well in a natural or wildlife pond setting. The leaves on non-flowering shoots are heart-shaped, while those on flowering stems are narrower − reflecting the spearwort name. Each golden flower can be up to 5cm (2 inches) across, with the leaves reaching 20cm (8 inches) across. It will thrive in full sun or shade and can be propagated by dividing overgrown clumps. It flowers right through the summer.

Myosotis scorpioides
Water forget-me-not
⬍ *30cm (12 inches)*
✳ *Summer*

This vigorous plant will be one of the first to appear in spring and can soon become rampant. Its delicate blue flowers will put on a lengthy display in summer as its long green trailing stems continue to spread to uncolonized areas. Most effective when planted in clumps, it will grow up to 30cm (12 inches) high, and spread much farther. Depending on the situation, it can suffer from harsh winter conditions.

Veronica beccabunga
Brooklime
⬍ *20cm (8 inches)*
✳ *Summer*

This plant gets its name from its love of chalky, hard-water conditions, and is a colourful contribution to a wildlife pond with its tiny abundance of freely-seeding violet flowers. It is a quick-spreading marginal that can soon become untidy if not kept in check. It is a very hardy plant, which overwinters well.

◄ *Phalaris arundinacea*

Marginal plants: intermediate

Intermediate plants are in the moderate height range and rise up out of the ground cover, as occurs in nature. They often have broad leaves and colourful flowers and stand out against the vertical background plants. Most are suitable for any size pond.

Alisma plantago-aquatica var. *parviflorum*
Water plantain
🌿 3–11
⬍ 20–30cm (8–12 inches)
✳ Summer

The round, heavily veined leaves of water plantain have an almost puckered appearance. Sturdy spikes hold large sprays of flowers that strikingly resemble baby's breath. This is an outstanding plant that forms generous clumps of growth.

Alisma plantago-aquatica
Water plantain/water baby's breath
🌿 3–11
⬍ 30–46cm (12–18 inches)
✳ Summer

A heavy feeder with smooth, narrow, pointed foliage, water plantain is well suited for use in moving water to keep a flush of nutrients to the roots. It is susceptible to early dormancy in the absence of sufficient fertilizer. The flower stems are less dense than *A.* var. *parviflorum*.

Caltha palustris
Marsh marigold/cowslip
🌿 3–7
⬍ 20–30cm (8–12 inches)
✳ Early spring

The bright, sunny yellow flowers display themselves promptly after the snow melts. Marsh marigold forms dense clumps and is not aggressive or weedy. It will not tolerate a very warm climate but, rather, prefers the refreshing cool water in spring seeps, streams, and lightly-shaded bogs.

▲ *Alisma plantago-aquatica var. parviflorum*

▲ *Alisma plantago-aquatica*

▲ *Caltha palustris*

Iris – water iris

The iris has long been a staple plant in the garden pond. It is easy to grow, suffers from few pests or diseases, and offers various heights and flower and foliage colours. Because it will grow in or out of water, it is an excellent choice to mass at the perimeter of the water feature (planted both in and out of the water) to prevent the viewer from knowing where the water stops and the garden begins. This kind of diminishing edge will make a feature seem much larger than it really is.

Iris laevigata
Rabbit ear iris/Japanese water iris
- 4–10
- 60 cm (2 feet)
- Spring

This variety has jewel-tone purple blossoms with pure white beards. The absence of yellow makes this iris unique.

Iris laevigata 'Variegata'
Variegated Japanese iris
- 4–10
- 60 cm (2 feet)
- Spring

Without question, this is one of the most beautiful variegated plants. Each leaf appears to have been hand-painted on each side, blending the clear white and crisp green into a non-specific pattern of colour. The stunning purple flowers stand out beautifully against the bright variegated foliage.

Iris pseudacorus
Yellow flag iris
- 4–10
- 90–180cm (3–6 feet)
- Spring

Bold yellow flowers are visible from afar due to the grand size of this iris. Because of its highly successful seed germination, yellow flag has naturalized. Avoid it in earth-bottomed ponds, and remove seed pods to prevent unwanted germination.

Iris pseudacorus ▶

Iris versicolor
Blue flag iris
🌿 4–10
↕ 60–90cm (2–3 feet)
✳ Spring

An all-round favourite, the blue flag iris has a compact growing habit suitable for any size pool. The flowers are a delicate mix of purple, violet, yellow and white.

Mimulus ringens
Lavender musk/
lavender monkey flower
🌿 3–9
↕ 60cm (2 feet)
✳ Summer

Lavender flowers that resemble miniature snapdragons nestle among the foliage of this plant. It is an excellent choice to add some late summer colour to the water garden. Random pruning will encourage increased blooming and denser growth. *Mimulus* is a uniform and consistent performer. The generous root system makes it suitable for stream planting to produce additional filtration.

◀ **Iris versicolor**

▼ **Orontium aquaticum**

Orontium aquaticum
Golden club
🌿 5–10
↕ 30–60cm (1–2 feet)
✳ Early spring

The yellow, club-like flowers of this arum are held on bright white stems. The leathery, deep blue-green foliage repels water and is sometimes referred to as never-wet. Due to the compact, slow-growing habit of golden club, it rarely requires any care. It will prosper in deep water or moist soil and is seldom bothered by anything except a few spring aphids. Golden club thrives in moving water and tolerates high-iron situations. In the wild, it grows in part shade or full sun.

Peltandra virginica
Arrow arum/bog arum
🌿 5–10
↕ 60–90cm (2–3 feet)
✳ Summer

This outstanding plant forms a clump and requires little maintenance to thrive. Arrow arum blossoms are insignificant, but the foliage is shiny, bold and arrowhead-shaped. It will flourish in moist soil to a depth of 30cm (12 inches) in full sun or partial shade. It looks very attractive planted in a large container.

◀ **Peltandra virginica**

▼ **Mimulus ringens**

Pontederia – pickerel weed

Pickerel weed, which has glossy, spear-shaped leaves, is a well-known staple in the water garden. Depending on the variety, flowers are blue, lavender, pink or white, with heights ranging from 30 to 122cm (1 to 4 feet). The spiked summer flowers are a haven for bees and butterflies. The pickerel family is clump-habited and easy to care for, although they are heavy feeders and perform best with an adequate area in which to spread. Pickerel will grow well in light shade or full sun.

Pontederia cordata
Pickerel rush/pickerel weed
◊ 3–11
⬍ 60cm (2 feet)
✳ All summer

Bright lavender flowers bloom on a moderately sized plant. There is a strong variation of foliage sizes and shapes.

Pontederia cordata var. alba
White pickerel rush
◊ 6–11
⬍ 60cm (2 feet)
✳ All summer

White pickerel tends to get off to a slow start in the spring but flowers well once it is established.

▼ *Pontederia cordata var. alba*

▲ *Pontederia cordata*

Sagittaria japonica
Arrowhead
◐ *4–11*
⬍ *30–60cm (1–2 feet)*
✳ *Summer*

Crisp white flowers with bright-yellow centres appear on tiered stems above the arrowhead-shaped foliage. Variations in the foliage can often be attributed to the amount of nutrients provided. In a fertile environment, the leaves will be bold and deep green. When undernourished, the leaves are often small and pale, and the plant will likely become dormant prematurely.

Zantedeschia aethiopica
Calla lily/common calla
◐ *8–11*
⬍ *60cm (2 feet)*
✳ *Spring*

The stunning white flowers stand well above the glossy, dark-green, arrowhead-shaped foliage. Large established plantings have a stately presence in any garden pond. When started from dry tubers, the initial watering should be infrequent, maintaining moist soil until the plants have 15 to 20cm (6 to 8 inches) of foliage established. The tubers can then be placed in the pool with 6 to 8cm (2 to 3 inches) of water covering the container. As long as there is active healthy growth, the plants will adapt to being submerged; otherwise, they will rot. *Zantedeschia aethiopica* 'Green Goddess' shares all the same attributes, but the flowers have ruffled green edges.

Zantedeschia aethiopica ▶

Marginal plants: strong verticals

Strong vertical plants generally have sturdy, upright foliage that adds interest and texture to the water feature. A few have colourful flowers, but most simply offer a sound, stable backdrop to the plantings in front of them. Some of the variegated varieties are good for highlighting the bold foliage and flowers of the intermediate plants. Mass plantings help them accomplish their goal effectively. Keep height in mind when selecting these plants, as they firmly dictate scale in the garden.

Acorus calamus
Sweet flag
◑ 4–11
↕ 60–90cm (2–3 feet)

Sweet flag grows in much the same manner as iris but lacks significant flowers. The glossy, often gently rippled leaves sway gracefully in the breeze and have a distinct aroma when broken. Historically, sweet flag was used underfoot in doorways to release a welcoming scent as guests arrived. The roots and leaves have been used for food, as medicine, and to relieve the burn or itch from insect bites (as in calamine lotion).

Acorus calamus 'Variegatus'
Variegated sweet flag
◑ 4–11
↕ 60–90cm (2–3 feet)

This plant is well known for the creamy-white variegation that holds strong on the foliage throughout the season. Variegated sweet flag grows in light shade or full sun, and mature plants seek depths of up to 30cm (12 inches).

Arundo donax 'Variegata'
Variegated giant reed
◑ 6–11
↕ 1.5 to 3m (5–10 feet)

Tolerant of the confines of a sturdy container, this cultivar is better suited to an ornamental pond than the much more aggressive species *Arundo donax*. The strong, hollow reeds grow much like bamboo and warrants restriction. The creamy-white

▲ **Carex nigra**

▲ **Acorus calamus 'Variegatus'**

▲ **Arundo donax 'Variegata'**

striped, ribbon-like leaves are a striking backdrop to broad-leaved foliage plants.

Carex nigra
Black flowering sedge
◑ 4–8
↕ 30–60cm (1–2 feet)
✳ Spring

Black and yellow flowers emerge early in the spring, followed by weeping blue-grey foliage that sways gracefully in the breeze. Sedges require little care and can be used effectively standing alone or en masse.

Cyperus alternifolius
Umbrella palm/umbrella grass
◑ 8–11
↕ 150cm (5 feet)

This plant is named for its leaf formations. Dubbed "palm", it is actually a grass that does well in full sun to part shade, in moist soil, or submerged up to 30cm (12 inches) deep. It will winter easily indoors as long as it has bright light and plenty of water. It is an extremely heavy feeder and well suited to moving water for added filtration. *Cyperus alternifolius* 'Gracilis' is a dwarf variety reaching heights of 60 to 90cm (2 to 3 feet).

Cyperus haspan
Dwarf papyrus
◑ 9–11
↕ 60cm (2 feet)

Dense tufts of foliage resemble green powder puffs. Golden flowers form on the tips and turn brown towards the end of summer. The heavy viviparous plant heads cause the stems to arch downwards. Once in contact with moist soil or water, the heads will sprout new plants.

▲ *Cyperus alternifolius*

Cyperus papyrus 'King Tut'
Compact papyrus
🌡 8–11
↕ 90–120cm (3–4 feet)

This dwarf, uniformly upright papyrus is suitably sized for small and medium ponds. It is less tolerant of full sun than other members of the *Cyperus* family, unless it is placed in moving water. The plant winters indoors under low light, and it prefers to be moist rather than submerged while resting.

Eleocharis dulcis (syn. *Eleocharis tuberosa*)
Chinese water chestnut
🌡 8–11
↕ 60–90cm (2–3 feet)

Luminous, tissue-thin, hollow stems appear to glow in the sunlight. Water chestnut forms uniform columns of growth defined by the container. Edible tubers are formed in the autumn and should be collected and stored in the refrigerator for transplanting the following spring. Of course, a few should be reserved to peel, slice and eat raw for a crisp, milky sweet delight.

▲ *Cyperus haspan*

Equisetum – horsetail

Horsetail has graced the planet for millions of years and, due to its aggressive habit, doesn't appear to be leaving in the near future. It will grow comfortably in damp sand or moist soil and, once established, will venture into very deep water. On the upside, horsetail will adapt to the most confining situations, requiring little if any care for many years. The key is to keep it away from surrounding soil; once free, it is virtually unstoppable. Since the moisture requirements are so broad, horsetail can also be grown successfully in containers outside the pond. A pot with a slow leak to capture rainwater is best, but be certain to keep a solid tray beneath it to prevent it from escaping. Extended periods without any moisture may lead to the demise of the top growth but are unlikely to harm the spreading rhizomes. Remove any damaged foliage so it does not detract from new emerging stems.

▼ *Juncus glaucus*

▼ *Equisetum hyemale*

Equisetum hyemale
Horsetail/scouring rush

⬥ 5–10

↕ 46–60cm (18–24 inches)

Semi-evergreen cylindrical stems have vertical grooves. The periodic joints are encircled by black bands. The rigid, sturdy stems form a dense column of growth.

Equisetum hyemale var. robustum
Giant horsetail

⬥ 5–10

↕ 90–120cm (3–4 feet)

Tall, stiff stems become narrow towards the top and form delicate side shoots that give the plant a ferny appearance. Annual removal of the stems in spring will keep this horsetail from looking unruly. Cut stems laid flat in a pan of water sprout new plants quickly.

▲ *Equisetum hyemale var. robustum*

Juncus glaucus
Blue rush

⬥ 5–11

↕ 30–60cm (1–2 feet)

The slate-blue needle-like foliage persists throughout the winter. This becomes brown on the tips by spring in the far northern climate and should be trimmed or cut back to keep the vase shape looking clean. The russet-coloured blossoms weight the tops of the stems and broaden the vase in summer.

Phragmites australis 'Aurea'
Variegated Norfolk reed

⬥ 5–11

↕ 90–120cm (3–4 feet)

Stripes of gold and green are laid on the narrow leaves that grow horizontal to the stems. New growth is needle-sharp and can puncture the pond liner. Provide a sturdy container to prevent escape and limit the growth to create a lush, dense mass of colourful foliage. Should be avoided in earth-bottomed ponds.

Sagittaria lancifolia form *ruminoides*
Red-stemmed sagittaria

🌿 8–11

↕ 60–90cm (2–3 feet)

✳ Summer

Sturdy burgundy stems hold spear-shaped leaves at the top. Tiered stems are tipped with clear white flowers that have sunny yellow centres. A moderate grower, this plant forms a dense clump of stunning foliage and flowers all summer long.

▲ *Phragmites australis* **'Aurea'**

Scirpus (syn. *Schoenoplectus*) *lacustris* subsp. *tabernaemontani* 'Albescens'
White bulrush

🌿 5–9

↕ 120–150cm (4–5 feet)

Almost pure-white, pointed narrow stems emerge in early spring. As they mature, they become creamy with fine green lines that run vertically on the stems. Withholding fertilizer delays the eventual predominant greening of the foliage in the late summer months. The long, bright, hollow foliage sways gracefully in the breeze for added interest.

▲ *Scirpus lacustris* subsp. *tabernaemontani* **'Zebrinus'**

▲ *Scirpus lacustris* subsp. *tabernaemontani* **'Albescens'**

Schoenoplectus lacustris subsp. *tabernaemontani* 'Zebrinus'
Zebra rush

🌿 5–9

↕ 120–150cm (4–5 feet)

Like white bulrush, the new growth of the zebra rush shows the most prominent variegation. The white bands are horizontal along the green stems. The variegation can be re-inspired by a midsummer division of the plant to a fresh pot of soil. The absence of fertilizer helps maintain more prolonged colour.

▲ *Sagittaria lancifolia* form *ruminoides*

Typha – cat-tail

Cat-tails are commonly associated with water gardens, spreading quickly by underwater rhizomes and seed. The larger varieties are much more aggressive in earth-bottomed ponds than their dwarf counterparts. All have very sharp growing tips and should be confined in the lined pond to prevent puncture of the pond lining, especially when grown in planting pockets around the perimeter. The container can be buried in gravel to disguise its presence.

Typha angustifolia
Narrow-leaf cat-tail
🌢 3–10
⬍ 180cm (6 feet)

Suitable for large ponds only, narrow-leaf cat-tail should be given generously sized containers. The foliage is deep blue-green with long narrow seed heads. The flexible ribbons of foliage move freely in the breeze.

Typha latifolia
Common cat-tail
🌢 3–10
⬍ 120–150cm (4–5 feet)

The broad leaves of the common cat-tail are bright green and sweep away from the main stem in a vase shape. The seed heads are tall but stout. The bold foliage of the common cat-tail should be reserved for larger ponds.

▲ *Typha angustifolia*

▲ *Typha latifolia*

Typha latifolia 'Variegata'
Variegated great reed mace

◐ 4–11

↕ 120–150cm (4–5 feet)

This cat-tail is most frequently grown for the outstanding vertical green and white stripes that run up and down the leaves. The foliage forms the same vase shape as the common cat-tail. The crisp white variegation remains strong throughout the season.

◀ ***Typha latifolia* 'Variegata'**

Typha laxmannii
Slender reed mace

◐ 3–10

↕ 90–120cm (3–4 feet)

Slender-leaved with a tight growing habit, the graceful cat-tail does not spread as rampantly as the larger varieties. The pokers are tall and narrow.

Typha minima
Dwarf Japanese bulrush

◐ 3–10

↕ 46–60cm (18–24 inches)

The extremely compact blue-green foliage of the miniature cat-tail is complemented by nearly round seed heads. Plants that are pot-bound produce the most abundant catkins. Division should take place shortly after flowering.

▲ ***Typha laxmannii***

◀ ***Typha minima***

Marginal plants: specimens

Specimen plants are best suited to a single large container or stand that becomes a focal point in the water feature. They are generally tall and/or offer unique or bold foliage texture. In large ponds, substantial plantings of specimen plants are important to keep the arrangement in scale.

Canna – canna

Most cannas will grow in the water, though some varieties are true aquatics. Those that are not (considered terrestrial) need to have at least 15 to 20cm (6 to 8) inches of foliage growth before they can be submerged into the pond to prevent them from rotting. Terrestrial cannas must be removed prior to dormancy and used as houseplants or stored dry for winter. Aquatic cannas will winter in the water as long as they are hardy in that climate. All of these plants offer bold foliage textures, colours and season-long blooms that will add excitement to the water garden. Dead-heading the spent flowers encourages blooming and helps keep the plants looking fresh.

Canna 'Australia'
◐ 8–11
↕ 120–150cm (4–5 feet)
✳ All summer

This variety has lance-shaped, burgundy-black foliage, complemented by intense red flowers. The leaves of this canna are so saturated with colour that they are shiny.

Canna flaccida
Native yellow water canna
◐ 8–11
↕ 120–150cm (4–5 feet)
✳ All summer

A true aquatic canna species, this plant has narrow, medium-green leaves and delicate, bright-yellow flowers.

Canna 'Pink Sunburst'
◐ 8–11
↕ 120–150cm (4–5 feet)
✳ All summer

Burgundy foliage is striped with pink, red and orange. The flowers are a crisp pink.

Canna 'Striata'
Variegated water canna
◐ 8–11
↕ 120–150cm (4–5 feet)
✳ All summer

The striped leaves are bold and colourful. The flowers are orange tinged with red.

Canna 'Stuttgart'
◐ 8–11
↕ 120–150cm (4–5 feet)
✳ All summer

The medium-green foliage has uneven broad white patches. It requires some shade to keep the foliage from scorching.

▲ *Canna* **'Australia'**

***Canna* 'Striata'** ▶

Colocasia – taro/elephant ear

The bold leaves of taro add dramatic texture and colour to the water garden. Most varieties grow quickly and put on an awesome display. A longtime staple food in Asian culture, most parts are eaten but must be cooked thoroughly to destroy irritating toxins in the plant. Taro is easily wintered indoors as a houseplant, or the corms may be stored dry and restarted in the spring.

Colocasia antiquorum 'Illustris'
Imperial taro
🍃 8–11
↕ 60–90cm (2–3 feet)

The green leaves have varying degrees of dark purple patterned between the green leaf veins. This compact grower generates numerous young plants on runners and will quickly fill out the container.

Colocasia esculenta
Green taro/wild taro
🍃 8–11
↕ 120–180cm (4–6 feet)

The particularly large green leaves of this plant are gently ruffled along the edges. A very fast grower, the green taro provides almost instant impact.

Colocasia esculenta 'Fontanesii'
Violet stem taro
🍃 8–11
↕ 150–180cm (5–6 feet)

Black stems hold the large shiny green leaves well above the water. The silky texture of the leaf surface magnifies the gentle ripples.

▲ *Colocasia esculenta* **'Fontanesii'**

▲ *Colocasia antiquorum* **'Illustris'**

Colocasia esculenta 'Black Magic'
Black magic taro/black taro
🍃 8–11
↕ 90–120cm (3–4 feet)

Dusty black leaves sit on dark purple-black stems. Likely most popular taro due to its moderate stature and unique colour.

▲ *Colocasia esculenta*

▼ *Thalia dealbata*

Colocasia esculenta 'Violet Stem'
Violet stemmed taro
◧ 8–11
⬍ 150–180cm (5–6 feet)

This plant is similar to 'Fontanesii', but the leaves are dusty green rather than glossy. Both plants achieve towering heights quickly as the summer warms.

Cyperus papyrus
Egyptian papyrus
◧ 8–11
⬍ 240cm (8 feet)

Brooms of needle-like foliage become heavy as they mature and cause the stems to arch gracefully towards the water's surface. Egyptian papyrus needs plenty of surrounding space so the broad weeping habit of this plant can be fully appreciated. Could stand outside over the summer.

Taxodium distichum
Swamp cypress
◧ 4–11
⬍ Up to 30m (100 feet)

Bald cypress is famous for the "knees" that are formed by the tree roots when it is grown in shallow water. It is a deciduous conifer that will grow in or out of the water. It is an extremely slow grower that will tolerate severe pruning to keep it uniform and compact. It will also tolerate being confined to a moderate-sized container for extended periods of time, as long as it is submerged in shallow water. Knees will even form in the pots and protrude out of the water, creating added interest.

Thalia dealbata
Hardy water canna/powdery thalia
◧ 6–11
⬍ 180–210cm (6–7 feet)
✳ Summer

Thalia provides dense, bold foliage to create a tropical feel in the northern garden. The clump-habited growth makes it a wonderful addition to earth-bottomed ponds, where it will likely winter further north if placed deep enough to avoid a total freeze of the rootstock. In lined ponds, the container needs to be quite large so that it can ballast the broad foliage from the wind. The dark-purple blossoms are formed in tight clusters at the top of narrow stems that extend well above the foliage. The flowers and seeds that form on the stems are heavy and sway gracefully in the breeze. Together the foliage and flowers produce a striking display.

▲ *Taxodium distichum*

Lily-like plants

These plants have leaves that primarily float on the water's surface like water lilies – hence, "lily-like". The flowers range from 2 to 5cm (1 to 2 inches) across, depending on the variety. They will grow in sun or part shade and prefer water that is 30 to 60cm (1 to 2 feet) deep. Useful in lined garden ponds of any size, lily-likes offer quick cover and an excellent foraging area for koi and goldfish. Most plants spread by runners or seed and can become an invasive nuisance in earth-bottomed ponds.

Aponogeton distachyos
Water hawthorne
🌿 4–11
✳ Autumn and spring

This delightful bulb generates strap-like leaves and beautiful white blossoms during autumn and spring. When water temperatures are below 15°C (60°F), water hawthorne is in peak performance, pausing only when the water is frozen. Where water temperatures remain warm, it may flower throughout the winter. It should not be planted in earth-bottomed, spring-fed ponds, where it can become invasive from seed. In a lined pond, it can share the same containers as water lilies, as it is dormant during the warm summer months. The flowers have a heavenly fragrance and will last in a vase for almost two weeks.

Hydrocleys nymphoides
Water poppy
🌿 8–11
✳ Summer

Poppies begin to flower when the water temperatures are consistently warm. The sunny yellow blossoms stand out beautifully against the glossy, round, deep-green leaves that stand upright in shallow water, transitioning to floating as the water gets deeper. In the fall, prune any frost-damaged upright foliage, and the floating leaves that remain will turn into a patchwork of mottled burgundy and green that will persist until the pond freezes over. *Hydrocleys nymphoides* is much smaller than its giant cousin, whose leaves are 5 to 10cm (2 to 4 inches) across.

Nuphar japonica
Japanese pond lily
🌿 6–10
✳ Summer

Leaves are arrowhead-shaped and slightly ruffled, forming above and below the surface. They often have a burgundy cast. The flowers are an orange-yellow mix and open fully to reveal the centres.

▼ **Hydrocleys nymphoides "Water poppy"**

▲ **Aponogeton distachyos**

Nuphar lutea
Yellow spatterdock
✳ *Summer*

A very vigorous, potentially invasive plant that is best suited to large ponds. Bright yellow, brandy-bottle flowers appear in summer, producing flask-shaped seed pods. Although not to be confused with normal water lilies, this deep water plant does produce lily-shaped leaves up to 30cm (12 inches) across. Ideally it should be planted 1.5m (5 feet) deep, although it can be found in water as deep as 4.5m (15 feet).

Nuphar lutea ▶

Nymphoides – water snowflake/floating heart

All the *Nymphoides* have leaves that resemble miniature water lilies with varying textures and colours. They spread by runners, seed or plantlets that form on the leaf stem near the flowers. The leaves are smaller and more numerous than those produced by water lilies, forming dense areas of surface growth. They are very adaptable and also find themselves at home in container gardens. Excessive growth may be pruned out regularly to maintain areas of open water. All varieties should be avoided in earth-bottomed ponds.

Nymphoides peltata
Yellow floating heart
🍃 *5–11*
✳ *Summer*

Yellow, ruffled flowers sit above ruffled-edged green foliage. *Nymphoides peltata* spreads aggressively by seed. The pods are large and numerous with a high germination rate.

▼ *Nymphoides peltata*

Water lilies
Nymphaea

Water lilies produce large, colourful flowers throughout the summer months, and many have mottled or speckled foliage. They are quick to establish, providing shade and cover for the fish. Most varieties perform well in 45 to 90cm (18 to 36 inches) of water. Dwarf varieties prefer to be in the range of 45 to 60cm (18 to 24 inches). In colder climates and ponds with limited sunlight, lilies can be raised off the bottom to the warmer surface water – 15 to 25cm (6 to 10 inches) deep – in the summer months to trick them into believing they are closer to the sun; this will extend the growing season and induce more flowering. All perform best in generous containers with plenty of fertilizer. Undersized containers lead to diminished leaf size and reduced flowering. As with most plants, if water lilies are weak and undernourished, they will be more susceptible to pests and diseases that healthy plants resist.

▲ *Nymphaea* **'Barbara Dobbins'**

Water lilies: hardy

Hardy water lilies reward the owner year after year with abundant foliage and flowers coloured white, yellow, peach, pink and red. They can be categorized into three groups. Dwarf lilies have a spread of 30 to 90cm (1 to 3 feet) in diameter. Medium-sized plants will spread 90 to 150cm (3 to 5 feet) in diameter, and large varieties spread upward of 180cm (6 feet) in a season. There are a number of different tuber types, the favoured being those that have compact, clump-forming, or marliac-type tubers. They are more content in a container and less likely to jump the pot and keep going. Many new hybrids are bred to have a compact growth habit that isn't always recognizable from the broad foliage spread. Listed here are a few of the popular varieties, old faithfuls and new hybrids. All have proven to be outstanding performers and have a compact to moderate growth habit.

▲ *Nymphaea* **'Attraction'**

Nymphaea 'Attraction'
🌿 *3–11*
✳ *All summer*
⬌ *Medium*

This variety has flowers with wine-red centres that subtly fade to the white outer sepals.

Nymphaea 'Barbara Dobbins'
🌿 *3–11*
✳ *All summer*
⬌ *Medium*

This outstanding bloomer has apricot flowers touched with yellow. The foliage is speckled lightly with burgundy.

▲ *Nymphaea 'Denver'*

Nymphaea 'Colorado'
◐ 3–11
✳ All summer
⊟ Medium

The pink petals have yellow tips when viewed closely. From a distance, the flowers look peach-coloured. The blooms are produced continually, standing well above the water.

Nymphaea 'Denver'
◐ 3–11
✳ All summer
⊟ Medium

The creamy-white blossoms have a hint of yellow. The foliage is lightly speckled with burgundy.

Nymphaea helvola
◐ 3–11
✳ All summer
⊟ Dwarf

Perfect for small ponds and patio-container gardens, this is an excellent bloomer, with delicate yellow flowers and lightly mottled leaves.

Nymphaea 'Colorado' ▶

▲ *Nymphaea helvola*

Nymphaea 'Joey Tomocik'
◐ 3–11
✳ All summer
⊟ Medium

Lemon-yellow flowers stand high above the water. This variety is an outstanding bloomer.

▲ *Nymphaea marliacea 'Albida'*

Nymphaea marliacea 'Albida'
◐ 3–11
✳ All summer
⊟ Medium

This old hybrid has stood the test of time. Clear white flowers sit above crisp green leaves.

Nymphaea 'Perry's Baby Red'
◐ 3–11
✳ All summer
⊟ Dwarf

Wine-red flowers open above deep-green foliage. This variety is a good bloomer for small ponds and patio gardens.

▲ *Nymphaea* **'Perry's Baby Red'**

▲ *Nymphaea* **'Pink Sensation'**

▲ *Nymphaea* **'Steven Strawn'**

Nymphaea 'Pink Sensation'
🌿 *3–11*
✳ *All summer*
↔ *Medium*

The crisp pink blossoms are tipped with silver. The flowers open early and stay open late in the afternoon.

Nymphaea 'Steven Strawn'
🌿 *3–11*
✳ *All summer*
↔ *Medium*

'Steven Strawn' is possibly the best red bloomer ever. The rich, deep-red flowers have white sepals.

Nymphaea 'Sunny Pink'
🌿 *3–11*
✳ *All summer*
↔ *Medium*

The peach flowers are very large in relation to the medium-sized speckled foliage. The flowers sit well above the water level.

▲ *Nymphaea* **'Sunny Pink'**

Nymphaea **'Joey Tomocik'** ▲

Water lilies: tropical

Tropical water lilies have large leaves, often with serrated edges and bold markings. They hold their flowers well above the water's surface. Tropical lilies can be wintered indoors, or the tubers can be collected after frost and stored in damp sand at 7 to 10°C (45 to 50°F).

Day bloomers open mid-morning and close in the late afternoon. Flower colours include white, yellow, pink, peach, blue, blue-green, lavender and purple. Day-blooming tropical lilies generally outperform hardy lilies and night bloomers. They usually spread 90 to 120cm (3 to 4 feet) in diameter in a growing season. Many are viviparous, forming new plantlets where the stems meet the leaves. Night bloomers have larger flowers than day bloomers but are only available in white, red and pink. White and pink night bloomers are the best at catching the moonlight, but reds remain popular for their intense colour. Night bloomers are usually the last lilies to begin flowering for the season. Their flowers open in the late afternoon and close the following morning. Tropical lilies generally continue blooming through several light frosts. Plants spread 120 to 180cm (4 to 6 feet) in a growing season. Listed varieties are day bloomers, unless otherwise noted, and represent just a few of the many outstanding varieties available.

▼ *Nymphaea* **'Green Smoke'**

Nymphaea 'Albert Greenberg'

🌿 *8–11*

❋ *All summer*

Peach-coloured blooms sit above gently mottled foliage. This is an excellent bloomer that tolerates the confines of a generously sized container garden.

▼ *Nymphaea* **'King of Siam'**

◀ *Nymphaea* **'Panama Pacific'**

Nymphaea 'Green Smoke'
▮ *8–11*
✳ *All summer*

Each petal is a combination of yellow, white and blue, so the overall appearance of the flower is light green. This variety is very unusual.

Nymphaea 'King of Siam'
▮ *8–11*
✳ *All summer*

The double, dark-purple flowers are large in relation to the foliage. Many day-blooming hybrids have stamens that take on a petal-like appearance.

Nymphaea 'Panama Pacific'
▮ *8–11*
✳ *All summer*

A purple day bloomer with a proven track record, 'Panama Pacific' remains a favourite of water gardeners.

◀ *Nymphaea* **'Albert Greenberg'**

Lotus
Nelumbo

Lotus flowers sit above magnificent, huge, round waxy leaves and carry a delightful fragrance. Lotus favours a sunny, hot, humid summer without excessive rainfall. It is a tuber-forming plant; the tubers are harvested in the spring, if necessary. Plants in adequately sized containers may not require harvest or maintenance for 3 to 5 years or more.

Runners can grow from 6 to 10m (20 to 60 feet) a year. Lotus should always be contained unless you intend to allow them to consume the entire body of water. They can be grown successfully in or out of the water garden, but an adequate reservoir must be maintained. In cold climates, lotus grown in containers above-ground should be wintered in an area protected from freezing, such as a garage or cold basement.

Lotus are particularly heavy feeders. Provide fertilizer at least every 3 to 4 weeks to maintain the colour of the foliage and encourage flowering. Fertilizer should not be added in spring until the plant has several aerial leaves, or too many salts may accumulate in the soil. The dormant tubers carry no roots, and until active runner growth establishes itself, the plant cannot consume nutrients. Push fertilizer deep into the soil to make it accessible to the roots.

Nelumbo 'Baby Doll'
◐ 4–11
↕ 30–60cm (1–2 feet)
✳ Summer

Single white flowers sit on a dwarf plant. This variety is ideally suited to small ponds or container gardens.

Nelumbo 'Chawan Basu'
◐ 4–11
↕ 60–90cm (2–3 feet)
✳ Summer

Bright-pink edges fade to pure white on delicate single blossoms. This medium-sized plant is suitable for large containers or medium ponds.

▲ *Nelumbo* 'Momo Botan'

▲ *Nelumbo nucifera*

▲ *Nelumbo* 'Mrs. Perry D. Slocum'
◀ *Nelumbo* 'Chawan Basu'

▲ *Nelumbo* 'Baby Doll'

Nelumbo 'Momo Botan'
▮ *4–11*
⬍ *60cm (2 feet)*
✳ *Summer*

One of the longest blooming hybrids, 'Momo Botan' has double pink blooms that generally persist until heavy frost.

Nelumbo 'Mrs. Perry D. Slocum'
▮ *4–11*
⬍ *120–150cm (4–5 feet)*
✳ *Summer*

A true changeable; double flowers emerge a brilliant pink. By the second day, they are a delicate mix of pink and yellow. On the third day, flowers are primarily yellow. It is quite common to have all three stages on display at the same time, making this a popular hybrid.

Nelumbo nucifera
Hindu lotus
▮ *4–11*
⬍ *120–150cm (4–5 feet)*
✳ *Summer*

The petals of this single flowering species are a soft cream towards the centre, with bright pink tips. It is an excellent and sturdy species for the novice lotus grower.

Bog plants

Bog plants generally prefer their crown, tuber or rhizome to be elevated above the water level. The plant roots are then able to seek their favoured moisture level. They tolerate temporary flooding and should not dry out for extended periods. There should always be some moist soil beneath them. Bogs are easy to create and well suited to areas that are streamside or adjacent to the pond. Bog plants are more appropriate than drought-tolerant perennials, which often appear out of place and look awkward at the water's edge. Bog plants like to creep around the moist areas at the edge of the water feature, and are excellent for making the transition from dry to wet areas.

Bogs present an exciting opportunity to incorporate the unique and unusual foliage shapes and colours of carnivorous plants to the delicate textures of fern and cranberry into the surrounding garden area.

▷ *Dryopteris erythrosora* 'Brilliance'

▽ *Astilbe*

Alchemilla
Lady's Mantle
⬍ *30cm (12 inches)*
✳ *Summer*

A very common garden plant; it can grow in damp soil with an open structure. The large, serrated leaves have a downy surface that collects moisture. Tiny, yellow-green flowers are held in umbrella-like clusters throughout the summer. It is capable of spreading quickly in moist, humus-rich soil.

Astilbe
⬍ *90cm (35 inches)*
✳ *Summer*

Astilbe is a versatile plant that thrives in a bog garden and produces intensely-coloured flowering stems. A wide range of colours is available – from pinks to crimsons. The flowering plumes are long-lasting and may be dried. The foliage will reach as high as 90cm (35 inches), but dies back completely in the winter.

Dryopteris erythrosora 'Brilliance'
Brilliance autumn fern

🌡 *5–8*

⬍ *46–60cm (18–24 inches)*

The new growth on this delicate, slow-spreading, evergreen fern is coppery pink and apricot. The glossy fronds of 'Brilliance' retain their vibrant colour much later into the summer than the standard autumn fern.

Filipendula
Meadowsweet

⬍ *2m (6.5 feet)*

❋ *Late summer*

A tall, moisture-loving, bushy plant that will suit most bog gardens. The individual pink or white blooms are tiny, but create a colourful mass of feathery flowerheads. All dead foliage and stems should be cut back in autumn.

Gunnera
Giant rhubarb

⬍ *Over 2m (6.5 feet)*

❋ *Early summer*

Most commonly seen in large bog gardens, a display of impressively large leaves will emerge each year. It prefers partial shade, and suits a position at the edge of a large pond. Conical clusters of brown flowers appear early summer, themselves reaching 1.5m (5 ft) in height. The plant will require a covering of protective mulch in winter.

▲ *Filipendula*

▲ *Gunnera*

▲ *Pratia pedunculata*
◀ *Hosta*
▼ *Lobelia cardinalis*

Hosta

⬍ 30cm (12 inches)
✳ Summer

Hostas are popular, undemanding bog plants, available in many different varieties. They have large, lush leaves that can be found in different shades of green. Well-fed specimens produce lily-like flowers – in shades from white to purple. Flowers emerge in summer, and can reach a height of 100cm (39 inches).

Lobelia cardinalis

⬍ 90 cm (35 inches)
✳ Midsummer to early autumn

This aquatic lobelia is hardier and taller than other lobelias. Clusters of deep red flowers appear above the foliage. These plants overwinter well, flowering from midsummer to early autumn. They can be propagated by dividing clumps or through cuttings.

Mazus reptans
Creeping mazus
◑ 5–8
⬍ 2.5–7.5cm (1–3 inches)
✳ Summer

This tidy little ground-cover plant spreads quickly and loves to wander through stonework. The uniform growth sports lavender-blue or white flowers for 6 to 8 weeks. It tolerates light foot traffic and grows well in full sun or part shade.

Pratia pedunculata
Blue star creeper
◑ 7–10
⬍ 2.5–7.5cm (1–3 inches)
✳ Summer

Delicate tiny leaves on trailing stems root readily wherever the soil is moist. Star-shaped blue flowers appear for most of the summer. Established plantings have an almost mossy look.

Tulbaghia violacea ('Silver lace')
Variegated society garlic
🌶 7–11
⬍ 25–38cm (10–15 inches)
✳ Summer

'Silver lace' has outstanding white leaves with blue-grey striping that runs vertically along the foliage. The bulbs colonize quickly to form dense clumps of narrow leaves that stay variegated throughout the season. Light lavender flowers bloom in open clusters on stiff stems. Remove spent flowers to encourage reblooming all summer long.

Vaccinium macrocarpon
Cranberry
🌶 3–7
⬍ 15–30cm (6–12 inches)
✳ Spring

This low-growing rambling shrub roots freely in moist soil, creating a dense evergreen ground cover. Regular pruning will contain the runners and encourage fuller growth. The delicate pink flowers are a lovely complement to the tiny leaves. Cranberries can be harvested when fully mature in the autumn.

Sarracenia – pitcher plants

Carnivorous plants add flair to the bog garden. The nectar-holding leaves are like upright trumpets or angled flutes with incredibly vibrant colours and veining. The flowers, held firm on stiff stems that arch at the top, are an added bonus. The foliage is so strikingly coloured, it attracts attention all season long, putting out a strong flush of growth in the spring, resting in the summer, and producing a second flush of growth in the autumn that persists well into winter. The leaves and seed pods may be used in cut or dried flower arrangements.

These remarkable plants are easy to grow. They only require consistently moist, acidic soil and at least a half-day of sun. They are generally only bothered by a few aphids in the spring and prefer not to be fertilized. Children find pitcher plants especially exciting, lifting their hoods daily to see how many bugs have been eaten. They are considerably hardier than once thought and widely available, thanks to tissue culture production.

Sarracenia purpurea
Northern pitcher plant/ purple pitcher plant
🌶 3–8
⬍ 15–30cm (6–12 inches)
✳ Spring

Stout bulbous pitchers hold more water than most other pitcher plants because the hoods stand upright on the leaves. The foliage is a combination of deep red and green, causing the leaves to take on a purple cast. Mature plants have numerous blood-red flowers.

▼ *Sarracenia purpurea*

Submerged plants

Like other plants, submerged plants produce oxygen in daylight hours and reverse the process at night. Their defining difference is that they absorb food directly from the water by attracting nutrient-laden sediment from which they feed. Most of the roots produced by these plants are for stabilization rather than absorption. Some species are even rootless. In lined ponds, they should be planted in containers of sand or small gravel. They will take their nutrients directly from the water. Several bunches can be placed in the same container. It is not necessary to space them evenly on the pond bottom.

Callitriche verna
Starwort
✳ Summer

The various species are difficult to identify as their form and colour will vary according to environmental conditions. They will all tend to have delicate green foliage, forming rosettes that could become invasive if not kept in check. This plant does flower in summer, but the flowers are easily missed.

Ceratophyllum demersum
Hornwort
▨ 4–11

Ceratophyllum has been shown to release allelopathic chemicals that naturally inhibit some forms of algae growth, making it a prime addition to the water garden. This rootless plant nestles itself on the pond bottom in 30 to 90cm (1 to 3 feet) of water. Depending on the water's hardness, hornwort may form very soft, delicate leaves or rather stiff, bristled leaves. This texture makes it less prone to fish and snail predation. It is tolerant of a broad range of conditions and does not require planting. Since it is unrooted, excessive growth is easy to eradicate.

Elodea crispa

A quick-growing, submerged oxygenating plant that grows up from the pond bottom. It can become quite leggy and untidy with age and should be regularly thinned –

replant new shoots to replace the old ones. This plant prefers to be potted. The curled leaves differentiate it from other oxygenators. Elodea is usually sold in bunches, and rarely flowers.

Myriophyllum aquaticum
Milfoil

This plant is typified by finely divided leaves and fares best in clear, well-filtered ponds. There are many different species, some of which are only suitable for temperate ponds. It provides fish with an excellent spawning medium, and later on, a protective nursery for fry. It will die back over winter, and re-emerge in spring from dormant crowns. Of all the oxygenators, it is probably the most delicate and least hardy.

▼ **Ceratophyllum demersum**

Sagittaria subulata
Dwarf sagittaria
▨ 4–11

This delicate plant is like turf grass for the pond bottom. It has a mild-mannered nature and can be slow to establish. It will not exceed 15cm (6 inches) in height. Its low-profile stature suits both earth-bottomed and lined ponds. In lined pools, a large shallow pan will enable the establishment of a nice healthy bed. Dwarf sagittaria tolerates varying water depths and will tolerate light shade.

▲ **Sagittaria subulata**

▲ **Callitriche verna**

▼ **Myriophyllum aquaticum**

FISH DIRECTORY

The majority of pond fish available are different varieties of ornamental carp. But there is also a smaller range of native fish that might work equally well in your pond. Fortunately, it is possible to choose varieties of ornamental pond fish from the range available that are compatible with factors such as your pond's size and filtration – with koi being the most demanding.

Goldfish

The goldfish can be regarded as the standard bearer of all ornamental pond fish, yet it apparently has an identity crisis. It is a fish with many guises, some so extreme that they seem to belong to different species.

◄ Sarassa comet

Initially prized by the wealthy rulers of China over 1,500 years ago, today the goldfish is the world's most widely kept pet. Through the meticulous attention to detail associated with the advanced Chinese civilization, goldfish were selectively reared from the dull, brown native crucian carp to produce the simply beautiful fish we have today.

Goldfish are available in a range of sizes from 2.5 to 40cm (1 to 16 inches) long. It can be very rewarding (and better value) to buy smaller specimens to nurture, which will grow to suit the size of your pond. Buy around six at a time, as goldfish are quite gregarious.

Variations

Selective breeding has resulted in more than 100 varieties. Commercial breeders have concentrated on producing different varieties of goldfish by changing their physical features. Eye shape and position, body coloration and scalation, body shape, fin size, shape and number have all been mutated to produce variations.

These varieties do not resemble each other, and it is easy to believe that the fish are different species, which is not the case. Biologically, all varieties of goldfish can be successfully interbred to produce viable offspring of amazing diversity. Varieties of goldfish can be divided into two groups: those that will live and thrive in a garden pond, including overwintering, and those that are best kept in an aquarium full time or brought in from the pond to overwinter inside. In the trade, this latter group is referred to as fancy goldfish and will generally be displayed for sale in aquariums rather than open-topped display tanks.

▲ London shubunkin

▲ Shubunkin

▲ Fantail goldfish (Carassius auratus)

▲ **Goldfish**

Goldfish characteristics

Compatibility: Goldfish are compatible with all other pond fish.

Temperature: They tolerate temperatures from near freezing to 30°C (86°F). It is the goldfish's tolerance of temperatures that makes it such a widely kept fish.

Hardiness: Goldfish are tolerant of a wide range of water chemistries (as long as they are stable). They are relatively tolerant of low dissolved oxygen levels. They are also less prone to disease than other ornamental pond fish.

Food and feeding: Goldfish are omnivores, requiring both animal and vegetable components in their diets. They thrive on floating artificial foods.

Coloration: From deep orange of the classic goldfish through to red, white and even black on some variants. Will produce olive-brown offspring in a pond, some of which may turn into "goldfish".

Size: Good pond specimens grow up to 30cm (12 inches). Some may reach 40cm (16 inches).

Habitat/pond requirements: Goldfish prefer a well-planted, slow-moving pond in which they can browse.

Spawning and breeding: Goldfish are flock spawners, scattering thousands of tiny adhesive eggs into surface weed. Spawning takes place in late spring/early summer and can appear to be quite an aggressive process.

Goldfish can tolerate a wide range of temperatures and conditions. To recognize whether a variety is suitable for a pond, check that it resembles the typical shape – even if it shows differences in colour or fin length, then it is likely to tolerate icy winters and be fast enough to compete for food.

Goldfish are omnivorous and accept both flaked and pelleted foods. Fresh food treats can also be offered, and skin pigmentation can be improved by feeding a colour-enhancing diet.

Comets

Comets have been bred for their long tail fins, which in larger specimens may be half the length of the body. Comets are rarely one colour but will regularly display white-and-red patterns that are more pronounced when viewed from the top. Furthermore, the comet's colour is usually more red than gold.

Shubunkins

Shubunkins are extremely distinctive in their coloration, with much variation between individual fish. They are essentially goldfish in different clothing. Rather than being gold, they are blue, with colour appearing to come from beneath the scales rather than from above, as is the case with traditional goldfish. Shubunkins lack the silvery reflective scales, giving them a non-metallic sheen. They have a black, red and orange mottling set on a bluish "mother-of-pearl" background.

Fancy goldfish

▲ Redcap oranda

These more distant relatives of the goldfish have been selected to exhibit some extreme physical features. Fancy goldfish are so inbred that they lack the vigour of their distant relatives and will not tolerate an icy winter in a pond.

▲ Black moor

▲ Bubble eye

Typically more rounded, often with a "humped" back, fancy goldfish have longer, more elaborate fins than goldfish. They can suffer from a loss of circulation in colder temperatures, resulting in the fin tissue dying and becoming infected; even varieties with more conservative finnage will not overwinter well. The weird body shapes selected for external "beauty" have also led to some extreme internal physiological developments, especially with the swim bladder. This internal gas-filled sac keeps fish neutrally buoyant. If it becomes off-centre or over-inflated, fancy goldfish can have difficulty swimming or keeping upright. They are also very slow and awkward swimmers, making them easy prey for herons.

Oranda

When viewed from above, orandas' double tails look like butterflies. They can adopt a variety of colours, including calico, which resembles a shubunkin.

Black moor

Similar in shape to an oranda, this black moor has bulbous eyes that project from its head.

Lionhead

The lionhead has a development on its head that looks like a lion's mane. It has twin tails but lacks a dorsal fin.

Other variations

Bubble eyes, pompons and celestials are fancy goldfish in the extreme, where breeders have selected for extreme variations in head and eye developments.

▶ Pearlscale

▲ Calico veiltail

▲ **Celestial**

Fancy goldfish characteristics

Compatibility: Fancy goldfish will survive in a pond where they are not outcompeted by faster fish.

Temperature: Fancy goldfish prefer temperatures above 10°C (50°F) and must be moved inside when it's colder. They do not tolerate rapid changes in temperature.

Hardiness: Even though fancy goldfish originate from the hardy goldfish, these inbred variants require excellent water quality and are more prone to disease, especially fin rot.

Food and feeding: Fancy goldfish require an omnivorous diet. Try offering a slow-sinking food, as ingested air from feeding at the surface can lead to swim bladder and buoyancy problems.

Coloration: This depends on the variety. Almost anything is possible!

Size: This also depends on variety, but usually fancy goldfish will grow no bigger than 15cm (6 inches) in a pond.

Habitat/pond requirements: Fancy goldfish prefer a sheltered pond.

Spawning and breeding: Although fancy goldfish spawn like goldfish, they are less likely to do so in a pond. Crossing fancy goldfish can create very interesting offspring.

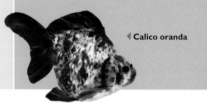

◀ **Calico oranda**

▲ **Orange veiltail**

▶ **Red lionhead next to "white" goldfish**

Koi (*nishikigoi*)
Cyprinus carpio

Many regard koi as the most prized of pond fish. Available in the widest range of colours and varieties of pattern, this sociable fish, although a voracious feeder and fast grower, will become tame and feed from the hand. Individual koi will show different "characters" and can live to be 20 to 30 years old in a pond. They are tolerant of other pond fish.

▲ **Koi Gin rin kohaku**

Koi used to be regarded as fish that were only accessible to the elitist end of the market. However, they are now bred more widely worldwide, and more outlets sell them. Inevitably, their price has dropped as their availability has increased.

Koi origins

Koi, or *nishikigoi* (Japanese for "coloured carp"), originate from the paddy fields of Asia and Japan. Like most ornamental pond fish, koi were discovered by accident as coloured genetic mutations from native black carp that the farmers had introduced from Asia to supplement their bland diet. However, the carp bred naturally, producing many thousands of offspring, some of which were not black like their parents but pale yellow.

For many generations, instead of being eaten, the cherished pale yellow koi were crossed with other similarly coloured genetic mutations, which eventually turned into the koi we know today. Different regions of Japan are reputed to have given rise to the different varieties that are found in ponds all over the world.

Koi are produced in several key areas where the climate is suitable for farming. Japanese koi offer the best quality or "pedigree", with deep red pigmentation and clean skin in metallic varieties. Koi from Israel offer excellent value and at times can be difficult to separate from the consistently excellent Japanese fish. Approximately 1 per cent

only of a typical spawn of koi in Japan reaches the market. The other 99 per cent don't survive, as they are not considered to have reached the desired grade and are culled as early as 3 weeks old.

Choosing koi

The vast array of patterns and colours available seems unlimited, as the pattern of each koi is unique. It is the knowledge that a truly excellent koi is irreplaceable that makes the top end of the market out-of-bounds for the majority of people. Nevertheless, one of the attractions of keeping koi is that there will always be a wide selection to choose from, irrespective of your budget.

The needs of koi

Koi have inherited many characteristics from their ancestors, being omnivorous scavengers often referred to as the pigs of the pond. The downturned mouth, or "snout", and barbels are perfect for rooting around on the pond bottom.

Like all members of the carp family, koi do not possess a stomach but a long, undifferentiated gut that is well equipped to digest the indiscriminate natural diet of this opportunistic omnivore. It is best to feed koi little and often, due to their natural feeding style.

Because of their tendency to root around on the pond bottom, showing no respect for planted baskets, koi are best kept in a plant-free pond.

 ▼ **Koi**

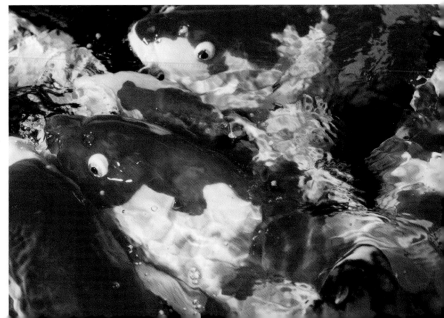

Typically, specialist koi ponds are clinical displays in a crystal clear, plant-free pond. However, koi are farmed in muddy clay ponds, conditions that these ornamental carp have shown they prefer. In true carp style, these scavengers feed using their strong sense of smell.

One of the most significant differences between koi and their robust "wild" carp ancestors is that koi are not as hardy. As koi are easily stressed and susceptible to disease, a well-filtered, deep pond is essential to keep them in top condition. They are also ravenous, fast-growing fish. A koi pond should be at least 7,250 litres (1,600 gallons) in volume and a minimum of 1 to 2m (3 to 6 feet) deep.

Essentially warm-water fish, koi prefer a stable pond temperature but can tolerate a wide range throughout the year, from just above freezing to 20°C (86°F), preferring and spawning in the 18 to 24°C (65°F to 75°F) range.

A wide range of commercially available premium-quality koi foods will provide the fish with all the nutrition they require, including selected ingredients that will boost colour. It is wise to change diet with the season, from a high-protein growth food in summer to lower-protein vegetable-based food in spring and autumn.

Other varieties

Two very popular "varieties" are ghost koi and butterfly koi. These are not officially recognized, however, and you will not find them in a koi show. They have become very popular with pondkeepers due to their unique characteristics.

Varieties of koi

Different varieties of koi are classified by their coloration, pattern and scalation, as in the following examples.

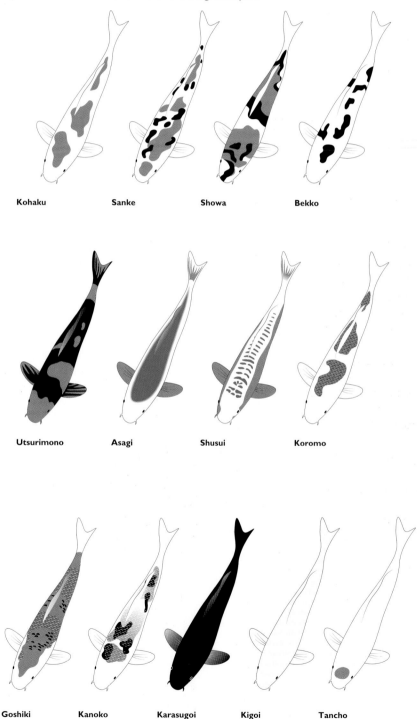

Kohaku   Sanke   Showa   Bekko

Utsurimono   Asagi   Shusui   Koromo

Goshiki   Kanoko   Karasugoi   Kigoi   Tancho

Ghost koi

The ghost koi is a controversial pond fish. To the koi purist, it is regarded as a misfit that should have been culled, but to the average pondkeeper, it is one of the most desirable fish.

Ghost koi first "appeared" in the early 1980s as the result of a cross between a highly visible, metallic koi and a wild, dark-coloured carp. The offspring can exhibit a wide range of colour types but are generally dark, with a surface dusting of metallic skin. Usually, the most visible and striking areas of a ghost koi are the metallic head and flashy pectoral fins that glint in the sunlight.

Ghost koi are an excellent choice for the novice pond owner, as they are vigorous, tame and rewarding to look after. They are available in a wide range of sizes and shades and are very competitively priced. It is not surprising that they have become so popular.

Undemanding

These hybrids (crosses) between wild carp and metallic koi tend to show a characteristic "hybrid vigour"; they are as tough as nails, compared with koi, and have a tendency to grow very rapidly. They are very forgiving and undemanding, rewarding the pondkeeper with a healthy appetite for life and food, often becoming dominant fish in a pond and most likely to be the first up for feeding. They have a reputation for becoming tame very quickly, endearing themselves to the pondkeeper straightaway.

Good value

Ghost koi offer excellent value for money. Unlike high-grade koi breeding, where only a small percentage of the offspring from each spawn will show the desired markings and hence reach the market, the reverse is true for ghost koi. This means that more reach

the market and, as a result, are cheaper than traditional koi. In addition, they do not require the specialist culling or culturing expertise demonstrated by Japanese koi farmers.

Hardy

Ghost koi offer pondkeepers the opportunity to try koi keeping without the expense of creating a large koi pond. One of the spin-offs of their enhanced vigour, health and vitality is that "ghosties" don't require pampering to keep them in tip-top health. In fact, ghost koi have such a high natural resistance to disease that the need to treat them for ailments is very rare.

Attractive

Even though ghost koi are simple in their coloration, a range of metallic hues is available in aquatic shops. Golden metallic koi will produce golden

▲ **Ghost koi**

ghost koi, and the same follows from silver broodfish. Further variations can occur within a batch of ghost koi when looking at variations in scale patterns.

▲ **Ghost koi**

Koi characteristics

▼ Ghost koi

Compatibility: Koi are very compatible with other fish. They can outcompete smaller fish at feeding time, though, and will uproot plants in submerged planted baskets.

Temperature: Koi are essentially warm-water fish but will tolerate from near freezing to 30°C (86°F).

Hardiness: The higher the grade of koi, the less hardy it will be. Ghost koi show hybrid vigour through rapid growth rate and resistance to disease.

Food and feeding: Koi are omnivores and will thrive on commercial dry koi foods and readily accept moist treats such as worms, prawns and even oranges.

Coloration: The diverse coloration of koi is their chief appeal.

Size: Koi grow up to 1m (3 feet) in length but will reach 60cm (2 feet) in a sizable pond.

Habitat/pond requirements: Water must be well filtered and circulated to provide a stable pond environment. The pond should be 1 to 1.3m (3 to 4 feet) deep to provide adequate overwintering protection.

Spawning and breeding: Koi are boisterous flock spawners and release thousands of adhesive eggs in midsummer. If they are kept in an unplanted pond or without soft spawning media, spawning could result in physical damage.

Butterfly koi

Whereas ghost koi are very popular in Europe, butterfly koi have become the unconventional favourite in the United States. Just like standard koi, they are available in a wide range of colours, with other nonstandard variants as well. Metallic varieties are especially stunning. Defining features are long, trailing "butterfly" fins and tail and a long, slender body.

Butterfly koi were created in Niigata, Japan (the home of koi), by crossing native wild Indonesian river carp (with their naturally flowing fins) with koi varieties to try to restore vigor and hardiness to some inbred koi bloodlines. Some of the resultant fish showed the long-finned features of the butterfly koi (the Japanese called them dragon koi). They are also farmed in the United States to satisfy local demand.

Butterfly koi are not considered to be true koi varieties by Zen Nippon Airinkai (the organization that sanctions Japanese koi shows) because they do not conform to some key judging standards (notably, fin length and body shape).

▶ Butterfly koi

Orfe
Leuciscus idus

At times too swift for the eye to follow, the orfe
is a very popular and undemanding pond fish.

Although a member of the carp family,
the orfe (or ide) is a distant relative of
the common carp and more
accustomed to the dynamic life of a
flowing river. Its streamlined body
makes its life an easy one in rivers but
also makes it one of the fastest fish in
the garden pond. Typically a surface-
dwelling fish, its deep, muscular body
means that the orfe can often be
seen jumping, splashing and taking
flies from the surface.

Seen as a shoal of darting slices of
peach, flitting in and out of the shelter
of lilies and submerged plants, this shy
yet inquisitive fish can become quite
tame. Often the first to feed, it is the
orfe's darting activity during feeding
time that can alert other fish to the
food. An orfe's character seems to
change with age, developing from a
restless juvenile to a calmer, more
sedate adult, often seen lying in the
sun at the surface.

▲ **Golden orfe**

Appearance

Golden orfe are remarkably fast
growing, shooting on rapidly to suit the
size of the pond. Different "grades" of
orfe are available, with qualities ranging
from clear, blemish-free, golden skin to
the less stunning random arrangement
of "black pepper spots" on the dorsal
surface. This black pigmentation may
be so intense that a significant part of
the golden orfe is actually black.

A less common variety is the blue
orfe. Although the same species as the
golden orfe, it can be found in a variety
of blue tones, from pale grey to black,
where the darkest coloration is found
on the fish's top surface. A mixed shoal
of blue and golden orfe creates a
stunning display.

A highly impressive feature of golden
orfe in top condition is the blood-red
fins contrasted against the paler flanks.
It is only when you get really close to
larger orfe that you can appreciate the
depth and muscular nature of the body.
The coloration of both fins and skin
becomes even more vivid with a
colour-enhancing diet.

◀ **Golden orfe (top view)**

Spawning and growth

The orfe is one of the first fish of the year to spawn; being a river fish, it breeds at cooler temperatures, compared with other pond fish. Typical boisterous activity is observed in mature fish from April to May. Spawning can be such a physical affair that you can often hear the splashing caused by the activity before you see it. Hundreds of adhesive translucent eggs, once released, will smother submerged plants and hatch in about 10 days (depending on the water temperature). Both eggs and fry can be very tempting for other pond fish, which will feast on them before they can hatch.

Orfe can grow up to 60cm (24 inches) long and weigh over 2.7 kg (6 lb), but this size is rarely achieved in garden ponds; they will stop growing according to the size of the pond. They are carnivorous and will easily be tempted by flies and pond skaters, jumping clear of the water in the effort to catch a tasty morsel. They are easily catered to with a high-quality pond pellet or stick.

▼ **Blue orfe (top view)**

▼ **Blue orfe**

Orfe characteristics

Compatibility: Orfe are non-aggressive, fast-swimming fish.

Temperature: They tolerate temperatures from near freezing to above 30°C (86°F).

Hardiness: These hardy fish rarely seem to suffer from disease. Orfe are not as tolerant of low dissolved oxygen levels as goldfish and prefer to swim against a flow of water. They can be affected by some of the chemical pond treatments used for treating other fish.

Food and feeding: Orfe will take flies and other insects near the surface. It is a carnivore but will thrive on a typical dry pond food formulated for omnivores.

Coloration: Orfe have blood-red fins and tails. Golden orfe may develop black speckles. Blue orfe have a blue/black band that runs the length of the back, and their skin is not as orange as golden orfe.

Size: Orfe can grow to 60cm (24 inches) in a pond.

Habitat/pond requirements: Orfe prefer open space and a clear surface to swim in. They enjoy a strong current – a waterfall, for example.

Spawning and breeding: This typical carp-style egg-scattering flock spawner is the first of the *Cyprinids* to breed, doing so in early spring.

Tench
Tinca tinca

Every garden pond should have a tench – either the native green or ornamental golden tench. This sturdy bottom-feeding fish performs a perfect scavenging role, rooting around in the silt and sediment that may have accumulated over the seasons.

The tench's natural coloration offers superb camouflage, with a dark brown-green, olive-skinned back that blends extraordinarily well with the weedy depths it loves and inhabits. This makes the green tench an ideal addition to a wildlife pond.

Tench are likely to be sold from pale-bottomed tanks or troughs, where they can be easily viewed and selected. If they were not obviously displayed, they would be easily passed over, unnoticed. In addition, tench are a shy fish, better suited to the more protective garden pond than exposed retail tanks designed for ease of viewing and netting.

Valuable role

Tench are more valuable in a pond for the work they do than for their ornamental appeal. Performing the role of a catfish, the tench has a slightly downturned mouth equipped with a small pair of sensory barbels for detecting food in the murky depths. It's not surprising that its eyes are so small, as it must hardly use them. Tench will not pose a threat to other pond inhabitants, which can't be said for several catfish species that can wipe out entire ponds if stocked by mistake.

Caring for tench

Although little is seen of tench once they are stocked, a sinking food must be provided to allow this secretive fish to feed at leisure, under the protective comfort of the deeper water. Unless tench gain a regular source of quality food, this notoriously slow-growing fish will neither compete at the surface nor keep pace with the other pond fish, especially koi. If insufficient food reaches the pond bottom, it is possible that these fish will slowly wither away.

Although you should have no cause to touch or handle a tench, these fish have a reputation for being extremely slimy. Their tiny, firmly rooted scales are covered by what seems to be a

▼ **Green tench**

▲ Golden tench (top view)

liberal daubing of protective slippery mucus. In fact, folklore maintains that the application of this "magical" liquid to wounds or abrasions will help to heal the injury – hence the tench's nickname "doctor fish".

Golden tench

A naturally occurring though rare golden variant of tench is available sporadically in aquatic shops. It is very similar in colour to golden orfe, with the contrast being that the golden tench prefer to inhabit the lower rather than upper regions of the pond. Of course, golden tench are more visible in a pond than their naturally coloured relatives, and their popularity has a significant effect on their price and availability.

▼ Golden tench

Tench characteristics

Compatibility: This unassuming and peaceful fish keeps to itself at the bottom of the pond. Tench will not compete for food at the surface with busy, ravenous fish such as koi.

Temperature: Tench prefer cooler, deeper water but will tolerate near freezing to up to 30°C (86°F).

Hardiness: Naturally occurring green tench are more disease-resistant than other selected ornamental fish, although they can be affected by some chemical pond treatments used for treating other fish. They are tolerant of low dissolved oxygen levels.

Food and feeding: Tench must be offered a sinking food to ensure they get sufficient nutrition. They rarely surface to feed on floating foods offered to other fish.

Coloration: They are dark olive-green (which can vary, depending on the habitat), or else they resemble a golden orfe that prefers to stay at the bottom of the pond.

Size: Tench will grow to 30 to 40cm (12 to 16 inches) in a garden pond.

Habitat/pond requirements: Tench prefer a deep, shady pond that is well planted and has a little sediment on the pond bottom.

Spawning and breeding: The eggs are scattered and deposited in weed.

Sterlet
Acipenser ruthenus

Even though the sterlet is relatively new to garden ponds, it can be described as a prehistoric fish that dates back to the time of the dinosaurs. Its ancient ancestry is also evident when its body form is observed, as it appears alien in a pond, compared with other traditional pond fish.

A close relative of the sturgeon, the sterlet derives from rivers that feed into the Black and Caspian Seas; although it is a river fish, it can acclimatize well to life in a large garden pond.

Keeping sterlets

Instead of bearing the usual scales found on koi and goldfish, the sterlet is covered with five rows of armoured bony plates called scutes and displays a white edge to the fins and nose. The sterlet swims like no other fish, flexing its entire body into a series of lazy curves and moving in an ungainly, clumsy and "waggy" fashion. This weak swimmer has been known to become trapped in blanketweed.

Sterlets can have difficulty feeding in a pond for a number of reasons. First, their protruding snouts and downward-facing mouths really enable these fish to feed only off the bottom, so it is usually necessary to offer them sinking pellets. This can create a second problem: competition. In a typical garden pond of mixed fish, the frenzy experienced at feeding time may well result in no food reaching the sterlets on the pond bottom. They are carnivorous, naturally feeding on crustacea and invertebrates in the water column or on the riverbed. They use a set of four fringed barbels protruding from the mouth to feel, sense and locate food items such as sinking pellets.

▲ Star sturgeon

▼ Sterlet

▲ **Albino sterlet**

Timid nature

These caviar-producing fish can grow up to 1.2m (4 feet) long and weigh more than 16kg (35lb) in the wild; they are not known to spawn in garden ponds. Quiet and timid in relation to other pond fish, sterlets commonly go unnoticed. They are darkly coloured and blend in with the pond.

Although sterlets are appealing, they can be difficult to keep because they are unable to compete with goldfish and koi at feeding time. This can result in loss of weight, so special care should be taken to guarantee that they get sufficient food, especially because they prefer to lurk in the depths. Sterlets need more specific care and attention than typical pond fish do in order to thrive.

Sterlet characteristics

Compatibility: The quiet, peaceful sterlet will not attack other pond fish, even though it is a carnivore.

Temperature: Sterlets prefer a cool temperature of less than 20°C (68°F).

Hardiness: Not a very hardy pond fish, the sterlet demands special feeding attention. Once it starts to lose condition and body weight, it is difficult to rehabilitate. Like orfe and tench, sterlets can be affected by some of the chemical pond treatments used for treating other fish.

Food and feeding: Sterlets require a high-protein sinking food.

Coloration: Sterlets are dark grey with white edges to their fins.

Size: Sterlets will reach 60cm (24 inches) in a pond but grow to 1.2m (48 inches) in the wild.

Habitat/pond requirements: Sterlets require a large expanse of water that is free of blanketweed and other dense planting. Entanglement can be a problem.

Spawning and breeding: Sterlets are not known to breed in ponds.

▲ **Sterlet (underside)**

Other pond fish

Here is a selection of other fish that may be suitable for your pond.

▲ Three-spined stickleback

Three-spined stickleback
Gasterosteus aculeatus

The stickleback is an ideal fish for a wildlife pond. It has not been selectively bred to produce ornamental variants and blends in well with the native flora in a natural pond. It is undemanding, thriving in still-water ponds, where it scavenges, pecking away at silt and other pond debris. It is a temperate fish, overwintering well, even under ice.

The three-spined stickleback is very common and is protected from predation by its spines. It can also fend off other fish by nipping quite fiercely at any that enter its territory.

Growing to about 10cm (4 inches), the male stickleback develops a bright red coloration around its throat and builds a nest from vegetation on the pond bottom.

The three-spined stickleback is not generally sold in garden centres (there are no stickleback farmers), so you may have to introduce some from a friend's wildlife pond (but never from a wild pond).

◄ Three-spined sticklebacks (top view)

Fathead minnow
Pimephales promelas

Occasionally, though rarely, available in the UK, the ornamental golden form of the fathead minnow resembles a miniature golden orfe. Viewed close up, this golden variant appears to glow. Its beauty is matched by its hardiness, as it overwinters well in a frozen pond. Like the stickleback, the fathead minnow is territorial at spawning time, laying eggs in and among rocks that it then guards with great tenacity. Initially reared and marketed as bait fish for angling, this naturally diminutive fish – up to 10cm (4 inches) – is a great addition to a pond, especially if you have limited space.

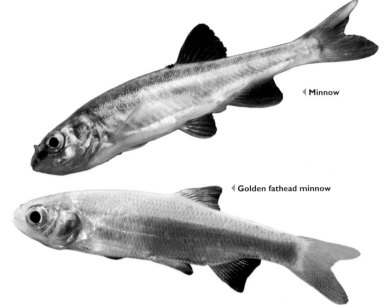

◀ **Minnow**

◀ **Golden fathead minnow**

Pumpkinseed
Lepomis gibbosus

This naturally ornamental fish is at home in wildlife ponds in North America, typically reaching 20cm (8 inches in a pond). It grows larger in the wild. Like the stickleback, it is protected by spines but is far lovelier to look at, displaying natural ornamental beauty with an assortment of green, orange, yellow and blue speckles. It overwinters well in a temperate pond, preferring a well-planted habitat. Like the fathead minnow, the pumpkinseed will prepare a spawning site (gravel/stones), with the male aggressively protecting the eggs and then the fry. A beautiful and fascinating fish to add to a wildlife pond, pumpkinseeds can prove a nuisance with smaller fish.

▼ **Pumpkinseed**

POND MANAGEMENT

A healthy, thriving pond is a living entity – in balance with nature. How you manage your pond will determine how successful it will be, and an understanding of how key processes affect your pond's performance will allow you to spot problems before they arise and to avoid expensive mistakes. It is essential to appreciate why a natural pond is the perfect model for your own garden pond, and what is likely to happen if you deviate from that ideal. A little background chemistry and biology are essential to enable you to interpret and respond wisely to what is happening in your pond, along with a little practical advice on how to maintain your pond through the different seasons.

Ideal environment
Most ornamental pond fish are related to the carp. Carp are created and adapted for a lowland lake existence, and that is the type of environment you should aim to provide for your fish in your own pond.

Understanding the pond

Effective pond management is the difference between creating a water-filled hole and a healthy, balanced and beautiful water garden. If you can get the water right, the pond will largely look after itself.

Your pond's purpose

The philosophy behind your pond will determine how you manage it and how it performs. You may want it simply to look stunning, or to be a haven for your fish to breed in, or to be a naturally planted wildlife pond left alone for nature to colonize. Whatever your priority, it will become clear that in order to satisfy all of the pond's "stakeholders" (fish, plants, other wildlife and you), you will have to make some compromises.

In attempting to provide your plants and pond fish with the environment that they thrive best in, you face a number of key decisions and challenges. The farther you depart from their natural environment, the more problems you are likely to face.

The natural model

You may have decided to create a structure that appears natural. This approach to creating a pond is probably the best; most successful ponds are based on the natural model. Plants and wildlife thrive in their natural environment because it meets their physiological requirements. Your biggest challenge will be to create the perfect environment that is also visually stunning and a worthy addition to your garden.

Conditions for fish

The most demanding inhabitants of a pond are the fish. Ask yourself "What do my fish need in their environment?" The majority of pond fish (goldfish, shubunkins, comets and koi) are man-made ornamental variants of the carp family, so you can use the standards required by carp as your guide for creating the perfect environment in your pond; however, due to inbreeding and their weakened genetic make-up, ornamental pond fish are less hardy than their natural ancestors.

A stable environment

Carp are one of the world's most adaptable fish species (which is why they are widely kept), yet they require a stable environment. They can tolerate a wide range of temperatures – from near freezing to over 30°C (86°F) – but you should avoid exposing them to such extremes. They grow most efficiently at around 26.5°C (80°F).

A stable pond environment is one in which water-quality parameters naturally resist change. Any change that does occur will be within limits to which your fish are adapted. For example, the larger the volume of water, the less likely your fish are to experience rapid and extreme changes in temperature and dissolved oxygen concentration.

A lowland lake will experience seasonal temperature changes; carp breed, grow and rest in response to these cues. You should aim to provide your fish with these variations, within your stable setting.

Water quality

Carp are not adapted to tolerate poor water quality, such as high ammonia and nitrite levels, and should not be subjected to it. Lowland waters will naturally experience some of the highest levels of other dissolved substances, compared with other freshwater environments. A lowland system is the area that receives the run-off (and the minerals dissolved in it) from the land that drains into it. Consequently, these lakes are typically hard-water areas, high in minerals, with slightly alkaline water. Each drainage basin will have its own specific characteristics different from the others, but the levels in the system will be relatively constant. Pond fish also require mineral-rich, slightly alkaline water, stable within the boundaries of acceptability. Compared with other species of fish, carp can be kept quite successfully within a wide pH range (7.5 to 8.5) as long as that pH remains stable.

Food

Food is one of the most difficult areas with which to match the natural experiences of carp. The artificial dry diets offered to pond fish are formulated to meet their nutritional needs and the environmental needs of an artificially stocked pond. A carp's natural diet contains between 50 and 60 per cent protein. Carp would happily live off a similar diet in captivity, but that runs the risk of affecting the water quality (see page 82, "Food and feeding").

An artificial diet allows them to receive precise nutrition every day. Offering pond fish such a highly digestible and low-waste diet is not natural, but it is a compromise between what you want (cleaner filters) and what carp are adapted for (a high-fibre diet).

Water clarity

Perhaps one of the starkest differences between an artificial pond and a carp's natural environment is the water clarity. Carp are most secure in the turbid, clay-rich conditions found in lowland waters. They rely on their keen sense of smell for rooting around and finding food on the completely dark pond bottom. (Their eyes are comparatively small because they don't rely on them.) Yet pondkeepers endeavour to keep fish in ever cleaner and clearer water that allows them to see down to the bottom of the deepest garden pond, as well as keeping filter maintenance to a minimum. But this is not ideal for the fish.

DIFFERENCES BETWEEN AQUATIC ENVIRONMENTS

Natural (lowland lake)
- Pond volume is huge; water quality is relatively stable
- Stocking densities are low
- The water is naturally turbid
- A naturally high-protein, high-roughage diet is available
- There is a balance of plants which utilize sunlight and nutrients.

Artificial (man-made pond)
- Pond volume is limited; water quality will vary
- Stocking densities are high—consequently fish may be stressed
- Filtered water is clearer; this may stress the fish and encourage algae
- A low-protein diet is offered, where the emphasis is on digestibility
- The pond's balance largely depends on filtration and the number and variety of plants relative to the size of the pond.
- The pond may suffer from algae, especially in sunny locations and where the pond is heavily stocked with fish, due to the associated high nutrient levels.

Feeding in captivity
Carp are naturally mid-water and bottom-feeding fish but in captivity are offered floating food, which brings them to the surface.

POND FOOD CHAIN
The food-chain diagram below represents a typical web of relationships in a freshwater pond ecosystem.

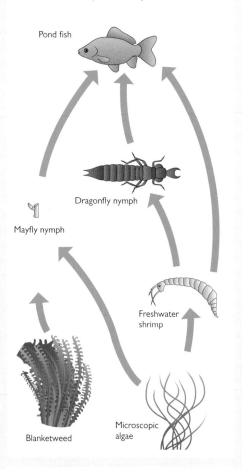

Pond fish

Dragonfly nymph

Mayfly nymph

Freshwater shrimp

Blanketweed

Microscopic algae

THE IMPORTANCE OF A FILTER
Installing a filter is the price you must pay for wanting to keep fish in an artificial pond. It performs the functions that would occur naturally in a lake or river ecosystem within a compact unit and is arguably the single most important factor that makes keeping fish in an artificial pond a possibility. (See pages 36 to 37 for more on filters.)

The pond ecosystem

To make your pond successful, you need to work with the principles of nature rather than against them. Even though your pond is an artificial creation, made from man-made materials and to your own design, it is transformed into a healthy aquatic environment by the same bio-processes that are found in any natural pond.

Balanced relationships
In an ecosystem, the number of producers and consumers is balanced, and each exploits a niche within a web of interactive relationships. Energy (food) flows through the food chain; each link in the chain is balanced in a sustainable relationship with the next. A natural aquatic environment such as a pond is able to support a limited number of fish through the food it provides and the amount of waste it is able to handle.

Deviating from nature
In a natural pond, there is no need for a pump, a filter or regular partial water changes to maintain a balance; the ecosystem meets the needs of the plants and fish, enabling them to thrive. But you will probably want to stock an unnaturally high density of fish in your own relatively small, crystal-clear pond, feeding them more food than would ever be available in the wild. In this case, you cannot leave it to nature alone to sustain the pond; you will need to intervene with pumps and filters to maintain a healthy environment.

Pond metabolism
It's useful to think of a pond as a living organism. Every pond receives various inputs (food, sunlight, nutrients and so on) and processes them to produce a range of different outputs. Just as our own metabolism determines how we function, how well a pond handles its varying inputs and outputs will determine the quality of the water and the health of the organisms it supports.

Temperature affects the pond's "metabolism", or how rapidly micro-organisms such as bacteria break down by-products. In a self-sustaining, balanced, natural pond, the metabolic processes of algae, bacteria, protozoa, invertebrates, insects and vertebrates (including fish) will be tightly interlinked, ultimately producing a stable pond environment. The micro-organisms are similar in an artificial pond but rely on the extra space provided by a filter to cope with the additional workload. Where the level of inputs and outputs of a natural pond are balanced, in an artificial pond, the pondkeeper must add inputs (such as food) to sustain the fish and manage the extra outputs (with regular partial water changes) to keep things balanced.

Oxygen/carbon dioxide balance

In a natural pond, the production of oxygen via plant photosynthesis and diffusion from the atmosphere governs the amount of aerobic life that the pond can sustain. The oxygen consumers (bacteria, invertebrates and fish) populate the pond to a level that can be sustained by the oxygen producers (plants). The consumers release a corresponding level of carbon dioxide back into the water, which is taken up by aquatic plants as they photosynthesize in daylight, to complete the cycle.

However, in a newly planted garden pond, the balance between plant photosynthesis and oxygen consumers cannot be achieved instantly, so more oxygen must be added. Aeration (by an air pump) and water movement (by a waterfall or fountain) meet this need and also help to "gas off" any excess carbon dioxide that cannot be absorbed from the water in a sparsely planted system.

Annual cycle

A pond has a natural annual cycle. During the winter months, the cold water temperature dictates a slow metabolic rate; by contrast a summer pond has a hyperactive, rapid-cycling metabolism that corresponds to the higher temperature.

All pond organisms are cold-blooded and their rates of metabolism fluctuate at the same rate, depending on the water temperature. Consequently, algae growth and the production of live food in a natural pond are negligible in winter, but so is the demand for these food organisms by the fish. If for some reason a winter pond is inundated with food, this leads to problems. In summer, the fish require a regular supply of food, but the metabolic rates of algae and other food organisms are correspondingly high.

Transferring this scenario to an artificial garden pond, water temperature again determines the metabolic rates of your fish and those of your beneficial filter bacteria that break down and reprocess toxic by-products such as ammonia. Fortunately, as the fishes' appetite and demand for food increase (with the resulting effect of increased excretion of ammonia), so does the metabolic rate of beneficial bacteria (and their ability to divide and populate), meaning that there is no build-up of toxic ammonia in the pond. But problems will occur if the fish are given too much food. Unlike a natural, balanced pond, in a garden pond there is a real risk that the quantity of supplementary food will be too great and out of balance with the pond's size and metabolism. It is unlikely that the filter bacteria will be able to cope with the inevitable consequences for water quality — presenting a real problem and source of stress for your fish.

BLANKETWEED

Blanketweed is a problem suffered by most artificially filtered ponds. It is caused by an imbalanced pond metabolism and occurs because the rate at which nutrients such as phosphates and nitrates enter the pond is unnaturally high and out of balance with the rate at which they are broken down. Excessive food relative to pond volume results in an accumulation of nutrients on which blanketweed thrive, boosted by abundant sunlight in a clear pond. In a natural lake or pond, the growth of blanketweed is kept in balance by the restricted nutrients. In addition, many organisms graze on blanketweed, preventing it from growing out of hand. If a filtered garden pond was allowed to revert back to a natural stocking density, coupled with the associated turbidity of a natural clay pond, you would soon find the blanketweed starting to disappear.

Flourishing algae

In an unbalanced artificial pond, blanketweed can soon flourish and take over a pond — spoiling both its appearance and function.

POND CYCLES

Nitrogen
• Comes from leaf matter, fish food or nitrates in tap water
• Causes nitrate levels to rise, which in turn causes proliferation of algae
• Can be broken down through anaerobic processes by bacteria

Phosphorus
• Mostly found in the form of phosphates; introduced through fish food or tap water
• Phosphates can also cause a proliferation of algae

Oxygen
• Produced by aquatic plants as a result of photosynthesis (see below)
• Utilized by pond organisms during respiration
• Build-up is not detrimental; it will naturally return to the atmosphere

Carbon dioxide
• Closely linked to oxygen cycle
• May build up at night in an algae-rich, muggy pond
• Will cause a drop in pH but will readily "gas off" into the atmosphere

PHOTOSYNTHESIS

Plants produce oxygen during the day. At night they take in oxygen and give off carbon dioxide.

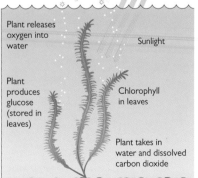

Plant releases oxygen into water

Sunlight

Plant produces glucose (stored in leaves)

Chlorophyll in leaves

Plant takes in water and dissolved carbon dioxide

Recycling nutrients

An artificial garden pond is a miniature representation of the wider aquatic world. This is particularly true when looking at how a pond processes the array of compounds that enters it, compared with the equivalent inputs to more "natural" environments.

The problem with a garden pond is that it has a great ability to accumulate things. You only have to observe an unstocked, newly built pond running for the first few weeks – a thin dusting of debris will soon settle, apparently from nowhere, on the pond bottom or in the filter. The same is true of levels of soluble substances that cannot be seen, which can soon accumulate to significant levels.

Elements that are recycled through a garden pond fall into two groups: those that remain in the water causing problems, such as nitrates and phosphates, and those that end up in the atmosphere, such as oxygen and carbon dioxide.

Nitrogen
The nitrogen cycle is at the heart of a healthy pond. It is driven by beneficial bacteria that reprocess different nitrogenous compounds. In a natural pond, these bacteria are found on all hard surfaces and in the soft sediment. In a densely stocked artificial pond, you should install a biological filter filled with suitable media that bacteria can colonize.

Most nitrogen enters a natural pond in the form of proteins found in organisms such as daphnia, snails and worms. In a garden pond, nitrogen will also enter in the form of leaf matter or fish food or as nitrates in untreated tap water.

Ammonia and nitrites
As a by-product of digestion, fish excrete ammonia (NH_3) through their gills. The only acceptable ammonia level in a pond is zero (meaning the ammonia is broken down at the same rate that it is produced). Bacteria break the ammonia down into nitrites (NO_2). These are also toxic; again the only acceptable level is zero. Finally, nitrites are broken down by the filter bacteria into relatively harmless nitrates. These aerobic bacteria require a steady flow of aerated water to be pumped through the filter.

Nitrates
Nitrates are either broken down further by anaerobic bacteria (requiring oxygen-deficient conditions) into nitrogen gas and then lost to the atmosphere or taken up by plants to form new plant proteins, completing the cycle. In an artificial pond, nitrate levels will

accumulate. They are far less toxic than ammonia and nitrites and can be allowed to rise to 50 ppm (the ideal, though, is zero). However, their accumulation is symptomatic of the pond being out of balance, and they should be removed by regular partial water changes. Nitrate levels will rise fastest in the warmer months when fish are actively feeding and excreting high levels of ammonia. The accumulation of nitrates in a pond can lead to the proliferation of algae − a sign that nature is trying to balance the pond but a real nuisance.

Phosphorus

Phosphorus is such a reactive element that, in the natural world, it is usually encountered in the form of phosphates, chemically bound to four oxygen atoms. Compared to nitrogen, the phosphorus cycle is simple, and levels of phosphorus found in a freshwater environment are generally low, though they can still promote the growth of algae.

Phosphates become incorporated into plant tissue; when this is eaten by a fish, it will excrete any excess phosphate that it can't absorb into the water. In a garden pond, phosphates are also introduced via fish food and tap water and are a primary cause of nuisance algae.

Oxygen

In a natural clay pond, oxygen is produced by aquatic plant life in the daylight hours through photosynthesis; they absorb carbon dioxide (CO_2) and eventually release oxygen in the form of bubbles. In turn, the oxygen is absorbed and utilized by organisms during respiration. The oxygen is then partially recycled as it is returned to the CO_2 "pot", dissolved in pond water, and released as a by-product of respiration. This may find its way into the atmosphere or be absorbed again by submerged photosynthesizing plants, to be released later as oxygen. The accumulation of oxygen in a garden pond is not a bad thing, and if levels increase too much, oxygen will soon return to the atmosphere as a gas.

Carbon dioxide

Carbon dioxide shares a very close relationship with oxygen and may accumulate during periods of excessive respiration and negligible photosynthesis. This may occur in an algae-rich mud pond at night or a heavily fed artificial clear pond at any time. An initial consequence of the build-up of CO_2 is a drop in pH (see page 166), but any excessive accumulation of CO_2 is short-lived as it, like oxygen, can simply "gas off" to the atmosphere. Excessive CO_2 production should be matched with an adequate supply of oxygen, otherwise all respiring organisms, including the pond fish, will experience an oxygen deficit.

THE NITROGEN CYCLE
The diagram below illustrates how the nitrogen cycle works in the context of a typical garden pond.

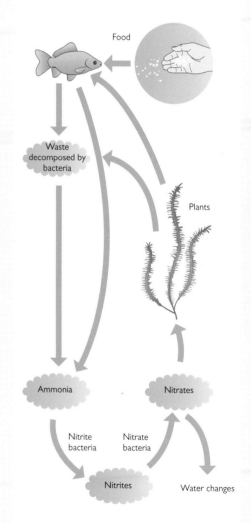

POPULATION EXPLOSION

If you let organic matter accumulate or offer excessive food, the resulting population explosion of heterotrophic bacteria will soon lead to problems. Bacteria are simple, single-celled organisms and digest organic matter by releasing their digestive enzymes into the surrounding pond water, then absorbing the products of digestion through their cell walls. So when there is an abundance of organic matter, the pond can soon deteriorate, with the release of lots of CO_2, methane, and ammonia resulting in an acidifying and oxygen-depleted environment. This cannot be tolerated by fish and other pond organisms – avoid it by removing any excess organic matter, including fish food.

WHAT'S IN THE SLIME?

It doesn't take long for a bacterial slime to coat anything in the pond. Bacteria soon colonize a hard surface, secreting a slime that eventually even covers themselves. Bacteria take in their food as it is absorbed into the slimy film. The slime has a life cycle of its own and gets thicker and deeper over time. It soon becomes attractive to heterotrophic bacteria, which target it as a source of food. Eventually, the film becomes so thick that the bacteria closest to the hard surface die off, causing the film to drop off and leave space for a new colonization.

Protozoa

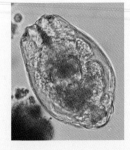

Only visible under a microscope, the protozoa in the slime perform an essential reprocessing role, breaking down any accumulated matter.

The web of life

Over time, all kinds of life will make a home in your pond. The older a pond gets, the more diverse its population of organisms, and the more stable and settled the environment.

By understanding the role that each organism has in maintaining a pond, you can apply this knowledge to your own artificial pond. Due to its age, location and type of construction your pond may not benefit from a natural, pond-sustaining population. You may need to intervene to ensure that the pond functions effectively.

Organism diversity

The population of organisms is different in every pond. As a pond matures and its organic content increases, it becomes more attractive to a wider range of organisms.

You can work with the pond-sustaining organisms; encourage them to do their jobs better than any piece of pond equipment. For instance, by installing a pond filter and supplying it with a constant flow of oxygenated water, you will encourage a massive population of beneficial bacteria to colonize it, augmenting the moderate bacterial activity that would otherwise have taken place, and enabling you to keep more fish and feed more food into a relatively small pond.

Bacterial functions

Bacteria are the reprocessors of the pond. Food items that pond bacteria break down can be divided into two groups – those that are organic (they contain carbon and are the product of life) and those that are inorganic (such as simple compounds containing nitrogen, sulfur and phosphorus).

Heterotrophic bacteria

Heterotrophic bacteria are concerned with organic compounds and digest them in order to absorb soluble nutrients. Heterotrophic bacteria have a much greater role to play in a natural pond, compared with a garden pond, as the environment is typically more organically rich. Natural mud ponds will readily accumulate organic matter in a silty, soft bottom, and these bacteria proliferate there.

Heterotrophic bacteria are known as "mineralizing bacteria" because they break down complex organic molecules into simple minerals. They demand a great deal of oxygen from the water, something that is directly proportional to the amount of organic matter. This does not pose such a problem in a lightly stocked pond, but a heavily stocked garden pond could soon become stressed with a heavy organic load, leading to a drop in dissolved oxygen.

Autotrophic bacteria

Autotrophic bacteria gain energy from the chemical bonds that make up inorganic compounds such as ammonia, phosphate and sulphates. Many different bacteria are involved in the breakdown of nitrogenous compounds in a pond. They require oxygenated water and the supply and removal of waste products.

Other bacteria break down other inorganic compounds, such as sulphates and phosphates. In the same way that nitrifying bacteria gain energy from processing nitrogenous compounds, sulphur bacteria and phosphate-loving bacteria process and recycle these nutrients. (For more on recycling nutrients, see page 162.)

Pond life in summer

When the pond is consistently above 12°C (53°F), your fish will feed, little and often, and grow. Fish must be fed regularly because there is insufficient natural food in an artificial pond to sustain a hungry, growing population. The food is digested, some of it is assimilated into fish tissue, and the remainder is excreted. The waste matter is then broken down by bacteria, fungi and protozoa.

The raised activity of all pond inhabitants will lead to an increased demand for dissolved oxygen. But as the pond water warms, its ability to dissolve oxygen is greatly reduced. In a natural pond, submerged plants produce oxygen as a by-product of photosynthesis. But in an artificial pond, there may be insufficient natural oxygen production (due to fewer submerged plants), so you must aerate the pond.

Algae and plant growth can become prolific under such nutrient-rich conditions. In the daytime, this results in the release of oxygen, but at night, when plants are net oxygen users, the pond can become oxygen depleted, leading to behavioural changes (such as the fish gasping at the surface). If the summer night is very warm, still and muggy, it can result in fish kills – good reason to provide aeration in the summer. The pond will benefit from fortnightly partial water changes to dilute excess by-products that it cannot process naturally.

Pond life in winter

Life in a pond in winter is the opposite of life in the summer. The cold water naturally holds lots of dissolved oxygen. The fish don't need feeding, so there's no waste for the micro-organisms to break down. (It's too cold for them to function effectively anyway.) Reduced sunlight also means that plants stop growing and photosynthesizing, with plants dropping their leaves and dying back. So in the winter, the pond is more balanced than in the summer, as it is not struggling to cope with the abundance of artificial food and an unnaturally large population of feeding fish.

Pond deterioration

A pond can deteriorate quickly in summer. Pondweed can proliferate and algae (green water) can soon bloom, requiring regular maintenance.

The role of a biofilter in the nitrification process

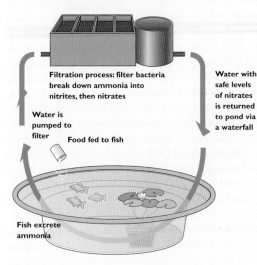

Filtration process: filter bacteria break down ammonia into nitrites, then nitrates

Water with safe levels of nitrates is returned to pond via a waterfall

Water is pumped to filter

Food fed to fish

Fish excrete ammonia

POND TEMPERATURE

All organisms within a pond are governed by the availability of food and sunlight and by the ambient temperature. It's useful to think of a pond as an oven – the warmer it is, the faster things happen (and may also deteriorate). Therefore, the upkeep of the pond requires more vigilance in the summer. In the colder months, the pond becomes inactive, and there is very little to manage.

DIFFUSION

The molecules of a fluid are constantly moving. They are so tiny that they are not visible, but evidence of their movement can often be seen. For example, if you turn off all the pumps and aeration in a pond, allowing the water to slow completely, and add a dye in one corner of the pond, it will diffuse from an area of high concentration to an area of low concentration through the whole pond until it is a uniform solution (it has reached equilibrium). It is by diffusion that the appetizing odour of food or the allure of pheromones travels across a lake. Diffusion is a "passive" process, which means that it does not require any input of energy from living organisms such as fish or filter bacteria and will occur whether life exists or not. The temperature of a fluid determines the speed at which the molecules move, causing faster movement (and rates of diffusion) to occur in warmer water.

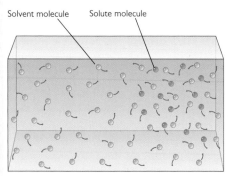

A localized concentration of solute molecules, soon after being added to a pond.

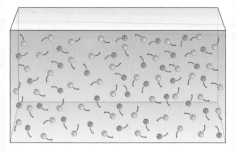

After sufficient time, the random movement of molecules has formed a uniform, dilute solution.

Pond chemistry

To fully appreciate, understand, and control your pond, you will benefit from knowing a little chemistry. Water is an amazing substance that makes life on earth possible. Besides making a pond "wet" and providing something for your fish to swim in, water enables all the necessary chemical reactions that help maintain a pond's health and balance.

Water is the world's best solvent. You can tell where water has been by analysing what is dissolved in it. The water in an upland mountain stream is relatively low in dissolved minerals, whereas the opposite is true for a lowland river or lake. A garden pond is best modelled on the chemistry and water quality found in a lowland lake, the natural habitat of the ancestors of most ornamental pond fish.

Water and ions

A molecule of pure water (H_2O) consists of two hydrogen atoms joined to one oxygen atom. In a pond, the water molecules dissociate (separate) into ions: positively charged hydrogen (H^+) and negatively charged hydroxyl (OH^-). These ions are constantly forming and reforming with any ion of an equal and opposite charge. It is this characteristic that makes water such an excellent solvent. For example, common salt — sodium chloride (NaCl) — will dissolve readily in water, forming sodium ions (Na^+) and chloride ions (Cl^-). This is true for many other elements and compounds, meaning that every aquatic environment has its own unique chemistry.

pH

An important measure for pond water is pH, a measure of the acidity or alkalinity of a substance. It is measured on a scale of 0 to 14, where 7 is neutral, below 7 is acidic and above 7 is alkaline. Pure water is neutral (neither acidic nor alkaline) and is the standard against which acidity and alkalinity are measured. The pH actually measures the quantity of free hydrogen ions (the H in pH). More hydrogen ions relative to hydroxyl ions will make the pond acidic, and more hydroxyl ions relative to hydrogen ions will make it more alkaline — so pH is a matter of balance. Taking lowland lakes as the model for water quality, your pond's pH should be alkaline, being stable between 7.0 and 8.5.

What if the pH becomes acidic?

If the pH is acidic, this means that there is an abundance of free H^+ ions. The following natural biological processes will put pressure on the pH of a garden pond to become acidic.

Solvent molecule   Solute molecule

Biological filtration: When fish release ammonia (NH_4), they are releasing nitrogen and hydrogen ions. When that ammonia is broken down by bacteria into nitrite (NO_2), the four free hydrogen ions are released into the water, causing a drop in pH. As ammonia excretion and biofiltration proceed unabated, there is a relentless downwards pressure on pH in every pond. If the pH drops below 7, you need to take action.

Respiration: Plants, fish and bacteria respire constantly, taking in oxygen and releasing carbon dioxide. The process of respiration can also cause the pH to drop as the carbon dioxide combines with water to form carbonic acid. Excessive plant growth can cause the pH to drop to extremes at night, rising again out of the danger zone in the day as plants utilize the carbon dioxide in photosynthesis.

A drop in pH in a pond to below 7 will lead to dramatic changes in the fishes' health, particularly if the changes are long-term. The fishes' colours are likely to fade through the deposition of excess mucus; in extreme cases, fish may be seen to gasp at the surface. Acidic pond water is also likely to be corrosive to plastic and metal surfaces, causing the pond water to become a toxic cocktail of contaminants.

What if the pH becomes alkaline?
An excessively high pH (above 9) appears to have a less extreme effect on fish than a low pH but should still be avoided. While a drop in pH is caused quite naturally, excessively alkaline water is likely to be a result of a pollutant, such as cement or builder's lime. An excessively alkaline pond will cause fish to secrete excess mucus and can also lead to them gasping at the surface − just as they do when they experience acidic conditions.

Buffers

A buffer is a chemical that, when added to a pond, will help stabilize a suitable pH. The natural tendency is for a pond's pH to become acidic. A buffer reacts with any excess hydrogen ions and releases them back again into the pond water should the pH rise too high. The most widely used buffer in and around ponds is calcium carbonate ($CaCO_3$) in the form of crushed shells, limestone gravel or similar material. By adding some to your filter, you can safeguard your pond against rapid and unhealthy swings in pH.

ACIDITY AND ALKALINITY
This diagram shows how the level of particular ions affects acidity and alkalinity − and where pond water sits ideally on the pH scale.

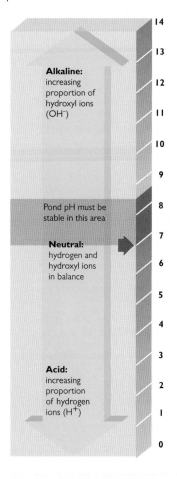

SOLUTIONS
Water is an excellent solvent. A substance that is dissolved in a solvent is called a solute − so salt (the solute) is dissolved in water (the solvent) to make a salt solution. A solution, if sampled at any number of points, will be made up of precisely the same proportions of solute and solvent.

BIOLOGICAL LOAD

A natural water body has a constant supply of fresh water and is stocked at a naturally low level. By contrast, a garden pond is a completely enclosed water body that must deal with an abnormally high biological load. You need to be aware of how to provide good water quality in an artificial pond. Fish are unable to escape from poor water quality. The resultant stress will make them more susceptible to disease, which is preceded by a tell-tale change in behaviour.

Influx of water
Natural water bodies benefit from the constant influx of freshwater. A garden pond relies on filtration and partial water changes to keep the water "sweet".

WATER CLARITY

Aim for a clear pond (even though clarity is no indication of the water's suitability for the fish). Water that is green due to an algae bloom will be liable to swings in pH and dissolved oxygen (DO) levels, which should be avoided.

Water quality

Water quality is a measure of the water's suitability for the fish and is the key to the maintenance of a healthy and successful pond. It directly affects the fishes' health.

Source water

Initially, water quality will be largely determined by the water source.

Using tap water

The chemistry of tap water will vary between regions. Water taken from a sedimentary area (such as limestone) is likely to be "hard" (high in dissolved minerals), whereas water taken from an igneous area (such as granite) will be "soft" (low in dissolved minerals). Water companies add neutralizing agents at the source, raising the pH to levels that fortuitously suit a pond. Tap water will also have disinfectants such as chlorine and chloramine added to make the water safe for human consumption. These can be toxic to fish and other pond life and must be removed before fish are added. Add a tap-water conditioner to the pond water, or pass all tap water through a water purifier. This will also remove or reduce high levels of other undesirable contaminants, such as heavy metals and pesticides.

Using well water

If you are fortunate enough to draw water from a well, chlorine and chloramine will not be a problem.

Testing the water

In the early days of a pond, you should test the water several times a week as you add fish and your filter matures. By testing individual parameters, you will soon build up a picture of the situation in your pond. With a little intuition, you can use your test results to predict future occurrences and also to learn from your experiences. As time passes and the pond matures, you can afford to test less often. In a more mature pond, you need only concern yourself with two or three different tests (pH, nitrite and perhaps nitrate) carried out every two weeks or so. But from day one, you should become familiar with all the useful tests, to establish your pond's unique characteristics.

Testing parameters

The seven useful parameters that you can test can be loosely divided into two groups: biological and chemical.

Biological parameters

Biological parameters include ammonia, nitrite and nitrate and are most significantly affected or controlled by life within the pond, and are processed by bacteria.

Ammonia (NH_3/NH_4^+): is toxic (which is why fish excrete it) and colourless and released from the gills, readily dissolving in pond water. The only guaranteed way of preventing fish from experiencing ammonia toxicity is to keep the level at zero.

Nitrite (NO_2): is a by-product of the biological (bacterial) breakdown of ammonia is also toxic. It has a reputation for being more stubborn and persistent than ammonia, with bacteria taking longer to break down and reduce nitrite levels. Nitrite can often rise out of control for long periods in a new pond, reaching levels where even a partial water change (30 per cent) does not appear to reduce the problem. If nitrite levels are allowed to become excessive, the nitrite itself can inhibit the nitrite-oxidizing bacteria, increasing even further the time taken for levels to drop. As with ammonia, the desirable nitrite level is zero.

Nitrate (NO_3), the least toxic of the three nitrogenous compounds, nitrate can be regarded as the nitrogen bank, where all the nitrogen from the pond system is ultimately deposited. Nitrates will accumulate within a pond over time and can be utilized through plant growth or diluted by a partial water change. Intervene with a partial water change if the level rises to 50 ppm.

Chemical parameters
These include pH, GH, KH (see "Testing parameters", right) and oxygen and are grouped together as chemical parameters because their levels are caused by chemical interactions (some of which may be directly related to other biological processes).

pH measures the acidity or alkalinity of pond water. A pond's pH should fall between 7.0 and 8.5, ideally being stable between 7.0 and 8.5. This slightly alkaline pH suits the environmental requirements of pond fish and should be relatively easy and inexpensive to maintain. Try to keep your pond's pH as stable as possible.

GH measures the general hardness of pond water, particularly the hardness-forming ions of calcium and magnesium. The level of GH should be medium to high (6 to 25 dH) to match the conditions that are preferred by the physiology of carp species.

KH is a measure of the soluble carbonate/bicarbonate ions that act as a buffer to maintain a stable pH. A medium to high KH is most desirable because it shows that the pH is not likely to fluctuate. This can be maintained by simply adding a mesh bag of limestone chippings or crushed shell to your filter. Aim for a KH of > 6 dH.

TESTING PARAMETERS
Pond water can be tested for the following parameters using test kits. You should aim for the following desirable ranges to achieve good water quality.

*pH (acidity and alkalinity)
7.0–8.5*

*GH (general hardness, expressed in dH)
6–25 dH (100–400 mg/L $CaCO_3$)*

*KH (carbonate hardness, or buffering material)
> 6 dH*

DO (dissolved oxygen)
> 6 mg/L

Ammonia
< 0.1 mg/L

Nitrite
< 0.1 mg/L

Nitrate
< 50 ppm

*It is essential that these parameters remain stable within the desirable range. Fish do not tolerate wide changes, which causes them stress.

DOCs
A garden pond is an enclosed system and will accumulate a range of by-products, or dissolved organic compounds (DOCs). These complex compounds come from fish food, soil and other organic matter. They give the water a yellow/brown tinge that discolours the white areas on fish. An accumulation of DOCs must be avoided, as they can lead to a drop in DO levels. Regular partial water changes will dilute them away.

Testing
Test your pond water regularly to ensure that parameters are met.

Poor fish health
Poor water quality is the single biggest cause of fish health problems. Remain vigilant by testing your pond water regularly.

Oxygen is required at a minimum level. It dissolves in water and can be added easily using diffused aeration, or moving water, or through photosynthesis from submerged aquatic plants. Warmer water holds less oxygen, so in summer (just when fish and bacteria require more oxygen), if a pond is excessively planted, it may well suffer from dawn depletion as DO levels drop at night through excessive plant respiration. DO must be at least 6 mg/L.

Testing frequency

Test your pond water regularly for pH to ensure that you can maintain it at the correct level. You should also test ammonia and nitrite very frequently during the running in of a new pond. These tests will show how the filter is maturing and whether it is keeping pace with the rate at which waste is produced. Once a pond is fully stocked and has been running satisfactorily for several months, there should be little need to use ammonia or nitrite test kits.

Types of tests

All test kits and testing equipment are made with the pond keeper in mind and are easy to use and interpret.

Colorimetric tests

Colorimetric test kits rely on a chemical reaction between the water and a reagent, which results in a colour change that can be compared against a colour chart. They come in several forms. Drops of liquid reagent may be added to a measured test sample of water and allowed to change, or dry tablets may be crushed and dissolved in the sample water and the colour change compared to a chart. Alternatively, plastic test strips, impregnated with reagent, are dipped into the sample water and allowed to react, causing a colour change.

Electronic tests

Electronic tests, available in a range of pocket-size digital meters, give a numerical reading. Digital meters are accurate and require regular calibration against known samples but are more expensive than colorimetric tests.

Interpreting results

The time and money you spend on testing water will be wasted if you do not act on the results. If, having tested your water, you discover that the quality is not as good as it should be, carry out appropriate remedial action immediately.

pH

If the pH is too high, carry out a partial water change with soft, acidic water (such as rainwater), and check for sources of buffer in your pond that could be raising the pH to extreme levels. If the pH is too low, add some treated tap water (which is usually neutralized by water companies) or add a source of lime such as limestone chippings or crushed shells.

Ammonia

The desirable ammonia reading is zero; if you have a positive reading (which suggests that the ammonia excreted by fish is not being broken down), you should stop feeding the fish immediately. Do not introduce any new fish, carry out a 20 to 30 per cent water change, and only start feeding again when the reading is back to zero (which may take a few days). Carry out a test each day for the next week.

If a positive ammonia reading reappears after daily testing, carry out steps 1 to 4 again. As the filter matures, a positive ammonia reading is less likely to occur.

Nitrite

The only desirable nitrite reading is zero, and if a positive nitrite reading is present, it is an indication that the filter is not coping with the amount of waste. Even a low nitrite reading is undesirable and, if present, the same remedial procedure as for ammonia toxicity should be followed.

Fish watching

Watching the behaviour of your fish is key to maintaining a healthy pond and will allow you to spot any problems before they escalate. A change in behaviour indicates that the water quality is not as it should be. At the first sign of a change in behaviour, stop feeding, and test for ammonia or nitrite to see if the filter is coping with the waste that the fish are producing.

The following changes in fish behaviour can be indicators of poor water quality:

1. Loss of appetite
2. Sulking on the pond bottom
3. Hanging motionless at the surface
4. Clamped fins
5. Gasping at the surface.

Any of these changes in behaviour usually indicate a deterioration in water quality, and you should perform follow-up water tests.

TOP TIPS FOR STABLE WATER QUALITY

1. Test regularly.
2. Build your pond as large as possible in the first place – the solution to pollution is dilution.
3. Carry out frequent smaller water changes rather than a few larger ones.
4. Add a source of calcium carbonate in your pond/filter to keep pH and KH levels stable and within acceptable limits.
5. When starting a new pond, add fish gradually and test regularly.
6. If you detect an unhealthy or surprise increase in ammonia or nitrite, stop feeding and carry out sufficient water changes to bring it down to zero immediately.
7. To avoid the risk of low DO, ensure your pond enjoys several reliable sources of aeration. Remember, you can't over-aerate.
8. Ensure that any new water is passed through a purifier or is treated with a tap-water conditioner after a water change.

Removing impurities
In-line water purifiers ensure the water that enters a pond is safe for fish by removing contaminants such as chlorine, chloramine and other impurities.

Getting started

Every new pond, whatever its size, must go through a maturation process that can put your fish at risk.

On completing a new pond, it can be tempting to try to stock it with its full complement of fish as quickly as possible. It is understandable that, having spent lots of time (and money) building a new pond, there is a great eagerness to see it as you intended – well stocked with thriving, beautiful fish. In the rush to achieve the finished result, it is easy to forget the basic principles of husbandry, with disastrous consequences. For the next three months, you will need to take patient, steady steps, progressing at the rate set by the natural biological processes in your pond. Don't forget that, even though your pond is man-made, you will still be relying on natural processes to manage and maintain it.

A brand-new pond is relatively lifeless – constructed of man-made and inert materials and filled with tap water that has been disinfected to make it suitable for drinking rather than for fish to live in. The pond and filter will not contain any of the beneficial organisms required to bring the pond to life or stabilize its water quality. Compared with a natural water body, a new pond is "dead" and certainly not ready to receive lots of fish at this stage.

Firing it up

You must turn the pump on to circulate water through the filter as soon as possible. This will provide the conditions for the beneficial bacteria to colonize and populate the filter. Plants can also be added to the pond immediately, using a diversity of plant types to help balance the pond as well as make it look beautiful.

There is a real risk of algae plaguing your new pond in the first few weeks due to its relatively poor plant coverage, high nutrient levels from the tap water, and excellent sunlight penetration through the crystal-clear water. If you do experience an algae problem, don't replace all the water with new, as you will be back to square one. Eventually, you should find that the growing algae will exhaust the abundant nutrients, causing it to die off.

Fish and filter

For bacteria to flourish in your biofilter, they will need a source of ammonia on which to feed, which is provided by the addition of your first few fish. As there will be no life in your filter at this stage, if you add too many fish, ammonia levels in the pond will soon rise, stressing your fish and leading to disease and even fatalities. Over the next

Newly planted pond
A newly planted pond may have the appearance of being established, but it will need time to mature before fish are introduced.

three months, it is essential that you only add fish gradually, at the pace set by the rate at which your biofilter matures.

Let the filter "cycle"

As a biofilter matures and the bacterial population increases, its ability to break down ammonia also increases, producing nitrites (which, unfortunately, are still toxic) as a by-product. In response to the increase in nitrites, a different population of bacteria will then start to colonize the filter, breaking down the nitrites into relatively harmless nitrates. This cycling of a biofilter is essential and will be repeated each time that more fish are added to a new pond, until the pond reaches its capacity and the filter has become fully mature. After about three months of adding fish, you will have established a fully matured filter, having passed through the risky period for your new pond. It will now have the capacity to withstand isolated peak inputs of ammonia or nitrite (caused by accidental overfeeding, for example).

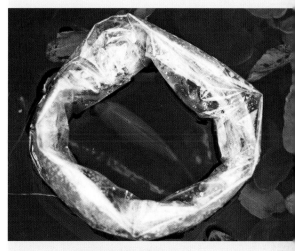

Introducing fish
New fish must be introduced gradually over the first three months of a pond's life to avoid stressful ammonia or nitrite peaks.

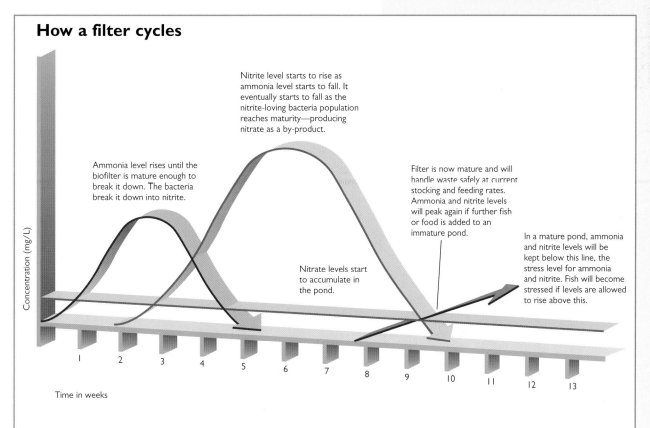

How a filter cycles

Nitrite level starts to rise as ammonia level starts to fall. It eventually starts to fall as the nitrite-loving bacteria population reaches maturity—producing nitrate as a by-product.

Ammonia level rises until the biofilter is mature enough to break it down. The bacteria break it down into nitrite.

Filter is now mature and will handle waste safely at current stocking and feeding rates. Ammonia and nitrite levels will peak again if further fish or food is added to an immature pond.

In a mature pond, ammonia and nitrite levels will be kept below this line, the stress level for ammonia and nitrite. Fish will become stressed if levels are allowed to rise above this.

Nitrate levels start to accumulate in the pond.

Concentration (mg/L)

1   2   3   4   5   6   7   8   9   10   11   12   13

Time in weeks

HOW THE FILTER COPES

A useful way of visualizing what is happening in your new pond as the filter matures is to imagine three barrels, each fitted with a tap. Barrel 1 collects ammonia from your fish, barrel 2 collects nitrite from barrel 1, and barrel 3 collects nitrate that is fed to it by barrel 2.
The more mature your filter, the more "open" the taps – allowing more waste to be processed. Ultimately, in a mature and balanced pond, the tap's capacity in barrels 1 and 2 will be far greater than the rate at which ammonia and nitrite are produced in the system; hence, ammonia and nitrite levels will always be zero.

Maturation process of a new filter

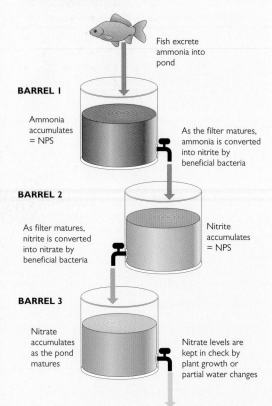

Fish excrete ammonia into pond

BARREL 1

Ammonia accumulates = NPS

As the filter matures, ammonia is converted into nitrite by beneficial bacteria

BARREL 2

As filter matures, nitrite is converted into nitrate by beneficial bacteria

Nitrite accumulates = NPS

BARREL 3

Nitrate accumulates as the pond matures

Nitrate levels are kept in check by plant growth or partial water changes

New Pond Syndrome

New Pond Syndrome (NPS) is often the first (and most expensive) problem encountered by new pondkeepers. In some cases, it can seem so extreme or final, with solutions seeming so long-term, that NPS could put you off keeping fish altogether.

You may first encounter NPS unknowingly in the form of diseased fish in a new pond and hope that you will be able to medicate the problem away. In fact, where NPS is the cause of health problems, treating fish is not the solution. By understanding the science behind the causes of NPS and responding accordingly, you can save considerable expense on pond treatments and, at worst, replacement fish. NPS can be serious – but it needn't be.

NPS is a term that describes what can happen if a new pond is stocked in haste. If too many fish are added too soon, then more ammonia is released into the pond than can be broken down by the immature filter. Ammonia and nitrite levels will rise, causing your fish stress and leading to disease and fatalities. Mild cases of NPS – with a slight ammonia peak, followed a few days later by a nitrite peak – are nearly always experienced, even with careful stocking and feeding. Fish can tolerate such periods as long as they are short-lived and at a low level. But if the levels of ammonia in a new pond are too low, then this will limit the population of bacteria that can be sustained in a filter, limiting its rate of maturation. By testing the water regularly and keeping on top of any ammonia or nitrite issues, you can prevent serious health implications.

Confirming NPS

If your pond is less than three months old, the symptoms of NPS can be recognized as follows:

1. High ammonia or nitrite readings
2. Fish gasping, sulking, swimming erratically or not feeding.

You can confirm NPS using test kits (see page 170). Ammonia and nitrite test kits will soon highlight the problem (if levels rise above 0.1 mg/L). Having confirmed that you have a problem caused by your immature filter, continue to test and observe the ammonia levels peak and then fall, followed by the nitrite level peaking and falling as it is processed by the filter (see "How a filter cycles" on page 173).

In a pond that is suffering from NPS, barrels 1 and 2 (containing either ammonia or nitrite – both toxic) will fill up more quickly than the taps allow them to empty. This will be evident by testing your water for ammonia and nitrite. The results will tell you where you are getting the bottleneck and which parts of your filtration are not coping. For example, if the ammonia level is high, then the ammonia-converting bacteria are not processing sufficient ammonia. Likewise, if you have a high nitrite level, then your nitrite-converting bacteria are also in an immature state. In extreme cases, you may get high readings for both ammonia and nitrite.

Stocking safely

As soon as your new pond is stocked with fish, ammonia is released by them, filling up barrel 1. The tap is virtually closed at this stage because there is very little bacterial activity, so the ammonia level will start to increase. You can reduce the amount of ammonia that your fish produce by stopping feeding immediately. You should also reduce the ammonia level by carrying out a partial water change with treated tap water, diluting the toxin away.

Ammonia or nitrites

Even by adding some mature media from an existing pond and filter, it is highly unlikely that you will be able to mature your filter and stock your pond without experiencing an ammonia or nitrite reading. Be prepared to accept low levels of these. However, should the level of either ammonia or nitrite rise significantly, you will need to react quickly, as follows:

1. Carry out a partial water change. This will reduce lethal levels of ammonia (and/or nitrite) but not remove it completely, allowing the bacteria population to increase as they continue to break down the residual levels of ammonia. The nitrite peak can also be diluted but, again, not totally removed so as to deny the bacteria a chance to mature but at the same time to find a safe limit for the fish.

2. Stop feeding the fish. As ammonia excretion is related to the level of protein in the diet, fish should not be fed while there is a positive ammonia reading. In addition, if the first partial water change does not reduce ammonia levels below acceptable levels, then a further water change will be necessary.

3. Proceed with caution. Subsequent stocking should only be continued when ammonia and nitrite levels have been at zero for a week, and then additions of new fish should be limited. Continue to test for ammonia and nitrite and ensure that the filter manages to handle the increased stock, intervening with water changes and a reduction in food if required (as highlighted by your water test results).

PREVENTING NPS

The most reliable method of preventing NPS is to stock your pond wisely and patiently. Add fish only a couple at a time, monitor ammonia and nitrite levels and observe and record levels so you can satisfy yourself that the filter is coping with its new workload.

You can help the maturation of your new pond and filter system by adding a source of bacteria. The more diverse and larger the bacterial population your filter can sustain, the quicker they can process the waste (passing it on to the next barrel). Traditionally, this has been a case of waiting for Mother Nature to colonize the filters with bacteria naturally (and slowly). However, you can add filter boosters (products containing beneficial filter bacteria) or some mature filter media from another pond filter to speed up the process. A pond-keeping friend may be in an ideal position to donate some highly desirable mature biomedia, introducing a wonderful breadth and diversity of bacteria to your new filter.

Controlling NPS
The number of fish and the amount of food will affect the water quality in a new pond. If you experience NPS, you will have to reduce feeding immediately to help control it.

Protective net
A fine-mesh pond net will prevent leaves and other blown debris from entering the pond. It also helps to protect your fish from herons.

Removing silt
Regular vacuuming of the pond will help to prevent the build-up of silt on the pond bottom.

General maintenance

Try to carry out any maintenance in a way that preserves pond stability. A little frequent maintenance is better than letting the pond deteriorate so much that it needs to be completely emptied.

Small ponds require more maintenance than large ponds because they accumulate debris and silt at a relatively faster rate. They also have a tendency to suffer more from algae problems.

Try to maintain a silt-free pond bottom. If you disturb a layer of silt when you drag a hand net along the pond bottom, this indicates that you need to carry out some maintenance. In a natural pond, the silt would be broken down by a host of microbes – something that is greatly reduced by your pond having an inert pond liner.

Preventive measures

If you can reduce the amount of debris that enters your pond, you can reduce the amount of pond maintenance.

Protective pond net

Stretch a pond net tightly across the pond to prevent leaves from dropping into the water in fall.

Hand net

Use a fine-mesh hand net to remove any floating leaf matter and debris. Choose one with a handle long enough to reach the other side of the pond.

Pond vacuum

A pond vacuum is used like a normal vacuum cleaner, and will enable you to suck silt and debris off the pond bottom. You can use the nutrient-rich silty water to fertilize your garden. Top the pond up with fresh water.

Maintaining hardware

The pond hardware must be maintained to remain effective.

Pond pump

If you have turned your pump off over winter, check that the impeller and seals are intact before turning it on in spring. Any prefilter should be removed and cleaned if the flow rate is impeded.

Filter

The filter media must be cleaned once it starts to collect debris from the pond. Your filter will have matured to be capable of handling waste produced by the pond, and this biological activity must be safeguarded when cleaning it.

Only clean out a portion – no more than one-third – of the total media in a biological filter at any one time, preserving some filter function to maintain good water quality.

Only clean out filter media using pond water. Avoid using tap water because the difference in water quality and the presence of chlorine (a disinfectant) can affect the delicate yet beneficial bacterial population.

UV clarifier
The UV clarifier will need a new bulb in spring. This should last the rest of the season and will ensure that it is most effective against algae through the height of the summer season. UV performance can be impaired by a dirty quartz sleeve (which keeps the UV bulb separate from the pond water passing through the unit). Quartz sleeves are notoriously brittle, so take care when handling and cleaning it, making sure that you remove any stubborn dirt and limescale.

Liner
It may be tempting to scrub away at your liner to expose its original clean surface, but by doing so, you will be removing some of the diverse pond life that works to maintain your pond's balance. You will also find that any exposed area of liner will soon become covered again by algae and other microscopic pond life.

Aeration pump
An air pump should run relatively silently. If it starts to vibrate loudly, it may be a sign that the internal flexible rubber diaphragm is wearing out. This may also be coupled with a drop in air output by the pump.

Diffusers
Airstones and other porous diffusers do have a tendency to block up, leading them to produce fewer, larger bubbles. When this happens, either replace them or scrub them to remove any blockages.

Emptying the pond
Despite your best efforts, you may still find that your pond needs to be completely emptied, cleaned out and refilled. Do this in autumn or winter, when the water temperature is above 8°C (46°F). You will not disturb fish or plant growth, and all leaf matter will have fallen. It also prepares the pond for spring.

Unfortunately, emptying the pond means a risky few months to regain the balance and maturity. You will also be subjecting your fish to an acute change in environment by returning them into a pond filled with raw tap water. Nuisance algae may proliferate in the new water.

Avoid cleaning the biofilter too well, to help it retain its maturity, and always keep the media wet to preserve the bacterial activity.

Clear blockages
A pump's performance will be greatly reduced by a blocked prefilter. Regular maintenance may be required to keep the pump running at full power.

EQUIPMENT YOU WILL NEED TO EMPTY YOUR POND

1. Temporary pool/vessel large enough for your fish
2. Hose and pump to empty the pond
3. Buckets, dustpan and brush to clear out the sludge
4. New planting baskets, gravel and soil for repotting overgrown plants
5. Pruners/knives for cutting back and thinning out plants
6. Tap-water conditioner for treating the new pond water
7. Test kits to check the stability of the pond for several weeks after re-introducing the fish

Seasonal maintenance

A pond will provide enjoyment and satisfaction throughout the year, even if it is frozen over during the winter months. Maintenance in cold-winter areas will focus around the more active periods, when you are either preparing your pond in late winter/spring or tidying up in the fall. Use the following maintenance guide if your pond freezes in winter.

EARLY WINTER

Care Consider erecting a pond cover over the pond if the winter proves to be extreme.

Fish Fish still on the pond bottom. Do not disturb them as they will now be in a state of torpor.

Plants Planted baskets will at times become frozen in the ice. Leave well enough alone until spring.

Enjoy Frost forms on marginal plants.

Tasks Guard against ice covering the pond by using a small pool heater.

MIDWINTER

Care Prevent ice from completely covering the pond by using a small pond heater.

Fish Fish won't feed for another few months.

Plants All plants will have died back. Start to spot any gaps on the pond shelf with a view to filling them.

Enjoy Water is at its clearest.

Tasks If the pond freezes, keep a hole in the ice.

LATE WINTER

Care Even at this early stage, keep an eye out for pond scum that may have managed to over-winter. Remove it before it can flourish in the warmer months.

Fish Fish may start to show some signs of activity. Don't feed. Start using a pond thermometer to measure the water temperature.

Plants Right any tipped-up baskets and replace gravel or repot as required.

Enjoy Frogs and toads will start to emerge, getting ready to mate and spawn.

Tasks Remove any traces of blanketweed.

EARLY SPRING

Care As the pond water starts to climb toward 10°C (50°F), if your pump has not been switched on, clean it out and check the moving parts. It will not be long before your fish will need filtration, so start up the pump and check that the flow is good through the filter.

Fish If your fish start to feed, offer them a low-protein wheatgerm-based food that is easy to digest. Check that all fish are swimming and feeding normally. Check that fins are intact and look for signs of fungus. Treat if necessary.

Plants Put the finishing touches on any planted baskets. Remove blanketweed and start adding a natural blanketweed treatment.

Enjoy Frogs will be spawning.

Tasks Turn on the pump, check the filter and replace the UV bulb.

MID SPRING

Care Once fish start to eat more food, check that the filter is coping by testing the water for ammonia and nitrite. Both must be zero.

Fish Continue to watch fish behaviour. Are they all feeding? Are any sulking in the corner or swimming erratically?

Plants New shoots will now start to emerge from the marginal baskets. This is your last chance to trim away any remains of last year's dead foliage without risking damaging this year's new shoots.

Enjoy Tadpoles appear – by the hundreds. Get the kids to count them!

Tasks Check that the biofilter is breaking down ammonia and nitrite and that levels are zero.

LATE SPRING

Care Keep the pump intake clear and stay on top of filter maintenance.

Fish Fish will now be feeding more and growing vigorously. As soon as the water temperature reaches 14°C (57°F), wean them off their low-temperature food onto a higher-protein growth food.

Plants The longer days and warmer weather will be causing the marginals to flourish and flower. Water soldiers will have risen to the surface. Remove blanketweed through manual removal and natural remedies (see page 57).

Enjoy A beautiful month in the pond. The first water lily leaves will now be at the surface. Tadpoles will be well on their way to becoming frogs – losing their tails.

Tasks Check for blanketweed.

Otherwise, you will need to remain vigilant throughout the year in maintaining water levels and filtration systems.

This chart is based on a temperate climate. The exact timings of activities listed will depend on the climate zone you are in. You may need to make adjustments for more extreme climates.

EARLY SUMMER

Care Top up for water lost through evaporation and water features. Carry out fortnightly partial water changes of 10 to 20 per cent.

Fish Fish will come into spawning condition at the end of June or the start of July, depending on the water temperature. Be sure to keep water well aerated by water movement in warmer weather, especially during hot, muggy nights.

Plants Dead-head any flowering marginals and remove any older lily leaves before they become diseased. Thin out any rampant oxygenating plants, and clear some space for the fish.

Enjoy Spawning fish and bright blue damselflies mate around your pond.

Tasks Clear excessive plant growth, especially older foliage. Keep a watchful eye on dissolved oxygen levels.

MIDSUMMER

Care Fish are feeding more than ever, so make regular checks on the filter maintenance.

Fish Keep a look out for fry. The best place for them to hide and forage is among your plants.

Plants Continue to keep at least half of the water surface clear to allow the pond water to "breathe". Regularly remove old foliage, including any duckweed or fairy moss. Now that the water is warm, for a little variety, why not add some delicate floating plants, such as water hyacinth and water chestnut?

Enjoy This may be the high point of the year in the pond. Look for tiny fry in among the dense plants in the pond. You'll have to look hard, as they are likely to be darker than their more ornamental parents.

Tasks Keep water circulating well. Clear excess foliage from the pond surface.

LATE SUMMER

Care Be vigilant for pond scum, and make regular checks on the filter, clearing the accumulated dead algae.

Fish Keep feeding to build up their winter reserves. Offer any fry a flake food.

Plants Continue to dead-head and thin out excessive floating plants. Start to review those plants that have really thrived this year, and split/repot as required.

Enjoy Lily flowers are in abundance – watch how they close up at night.

Tasks If you plan a vacation for a couple of weeks, show your neighbour the likely maintenance required, and put out daily rations of food to one side to avoid overfeeding.

EARLY AUTUMN

Care Prepare the pond for the autumnal leaf fall by purchasing a fine-meshed pond net.

Fish As the water temperature drops toward 10°C (50°F), start offering a lower-protein food.

Plants Plants will start to shed leaves quite dramatically as the temperature falls. Be vigilant about removing any decaying leaf matter before it becomes detached and sinks to the pond bottom.

Enjoy Water soldiers magically start to descend to deeper water as the weather turns colder.

Tasks Remove dead or dying foliage. Offer fish a lower-protein food.

MID AUTUMN

Care Once fish have stopped feeding, turn off the pump, remove it from the pond, and dry it out. Clean out the filter media and, if possible, keep it moist/wet over winter to retain the essential friendly bacteria for next year. Turn off the UV clarifier. Use the spare electric feed to install a 100-watt pool heater ready for the freezing temperatures.

Fish Stop feeding when fish show no appetite. Fish will descend to the pond bottom and overwinter in the silt. They will not feed until early spring next year.

Plants Remove any delicate floating plants such as water hyacinth that have died.

Enjoy See how the water becomes crystal clear as the cold water starts to kill off any remaining algae.

Tasks Turn off the pump/filter. Cover the pond against leaves.

LATE AUTUMN

Care Keep a check on any ice covering the pond. Use the heater if required. There's very little else to do within the pond itself.

Fish These will be inactive, resting on the pond bottom. Keep them netted or protected against predatory birds. This is when they benefit from your pond being at least 90cm (3 feet) deep.

Plants The frost will have killed off any remaining exposed foliage, which can be trimmed right back.

Enjoy Ice covers the pond.

Tasks Take action to keep a hole in the ice with a heater.

Hardiness zones

Remember that hardiness is not just a question of minimum temperatures.
A plant's ability to survive certain temperatures is affected by many factors,
such as the amount of shelter given and its position within your garden.

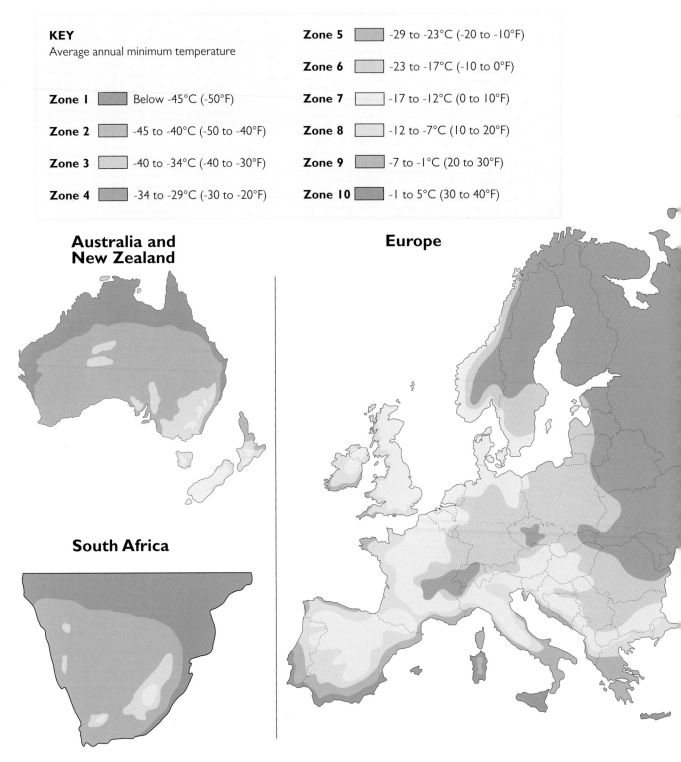

KEY
Average annual minimum temperature

Zone 1   Below -45°C (-50°F)

Zone 2   -45 to -40°C (-50 to -40°F)

Zone 3   -40 to -34°C (-40 to -30°F)

Zone 4   -34 to -29°C (-30 to -20°F)

Zone 5   -29 to -23°C (-20 to -10°F)

Zone 6   -23 to -17°C (-10 to 0°F)

Zone 7   -17 to -12°C (0 to 10°F)

Zone 8   -12 to -7°C (10 to 20°F)

Zone 9   -7 to -1°C (20 to 30°F)

Zone 10   -1 to 5°C (30 to 40°F)

Australia and New Zealand

South Africa

Europe

United States of America

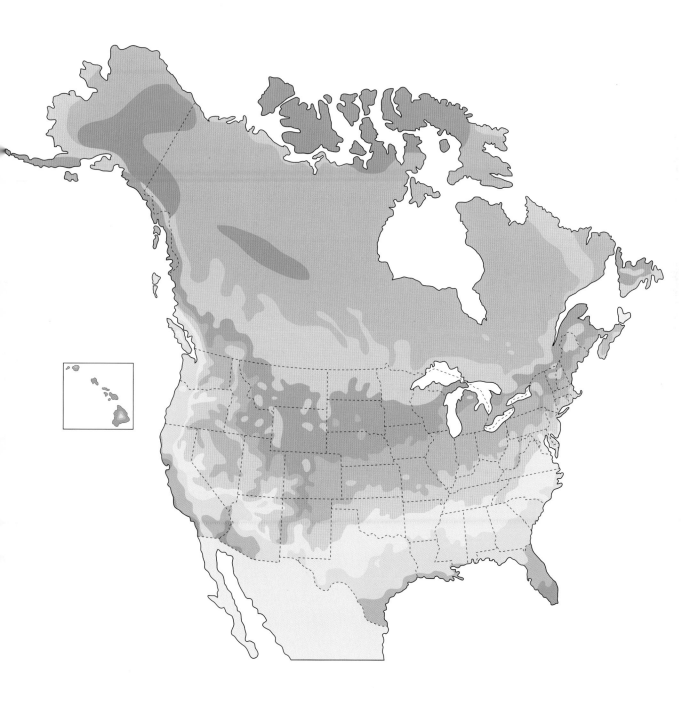

Glossary

A

Aerobic
In the presence of oxygen.

Air pump
A pump that delivers pressurized air into a diffuser to aerate the pond.

Algae
A primitive group of plants, very basic in structure and capable of rapid growth. Blanketweed and green water are examples of algae in ponds.

Allelopathic
One plant's ability to release toxic substances that inhibit the growth of another plant.

Ammonia (NH$_4$)
Toxic by-product of a fish's metabolism, excreted via the gills.

Anaerobic
In the absence of oxygen.

Anoxic
Oxygen-deficient or without oxygen.

Artificial food
Food for pond fish that is man-made. May take the form of floating pellets, sticks or flakes.

Autotrophic
An organism that gains its energy from chemical bonds within inorganic compounds.

Bacteria
Microscopic single-celled organisms that can be beneficial in a pond, by breaking down waste, or problematic, by causing disease.

Biofilter
A filter that is populated by beneficial bacteria, breaking down the pollutants and waste created by fish. Takes several months to mature.

B

Bog plant
A terrestrial plant that thrives in damp and moist soils.

Buffer
A chemical that will prevent undesirable pH swings. Calcium carbonate is widely used as a buffer.

C

Carbonate Hardness (KH)
A measure of the carbonate ions in water.

Carnivorous plants
Use insects as a source of food. Avoid commercial fertilizers.

Carotenoid
A group of compounds that will enhance the colour in ornamental pond fish.

Chlorine/Chloramine
Disinfectant agents added to water to make it safe to drink. They are irritants that need to be neutralized from tap water prior to fish being introduced.

Circuit breaker (RCD)
Electrical safety device that can protect from electric shock should electrical pond equipment be faulty.

Colour enhancer
A food additive that will enhance the colour of ornamental pond fish.

D

Daphnia
A small, mid-water crustacean; a popular live food in ponds.

Day bloomers
Tropical water lilies that bloom during the day.

Dead spot
An area in a pond where water circulation is restricted. Ponds should be planned and constructed to avoid creating any dead spots.

Degree of hardness (DH)
General hardness – caused by calcium and magnesium ions.

Diffusion
The movement of molecules in a liquid from an area of high concentration to an area of low concentration.

Dissolved organic compounds (DOC)
A group of organic compounds that accumulate in a pond over time to discolour the pond water.

Dissolved Oxygen (DO)
Oxygen that is dissolved in the water that is then available to fish and other aquatic organisms.

E

Ecosystem
A natural unit of plants, animals and micro-organisms that functions together to create a habitat.

External filter
A filter that sits outside the pond. Can range from a small biofilter to a large multi-chambered filter for a koi pond.

External pump
A water pump that is installed externally to the pond.

F

Fancy goldfish
A variety of goldfish with extreme variations in body shape or finnage.

Fish watching
An important part of pond keeping, to monitor the behaviour and therefore the health of the fish in your pond.

Floating plant
A pond plant that floats on the surface and is able to gain its nutrients direct from the pond water via its trailing roots.

Flock spawn
The natural type of spawning in a pond where males and females spawning freely together.

Food web
The system of interlinked relationships by which organisms in a pond gain their food.

Formal pond
A pond that is geometric or symmetrical in shape.

Fountain
A dynamic display of water, above the pond's surface. Fountains can take many forms, depending on the fountain head and size of pump used.

G

Gravity-fed filter
A filter that is fed from the pond via a bottom drain. Filtered water is returned to the pond via a pump.

H

Hard water
Water that has a high level of minerals dissolved within it.

Hardy water lilies
Hardy water lilies that bloom during the day and survive the cold winter temperatures of a northern climate.

Heterotrophic
An organism that requires an organic food.

Hybrid vigour
Increased strength as a result of the mixing of different genes.

I

Informal pond
A pond with no symmetry or geometric shapes; one that is freeform or natural in its shape.

Internal filter
A filter that sits inside the pond – usually only practical in smaller ponds.

Invasive plant
A plant that is capable of rapid, uncontrolled growth, with the potential of invading and upsetting the natural ecosystem. Many pond plants are potentially invasive and must be disposed of with care.

Ions
An atom (or group of atoms) that gains or loses an electron (becoming positively or negatively charged).

L

Low-voltage
Electrical equipment whose voltage has been reduced from the mains voltage by way of a transformer.

M

Marginal plant
A plant whose roots are submerged, but whose foliage is displayed above the water. It resides in shallow water.

Mature (filter or pond)
A filter or pond that has become stable over a period of months, and is able to process the wastes produced within it.

Mechanical filter
The part of a filter dedicated to removing solid material.

Metazoa
An organism consisting of more than one cell.

Mucus
A slippery, protective membrane secreted on to the skin of fish.

N

New Pond Syndrome (NPS)
When water quality deteriorates in a new pond due to too many fish or too much food being added, relative to a filter's processing ability. Leads to stress, disease and mortalities.

Niche
A position in an ecosystem that is exploited by an organism.

Night bloomers
Tropical water lilies that bloom at night; opening in the late afternoon and closing the following morning.

Nitrate (NO_3)
Beneficial bacteria in a filter break down nitrites into nitrate. Nitrate is not toxic to fish, but can cause algae to proliferate in a pond.

Nitrite (NO_2)
Beneficial bacteria in a filter break down ammonia into nitrite. Nitrite is toxic to fish.

Nitrogen cycle
The cyclical process by which nitrogen is processed by living organisms.

Nitrogen harbouring
The ability to uptake and store nitrogen.

O

Omnivore
An organism that eats both animal and vegetable matter.

Operculum
On fish, the bony covering to the gill chamber.

Oxygenating plants
A group of submerged plants that are stocked in ponds due to their ability to release lots of oxygen in the pond.

P

Pathogen
A disease-causing organism (such as a virus, bacteria, fungus or parasite).

pH
A measure of how acidic or alkaline a substance is. A pond's pH should be stable between 7.0 and 8.5.

Photosynthesis
The process by which green plants convert the sun's energy into sugars, utilizing carbon dioxide and releasing oxygen.

Planting baskets
Perforated pots, available in different shapes and sizes that can be used for planting marginal and submerged pond plants.

Pond liner
Flexible material that is used to line a pond, creating an impermeable layer. Pond liner is available in different materials, with varying guarantees.

Prefilter
A small attachment to the intake of a pump that keeps debris from damaging the pump. Tends to block frequently, requiring regular cleaning.

Preformed pond
A rigid or semi-rigid, preconstructed pond.

Pressurized filter
A filter that is completely sealed and can be buried out of sight.

Protozoa
A single-celled organism.

Pump-fed filter
A filter that is fed from the pond via a pump. Filtered water returns to the pond under gravity.

Q

Quarantine
Fish held in a separate quarantine pond system prior to being introduced to a pond to help acclimatize the fish and screen for disease.

S

Soft water
Water with low level of minerals dissolved within it.

Spawning
The release of eggs into the water for fertilization by the males.

Stress
Poor environmental conditions in a pond cause fish stress, which makes them more susceptible to disease.

Submerged plant
A plant that grows completely under water.

Submersible pump
A water pump that is installed below the surface.

T

Tap-water conditioner
A pond additive that makes tap water safe for fish.

Test kit
A simple-to-use kit to determine the quality of pond water.

Torpor
A period of hibernation or dormancy.

T-piece
A pipework fitting attached to the outlet of a pump that allows the flow to be regulated and separated into two pipes.

Tubercles
Tiny hard projections on the skin of male fish in spawning season to give the males purchase against the females during the spawning process.

Turbid
Water that is cloudy through the suspension of tiny particles.

U

Ultraviolet clarifier (UVC)
A piece of pond equipment that will kill algae that cause green water.

Resources

V

Venturi
A venturi offers a means of injecting air into a pond via a pumped water return.

Vertical head
The vertical difference in height between the pond's surface and the highest required point of delivery, such as the top of a waterfall. A useful measure of the "work" required of a pump.

Viewing point
The position from which your pond will be viewed the most, affecting how your pond should be oriented, landscaped and planted.

W

Water quality
A measure of how good the water is to create a healthy and supportive environment within the pond. It is the single greatest factor that affects the health of fish.

Waterfall
A stream or cascade allowing water to flow down into a pond.

Waterfall box
A box that feeds a waterfall, creating an even flow of water across the width of the waterfall.

Wildlife pond
A pond that is planted with native plants and fish and built to encourage natural wildlife. It will not be filtered or circulated by a pump.

Organizations

British Koi Keepers Society
www.bkks.co.uk

Ornamental and Aquatic Trade Association
www.ornamentalfish.org

International Waterlily and Water Gardening Society
www.iwgs.org

International Water Gardener
www.internationalwatergardener.com

Suppliers

Merebrook Pond Plants
www.pondplants.co.uk

Solesbridge Mill Water Gardens
www.solesbridge.co.uk

Maidenhead Aquatics
(stores throughout the UK)
www.fishkeeper.co.uk

World of Water
(stores throughout the UK)
www.world-of-water.co.uk

Bradshaws Direct
www.bradshawsdirect.co.uk

Watergardening direct
www.watergardeningdirect.com

Stapeley Water Gardens
www.stapleywgs.com

Books and magazines

Pond Owner's Handbook
John A. Dawes
Cassell Illustrated, 1998

The Master Book of the Water Garden
Philip Swindells
Interpet Publishing, 1999 (new ed.)

The Interpet Encyclopedia of Water Gardening
J Allison
Salamander

Water Gardening
Peter Robinson
Dorling Kindersley, 1997

The Water Garden Design Book
Yvonne Rees and Peter May
Barron's, 2003

Koi Magazine
www.koimag.co.uk

Practical Fishkeeping
www.practicalfishkeeping.co.uk

Koi Carp Magazine
www.koi-carp.com

Plant list
Italic numbers indicate illustrations

Index

Italic numbers indicate illustrations

Credits

We would like to thank and acknowledge the following for supplying photographs reproduced in this book.

Key: l left; r right; t top; b bottom; m middle

Ake Lindau/ardea.com 124t
Alamy: 170tl
Anne Green Armytage/Garden Picture Library 120br
Aquascape Designs Plc: 14tr
Ben Helm: 38m, 138, 144
Bob Gibbons/ardea.com 105r, 107b
Cloverleaf: 66l
Dan Rosenholm/GPL 118br
David Bevan: 2, 4b, 5t; 5bl, 5br, 6tr, 8m, 9, 14bl, 21tr, 22tr, 42, 47tr, 53b, 55t, 58–59, 60ml, 64tr, 65b, 67tr, 67br, 68–71, 73br, 74–75, 78tr, 81, 82b, 83tr, 84bl, 85r, 86–93, 94m, 95b, 105tm, 105br, 109, 110, 111tl, 111tr, 112br, 113r, 114br, 115, 117tr, 138, 140–141, 142, 143tl, 143mr, 144, 146–145, 156, 159br, 161br, 165r, 170bl, 173tr, 175br, 176tl, 177tr, 178m
Dreamstime: 79tr, 143br
Eric Crichton/GPL 107t
Fuat Kose/Shutterstock 113
Garden World Images/T. Sims 119br
George McCarthy/Corbis 103
Gordon Maclean/Garden Picture Library 135b
Harry Fox/OSF/GPL 100–101
Howard Rice/Garden Picture Library 124b
Hozelock Ltd: 24mr, 26b, 65c
Ian West/Garden Picture Library 106br
Illuminfx: 41b
Jan Baldwin/Narratives: 20m
Jeff Gynane/Shutterstock 135t
John Glover/Garden Picture Library 133b
John Mason/ardea.com 99tr, 104–105
J S Sira/GPL 112bl
Jurgen & Christine Sohns/FLPA 111br
Leo Batten/FLPA 137mr
Maryland Aquatic Nurseries, Jarrettsville, MD and Charleston Aquatic Nurseries, Johns Island, SC: 5bm, 6bl, 96, 98t, 98b, 99tl, 99bl, 99br, 102t, 102b, 105, 106t, 108bm, 108br, 111bl, 111m, 114tr, 114tmr, 114tm, 115br, 116bl, 116bm, 116tr, 117tm, 117m, 117br, 117tr, 119tl, 120bl, 121ml, 121br, 121bm, 121tm, 122t, 122b, 123m, 123b, 124b, 125t, 125b, 126tl, 126tm, 126tr, 126b, 127tr, 127b, 127mr, 128–129, 130, 131tl, 131ml, 131tr, 132bl, 132tr, 133t, 135t, 136t, 136b, 137bm, 137tr

Matala: 25mr Matala® fine bubble diffuser, 36tl Matala® progressive filter media courtesy Matala Water Tech., 164bl Rotifer living in Matala® biofilter
Michael Rosenburg/Shutterstock 134
NHPA: 120br, 121tl
Nishikoi: 67mr
Photolibrary.com: 113b, 120b
Photos Horticultural 118r, 119bl
Savio Engineering, Inc. (www.savio.cc): 25br, 29br, 33mr
Scott Pehrson/Shutterstock 132br
Shutterstock: 17tl, 23tr, 28t, 36b, 51c, 80tr, 83bl, 143bl, 158l, 168l, 172l, 177br, 178b, 179mr, 179br
Steven Hopkin/ardea.com 108
Steve Shoup/Shutterstock 137br
Theo Allofs/zefa/Corbis 105b
Triplex: 171br

Front cover image: Mike Garcia
Back cover and spine images: David Bevan

We would also like to thank Waterside Aquatics (www.watersideaquatics.co.uk) for supplying the plant specimens photographed on pages 46, 48, 52, 54 and 56.

All other illustrations and photographs are copyright of Quarto Publishing plc. While every effort has been made to credit contributors, Quarto would like to apologise should there have been any omissions or errors – and would be pleased to make the appropriate correction for future editions of the book.